Britain's Best
B&B

AA

Typeset by AA Lifestyle Guides

Printed in E.U by G. Canale & C

Editorial contributors: Alison Moore

Cover credits:
Front Cover: Soulton Hall, Shropshire
Back Cover: (t) Laskill Grange, North Yorkshire, (m) Lypiatt House, Gloucestershire, (b) Photolibrary Group

A CIP catalogue record for this book is available from the British Library

ISBN: 978-0-7495-6464-3

Published by AA Publishing, which is a trading name of AA Media Limited, whose registered office is:
Fanum House, Basing View, Basingstoke, Hampshire RG21 4EA
Registered number 06112600

theAA.com/shop

A04112

Britain's Best
B&B

Contents

Welcome

Britain's Best B&B is a collection of the finest Guest Houses, Farmhouses, Inns and Restaurants with Rooms offering bed and breakfast accommodation in England, Scotland, Wales, the Isle of Man and the Channel Islands.

A Place to Stay

This fully revised and updated guide makes it easy to find that special place to stay for a weekend or a longer break. There are more than 400 establishments to choose from, including smart town guest houses, contemporary city B&Bs, accessible country farmhouses and undiscovered gems in hidden-away locations.

Best Quality

Establishments in this book have received either a top star or a highly commended star rating following a visit by an AA inspector. This helps to ensure that you have a friendly welcome, comfortable surroundings, excellent food and great value for money. Further details about the AA scheme, inspections, awards and rating system can be found on pages 8–9.

Before You Travel

Some places may offer special breaks and facilities not available at the time of going to press – it might be worth calling the establishment before you book.

Using the Guide

Britain's Best B&B has been created to enable you to find an establishment quickly and efficiently. Each entry provides clear information about the type of accommodation, the facilities available and the local area.

Use page 3 to browse the main gazetteer section by county and the index to find either a location (page 394) or a specific B&B (page 398) by name.

Finding your Way

The main section of the guide is divided into five main parts covering England, Channel Islands, Isle of Man, Scotland and Wales.

The counties within each of these sections are ordered alphabetically as are the town or village locations (shown in capital letters as part of the address) within each county. The establishments are then listed alphabetically under each location name. Towns names featured in the guide can also be located in the map section at the back of the guide.

The Old Rectory *sample entry*

★★★★ ⓦ ⓠ 🞃 GUEST ACCOMMODATION

Address: Ash Road, SALISBURY,
             SA38 2PS
Tel: 00000 300124
Fax: 00000 300128
Email: info@oldrectory.co.uk
Website: www.oldrectory.co.uk
Map ref: 3 SZ32
Directions: Next to church at S end of Whitchurch
Rooms: 4 en suite S £85–120, D £95–£120
Parking: 8 Notes: ⊗ on premises ⋈ under 10 Closed: 25–26 Dec

Formerly a rectory and now a stylish and comfortable B&B, the perfect place for relaxing and recharging your batteries, whether staying just for a night or a few days. Guests have use of the spa, hot tub and a gym. Beautifully restored, with its character carefully preserved, The Old Rectory features contemporary furnishings that cleverly complements the spacious internal architecture. The comfortable studio bedrooms all have easy chairs, dining table and chairs, mini-fridges with complimentary fresh milk, fruit juice and yoghurt, hairdryers and remote-controlled TVs. Home cooked meals, including breakfast or a pre-booked evening meal, can be served in the dining room or conservatory.

Recommended in the area

Salisbury Cathedral; New Forest National Park; Stonehenge and Salisbury Plain

❶ Stars and Symbols

All entries in the guide have been inspected by the AA and, at the time of going to press, belong to the AA Guest Accommodation Scheme. Each establishment in the scheme is classified for quality with a grading of one to five stars ★. Each establishment in the Best B&B guide has three, four or five stars and many have a yellow star (highly commended) rating (see page 8 for further details). Establishments with a star rating are given a descriptive category : B&B, GUEST HOUSE, FARMHOUSE, INN, RESTAURANT WITH ROOMS and GUEST ACCOMMODATION. See pages 8–10 for more information on designators and the AA ratings and awards scheme.

continued

Egg cups 🍳 and Pies 🥧 – These symbols denote where the breakfast or dinner are really special, and have an emphasis on freshly prepared ingredients.

Rosette ◉ – This is the AA's food award. See page 9 for further details.

❷ Contact Details

The establishment address includes a locator or place name in capitals (e.g. NORWICH). Within each county, entries are ordered alphabetically first by this place name and then by the name of the establishment.

Telephone and fax numbers, and e-mail and website addresses are given where available. See page 12 for international dialling codes. The telephone and fax numbers are believed correct at the time of going to press but changes may occur. The latest establishment details are on the B&B pages at theAA.com.

Website addresses have been supplied by the establishments and lead you to websites that are not under the control of AA Media Limited (AAML). AAML has no control over and accepts no responsibility or liability in respect of the material on any such websites. By including the addresses of third-party websites AAML does not intend to solicit business.

❸ Map Reference

Each establishment in this guide is given a map reference for a location which can be found in the atlas section at the back of the guide. It is composed of the map page number (1–13) and two-figure map reference based on the National Grid.

For example: **Map 05 SU48**

05 refers to the page number of the map section at the back of the guide

SU is the National Grid lettered square (representing 100,000sq metres) in which the location will be found

4 is the figure reading across the top and bottom of the map page

8 is the figure reading down each side of the map page

Maps locating each establishment and a route planner are available at theAA.com.

❹ Directions

Where possible, directions have been given from the nearest motorway or A road.

❺ Room Information

The number of letting bedrooms with a bath or shower en suite are shown. Bedrooms that have a private bathroom adjacent may be included as en suite. Further details on private bathroom and en suite provision may also be included in the description text (see ❾).

It's a good idea to phone in advance and check that the accommodation has the facilities you require.

Prices: Charges shown are per night except where specified. S denotes bed and breakfast per person (single). D denotes bed and breakfast for two people sharing a room (double).

In some cases prices are also given for twin (T), triple and family rooms, also on a per night basis. Prices are indications only, so do check before booking.

Key to symbols

★	Black stars (see page 9)
☆	Yellow stars (Highly commended) (see page 9)
◉	AA Rosette Award (see page 9)
🍳	Breakfast Award
🥧	Dinner Award
3 TQ28	Map reference
S	Single room
D	Double room
T	Twin room
Triple	Triple room
⊗	No dogs allowed (guide dogs for the blind and assist dogs should be allowed)
🚼	No children under age specified
Wi-fi	Wireless network connection

⑥ Parking
The number of parking spaces available.
Other types of parking (on road or Park and Ride) may also be possible; check the descriptions for further information.

⑦ Notes
This section provides specific details relating to:

Smoking policy: Smoking in public areas is now banned in England, Scotland, Wales, Isle of Man and Channel Islands.

The proprietor can designate one or more bedrooms with ventilation systems where the occupants can smoke, but communal areas must be smoke-free.

Dogs: Although some establishments allow dogs, they may be excluded from some areas of the property and some breeds, particularly those requiring an exceptional license, may not be acceptable at all. Under the Disability Discrimination Act 1995 access should be allowed for guide dogs and assistance dogs. Please check the policy when making your booking.

Children: No children (🛇) means children cannot be accommodated, or a minimum age may be specified, e.g. 🛇 under 4 means no children under four years old. The main description may also provide details about facilities available for children.

Establishments with special facilities for children may include additional equipment such as a babysitting service or baby-intercom system and facilities such as a playroom or playground, laundry facilities, drying and ironing facilities, cots, high chairs and special meals. If you have very young children, check before booking.

Other notes: Additional facilities, such as access for the disabled, or notes about other services (e.g. if credit card details are not accepted), may be listed here.

⑧ Closed
Details of when the establishment is closed for business. Establishments are open all year unless closed dates/months are shown. Please note that some places are open all year but offer a restricted service in low season.

⑨ Description
This is a general overview of the establishment and may include specific information about the various facilities offered in the rooms, a brief history of the establishment, notes about special features and descriptions of the food where an award has been given (see ❶).

⑩ Recommended in the Area
This indicates local places of interest, and potential day trips and activities.

Best Quality

To achieve one of the highest ratings, an establishment in the AA Guest Accommodation Scheme must provide increased quality standards throughout, with particular emphasis in five key areas: cleanliness, hospitality, food quality, bedrooms and bathrooms.

The AA inspects and classifies more than 3,000 guest houses, farmhouses, inns and restaurants with rooms for its Guest Accommodation Scheme. Establishments recognised by the AA pay an annual fee according to the rating and the number of bedrooms. This rating is not transferable if an establishment changes hands.

Common Standards

A few years ago, the accommodation inspection organisations (The AA, VisitBritain, VisitScotland and VisitWales) undertook extensive consultation with consumers and the hospitality industry which resulted in new quality standards for rating establishments. Guests can now be confident that a star-rated B&B anywhere in the UK and Ireland will offer consistent quality and facilities.

★ Stars

AA Stars classify guest accommodation at five levels of quality, from one at the simplest, to five at the highest level of quality in the scheme. Each rating is also accompanied by a descriptive designator (further explained below).

Highly Commended

Yellow Stars indicate that an accommodation is in the top ten percent of its star rating. Yellow Stars only apply to 3, 4 or 5 star establishments.

The Inspection Process

Establishments applying for AA recognition are visited by a qualified AA accommodation inspector as a mystery guest. Inspectors stay overnight to make a thorough test of the accommodation, food, and hospitality. After paying the bill the following morning they identify themselves and ask to be shown around the premises. The inspector completes a full report, resulting in a recommendation for the appropriate Star rating. After this first visit, the establishment will receive an annual visit to check that standards are maintained. If it changes hands, the new owners must re-apply for a rating.

Guests can expect to find the following minimum standards at all levels:

- Pleasant and helpful welcome and service, and sound standards of housekeeping and maintenance
- Comfortable accommodation equipped to modern standards
- Bedding and towels changed for each new guest, and at least weekly if the room is taken for a long stay
- Adequate storage, heating, lighting and comfortable seating
- A sufficient hot water supply at reasonable times
- A full cooked breakfast. (If this is not provided, the fact must be advertised and a substantial continental breakfast must be offered.)

There are additional requirements for an establishment to achieve three, four or five Stars:

- Three Stars and above – access to both sides of all beds for double occupancy.
- Three Stars and above – bathrooms/shower rooms cannot be shared by the proprietor.
- Three Stars and above – a washbasin in every guest bedroom (either in the bedroom or the en suite/private facility)

- Four Stars – half of the bedrooms must be en suite or have private facilities.
- Five Stars – all bedrooms must be en suite or have private facilities.

Designators

All guest accommodation inspected by the AA is given one of six descriptive designators to help potential guests understand the different types of accommodation available in Britain. The following are included in this guide:

B&B: B&B accommodation is provided in a private house run by the owner and with no more than six guests. There may be restricted access to the establishment, particularly in the late morning and the afternoon.

GUEST HOUSE: Provides for more than six paying guests and usually offers more services than a B&B, for example dinner, served by staff as well as the owner. London prices tend to be higher than outside the capital, and normally only bed and breakfast is provided, although some establishments do provide a full meal service. Check on the service offered before booking as details may change during the currency of this guide.

FARMHOUSE: A farmhouse usually provides good value B&B or guest house accommodation and excellent home cooking on a working farm or smallholding. Sometimes the land has been sold and only the house remains, but many are working farms and some farmers are happy to allow visitors to look around, or even to help feed the animals. However, you should always take great care and never leave children unsupervised. The farmhouses are listed under towns or villages, but do ask for precise directions when booking.

INN: Traditional inns often have a cosy bar, convivial atmosphere, good beer and pub food. Those listed in the guide will provide breakfast in a suitable room, and should also serve light meals during licensing hours. The character of the properties vary according to whether they are country inns or town establishments. Check arrival times as these may be restricted to opening hours.

RESTAURANT WITH ROOMS: These restaurants offer overnight accommodation with the restaurant being the main business and open to non-residents. The restaurant usually offers a high standard of food and service.

GUEST ACCOMMODATION: This general designator can be chosen by any establishment in the scheme.

AA Rosette Awards

Out of the many thousands of restaurants in the UK, the AA identifies around 2,000 as the best. The following is an outline of what to expect from restaurants with AA Rosette Awards. For a more detailed explanation of Rosette criteria please see theAA.com

⍟ Excellent local restaurants serving food prepared with care, understanding and skill, using good quality ingredients.

⍟⍟ The best local restaurants, which aim for and achieve higher standards, better consistency and where a greater precision is apparent in the cooking. There will be obvious attention to the selection of quality ingredients.

⍟⍟⍟ Outstanding restaurants that demand recognition well beyond their local area.

⍟⍟⍟⍟ Amongst the very best restaurants in the British Isles, where the cooking demands national recognition.

⍟⍟⍟⍟⍟ The finest restaurants in the British Isles, where the cooking stands comparison with the best in the world.

Useful Information

There are so many things to remember when embarking on a short trip or weekend break. If you are unsure, always check before you book. Up-to-date information on all B&Bs can be found at the travel section of theAA.com

Codes of practice

The AA encourages the use of The Hotel Industry Voluntary Code of Booking Practice in appropriate establishments. The prime objective of the code is to ensure that the customer is clear about the price and the exact services and facilities being purchased, before entering into a contractually binding agreement. If the price has not been previously confirmed in writing, the guest should be handed a card at the time of registration at the establishment, stipulating the total obligatory charge.

The Tourism (Sleeping Accommodation Price Display) Order 1977 compels hotels, motels, guest houses, farmhouses, inns and self-catering accommodation with four or more

theAA.com

- Go to theAA.com to find more AA listed guest houses, hotels, pubs and restaurants – some 12,000 establishments.
- The AA home page has a link to a route planner. Simply enter your postcode and the establishment postcode given in this guide and click 'Get Route'. Check your details and then click 'Get Route' again and you will have a detailed route plan to take you door-to-door.
- Use the Travel section to search for Hotels & B&Bs or Restaurants & Pubs by location or establishment name. Scroll down the list of finds for the interactive map and local routes.
- Postcode searches can also be made on www.ordnancesurvey.co.uk and www.multimap.com which will also provide useful aerial views of your destination.

letting bedrooms to display in entrance halls the minimum and maximum prices charged for each category of room. This order complements the Voluntary Code of Booking Practice.

Fire precautions and safety

Many of the establishments listed in the guide are subject to the requirements of the Fire Precautions Act 1971. This Act does not apply to the Channel Islands or the Isle of Man, where their own rules are exercised. All establishments should display details of how to summon assistance in the event of an emergency at night.

Licensed premises

Whereas inns hold a licence to sell alcohol, not all guest houses are licensed. Some may have a full liquor licence, or others may have a table licence and wine list. Licensed premises are not obliged to remain open throughout the permitted hours, and they may do so only when they expect reasonable trade.

Children

Restrictions for children may be mentioned in the description. Some establishments may offer free accommodation to children when they share their parents' room. Such conditions are subject to change without notice, therefore always check when booking.

Complaints

Readers who have cause to complain are urged to do so on the spot. This should provide an opportunity for the proprietor to correct matters. If the personal approach fails, readers can inform AA Hotel Services, Fanum House, Basingstoke, Hampshire, RG21 4EA.
The AA may at its sole discretion investigate any complaints received from guide users for the purpose of making any necessary amendments to the guide. The AA will not in any circumstances act as a representative or negotiator or undertake to obtain compensation or enter into any correspondence or deal with the matter in any other way whatsoever. The AA will not guarantee to take any specific action.

Bank and public holidays 2010	
New Year's Day	1st January
New Year's Holiday	2nd January (Scotland)
Good Friday	2nd April
Easter Monday	5th April
May Day Bank Holiday	3rd May
Spring Bank Holiday	31st May
August Holiday	2nd August (Scotland)
Late Summer Holiday	30th August
St Andrew's Day	30th November (Scotland)
Christmas Day	25th December
Boxing Day	26th December

Booking

Advance booking is always recommended to avoid disappointment. The peak holiday periods in the UK are Easter, and from June to September; public holidays are also busy times. In some parts of Scotland the winter skiing season is a peak holiday period. Some establishments may only accept weekly bookings from Saturday, and others require a deposit on booking. Guest houses may not accept credit or debit cards. VAT (Value Added Tax) is payable in the UK and in the Isle of Man, on basic prices and additional services. VAT does not apply in the Channel Islands. Always confirm the current price before booking; the prices in this guide are indications rather than firm quotations. It is a good idea also to confirm exactly what is included in the price when booking. Remember that all details, especially prices, may change without notice during the currency of the guide.

Cancellation

Advise the proprietor immediately if you must cancel a booking. If the room cannot be re-let you may be held legally responsible for partial payment. This could include losing your deposit or being liable for compensation. You should consider taking out cancellation insurance.

International Information

If you're travelling from overseas, the following information will provide some useful guidance to help you enjoy your stay in Britain. The individual entries in this book will also give you information regarding travel and the best routes to take.

Money

Some establishments may not accept travellers' cheques, or credit or debit cards, so ask about payment methods when you book. Most European and American credit and debit cards allow you to withdraw cash from British ATMs.

Driving

In the UK you drive on the left and overtake on the right. Seat belts must be worn by every occupant of the car, whether they sit in the front or the rear. Speed limits are displayed in miles per hour.
Visit theAA.com for useful motoring advice, travel information and route planning.

Car rental

You will be required to present your driving licence and credit or debit card. You can also provide an International Driving Permit along with your driving licence. Further identification, such as a passport, may also be required. A minimum age limit will apply.

Trains

The UK has an extensive rail network. To find out about routes, special offers or passes, contact National Rail (www.nationalrail.co.uk, tel: 08457 484950; from overseas +44 20 7278 5240, and international rates apply) or a travel agent.

Medical treatment & health insurance

Travellers who normally take medicines or carry an appliance, such as a hypodermic syringe, should ensure that they have sufficient supply for their stay and a doctor's letter describing the condition and treatment required.

Before travelling ensure you have insurance for emergency medical and dental treatment. Many European countries have reciprocal agreements for medical treatment and require EU citizens to obtain a European Health Insurance Card (EHIC) before travel.

Telephones

Many guest houses have direct dial telephones in the rooms. Always check the call rate before dialling. Payphones usually take cash, credit or debit cards, or phonecards. Phonecards can be purchased from newsagents and post offices.

The telephone and fax numbers in this guide show the area code followed by the subscriber number. When dialling from abroad first dial the international network access code, then the country code (44 for the UK). Omit the first digit of the area code then dial the subscriber number. For example:

From Europe	00 44 111 121212
From the US	011 44 111 121212

When dialling from the UK, dial the international network access code, then the country code.

Electrical appliances

The British electrical current is 220–240 volts and appliances have square three-pin plugs. Foreign appliances may require an adaptor for the plug, as well as an electrical voltage converter that will allow, for example, a 110-volt appliance to be powered.

Online booking with **theAA.com/travel**

Book online...

Check in...

and Relax...

**Take the hassle out of booking accommodation
online with our new and improved site**

Visit

theAA.com/travel

to search by availability and book hundreds
of AA inspected and rated hotels and B&Bs in real time

Plus, find more information on:

Restaurants & Pubs • Caravan & Camping • Self Catering
• Holidays • Ferries • Airport Parking • Car Hire

Travel

AA For the
road ahead

ENGLAND

Dartmoor National Park

BERKSHIRE

River Thames and Windsor Castle

The Crown & Garter

★★★★ ⬅ INN

Address: Great Common, Inkpen,
HUNGERFORD, RG17 9QR
Tel: 01488 668325
Email: gill.hern@btopenworld.com
Website: www.crownandgarter.com
Map ref: 3 SU36
Directions: 4m SE of Hungerford. Off A4 into
Kintbury, opp corner stores onto Inkpen Rd, straight
for 2m **Rooms:** 8 en suite (8GF) **S** £69.50 **D** £99
Notes: Wi-fi ⊗ on premises 🐾 under 7yrs **Parking:** 40

Family owned and run, this 17th-century inn set in the beautiful Kennet Valley. The bar and restaurant are in keeping with the character of the building, with real ales, wines and a selection of malt whiskies. The restaurant offers an interesting range of country dishes freshly prepared mainly from local produce. The spacious bedrooms are in a courtyard around a pretty cottage garden. Each room has a bath and power shower, a hairdryer, flat-screen TV with Freeview, radio and Wi-fi access, plus tea and coffee facilities.
Recommended in the area
Newbury Racecourse; Combe Gibbet; Highclere Castle

The Swan Inn

★★★★ 🖥 ⬅ INN

Address: Craven Road, Inkpen,
HUNGERFORD, RG17 9DX
Tel: 01488 668326
Fax: 01488 668306
Email: enquiries@theswaninn-organics.co.uk
Website: www.theswaninn-organics.co.uk
Map ref: 3 SU36
Directions: 3.5m SE of Hungerford. S on Hungerford
High St past rail bridge, left to Hungerford Common,
right signed Inkpen **Rooms:** 10 en suite **S** £60-£70 **D** £80-£95 **Notes:** Wi-fi ⊗ on premises
Parking: 50 **Closed:** 25-26 Dec

The peaceful north Wessex downs provide an idyllic setting for this 17th-century inn. Inside there are oak beams, open fires and a warm welcome from the Harris family. The owners are organic farmers, and the restaurant and an adjoining farm shop feature superb produce. The spacious en suite bedrooms are firmly rooted in the 21st century, with direct-dial and internet connections.
Recommended in the area
Combe Gibbet; Kennet and Avon Canal; Avebury stone circle; Newbury Racecourse

In the distance, Brunel's 1864 Clifton Suspension Bridge

Downlands House

★★★★ GUEST ACCOMMODATION

Address: 33 Henleaze Gardens, Henleaze,
BRISTOL, BS9 4HH
Tel: 0117 962 1639
Email: info@downlandshouse.co.uk
Website: www.downlandshouse.com
Map ref: 2 ST57
Directions: 2m NW of city centre off A4018.
M5 junct 17, follow Westbury-on-Trym/City Centre
signs, pass Badminton private girls' school. Henleaze
Gdns on left
Rooms: 10 (7 en suite) (3 pri facs) (1GF) S £40-£55 D £70-£75 **Notes:** Wi-fi

This elegant Victorian property, situated between Westbury-on-Trym and Clifton in a quiet neighbourhood, provides all the charm, atmosphere and comforts of a large family home, and is a welcome relief from the anonymity of some larger establishments. It is conveniently located for enjoying many of the sights in and around Bristol, including walks on the Durdham Downs, shopping in Clifton village and the flora and fauna of Bristol Zoo, and is easily reached from the M4 and M5 motorways, making it a great base for a trip to the area. Inside, most of the attractive, individually decorated bedrooms, have en suite or private facilities, and all come with lots of extra touches to make you feel at home, such as free Wi-fi broadband, TV, hairdryer and hospitality tray. There is a smart lounge with a TV for guests to relax in or, weather permitting, a charming, leafy garden with table and chairs. The flavoursome cooked breakfasts are served in either the delightful conservatory or the stylish dining room. For evening meals, there are a number of restaurants within walking distance. On-street parking is also available.

Recommended in the area

Clifton Suspension Bridge; SS Great Britain; Harvey Nichols

Westfield House

★ ★ ★ ★ 🛏 BED & BREAKFAST

Address: 37 Stoke Hill, Stoke Bishop,
BRISTOL, BS9 1LQ
Tel/Fax: 0117 962 6119
Email: admin@westfieldhouse.net
Website: www.westfieldhouse.net
Map ref: 2 ST57
Directions: 1.8m NW of city centre in Stoke Bishop
Rooms: 3 en suite S £69-£79 D £79-£108
Notes: Wi-fi ⊗ on premises 👣 under 11yrs
Parking: 5

Set in several acres of private grounds, this large white Georgian-style, family-run guest house makes an ideal retreat from Bristol's city lights. Westfield House is close to Durdham Downs – a vast expanse of open common land, which stretches from Bristol's suburbs to the cliffs of the Avon Gorge – and the Bristol University Halls of Residence. The beautifully decorated and extremely comfortable bedrooms, either single or doubles, are all en suite, and have flat-screen TVs, DVD/CD players, free Wi-fi, fridges and tea- and coffee-making facilities. The living room centres round a cosy fireplace while large bay windows lead onto a large garden terrace. Owner Ann cooks more or less to order using quality local ingredients, and a typical meal may include dishes such as salmon en croûte with puréed spinach and hollandaise sauce accompanied by potatoes dauphinoise, followed by a delicious home-made apple pie – all the better in the summer months when served on the patio overlooking the lovely rear garden. The grounds are also a haven for a variety of wildlife including owls, badgers, newts, falcons, slow worms and hedgehogs. If you still hanker for the bright lights, Westfield House is just a short walk from Bristol city centre. There is ample off-street parking for guests.

Recommended in the area

Clifton Suspension Bridge; SS Great Britain; Bristol Zoo

Brunel's Clifton Suspension Bridge

BUCKINGHAMSHIRE

View from Beacon Hill

Nags Head Inn & Restaurant

★★★★ ⚜ INN

Address: London Road, GREAT MISSENDEN, HP16 0DG
Tel: 01494 862200
Fax: 01494 862685
Email: goodfood@nagsheadbucks.com
Website: www.nagsheadbucks.com
Map ref: 3 SP80
Directions: N of Amersham on A413, turn left at Chiltern Hospital onto London Rd signed Great Missenden **Rooms:** 5 en suite S £90-£120 D £90-£120 **Notes:** Wi-fi **Parking:** 40

The delightful Nags Head Inn has served as a location for a number of TV programmes and films, and has played host to many famous names over the years, including prime ministers and the children's author Roald Dahl – the animated film of Dahl's *Fantastic Mr Fox* actually features the inn. Located in the picturesque Chiltern Hills, in the valley of the River Misbourne, the establishment is within walking distance of the lovely village of Great Missenden and close to major road and rail routes. Inside, it has been tastefully refurbished to a high standard and retains its original 15th-century features, including low oak beams and a large inglenook fireplace. This carries through into the individually furnished en suite bedrooms, which are comfortable with a modern twist and come with flat-screen digital TVs and other thoughtful extras, ensuring a home-from-home experience. The gastro pub has a popular reputation locally thanks to its extensive menu of English and French fusion dishes made from high-quality local and organic produce, such as fish smoked on the premises as well as local saddle of lamb and cheeses. There's also an award-winning wine list and a selection of real ales. Ample parking and Wi-fi are available.

Recommended in the area

Hughenden Manor (NT); Bekonscot Model Village; West Wycombe Park (NT)

CAMBRIDGESHIRE

Punting on the River Cam, Cambridge

Newstead Abbey Lower Lake

The Crown Inn

★★★★★ INN

Address: 8 Duck Street, ELTON, PE8 6RQ
Tel: 01832 280232
Email: inncrown@googlemail.com
Website: www.thecrowninn.org
Map ref: 3 TL09
Directions: A1 junct 17 onto A605 W. In 3.5m right signed Elton, 0.9m left signed Nassington. On village green **Rooms:** 5 en suite (2GF) **S** £60-£80 **D** £80-£120 **Notes:** Wi-fi **Parking:** 15

Huddling beneath the conker-laden horse chestnut tree in the historic Wold's village of Elton is The Crown, an ancient inn constructed of sandstone and thatch. Guests can enjoy a tranquil night or short break in beautiful, individually appointed bedrooms, with king-size beds, en suite bath and shower, easy chairs, plantation shutters and mini fridges. Some rooms are located upstairs while two nestle in the courtyard on the ground floor. Breakfast is prepared to order by the chef landlord and served in the cosy farmhouse snug. The beamed bar has a huge oak mantel with a roaring fire.

Recommended in the area

Elton Hall; Fotheringhay Church & Castle (execution site of Mary, Queen of Scots); Burghley House

The Roaches

Cheshire Cheese Cottage

★ ★ ★ ★   BED & BREAKFAST

Address: Burwardsley Road,
BURWARDSLEY, CH3 9NS
Tel/Fax: 01829 770887
Email: r.rosney@yahoo.co.uk
Website: www.cheshirecheesecottage-bb.com
Map ref: 6 SJ55
Rooms: 2 en suite (2GF) **D** £75-£85
Notes: Wi-fi ⊗ on premises ⛄ ☺
Parking: 4

Rose and Roy Rosney extend a warm welcome to guests at their delightful little cottage set in extensive grounds. There are two en suite garden suites; one has a double bed and the other a king size, and each has a private lounge area. The rooms here are tastefully decorated and come with free Wi-fi, flat-screen TV with Freeview, CD and DVD players, hairdryer and tea- and coffee-making facilities. Breakfasts, full English or lighter options, are freshly cooked, and vegetarians can be catered for. On-site parking is available, and guests are welcome to make use of the patio and half acre of gardens.

Recommended in the area

Sandstone trail; Chester; Beeston Castle

The Pheasant Inn

★★★★★ ⌘ INN

Address: Higher Burwardsley,
BURWARDSLEY, CH3 9PF
Tel: 01829 770434
Fax: 01829 771097
Email: info@thepheasantinn.co.uk
Website: www.thepheasantinn.co.uk
Map ref: 6 SJ55
Directions: From A41, left to Tattenhall, right at 1st junct & left at 2nd Higher Burwardsley. At post office left, signed **Rooms:** 12 en suite (5GF) **Notes:** Wi-fi **Parking:** 80

This delightful 300-year-old inn is tucked away in a peaceful corner of rural Cheshire, yet is still within easy reach of the city. It is an ideal stop for walkers and ramblers, sitting high on the Peckforton Hills with views over the Cheshire Plain. Well equipped, comfortable en suite bedrooms are located in an adjacent converted barn or in the main building. Using fresh, local produce, creative dishes are served in the stylish restaurant or the traditional, beamed bar. In summer, guests can dine alfresco.

Recommended in the area

Cheshire Candle Workshops; Beeston Castle; Sandstone Trail

Sandhollow Farm B&B

★ ★ ★ ★ BED & BREAKFAST

Address: Harthill Road, BURWARDSLEY, Tattenhall,
Chester, CH3 9NU

Tel: 01829 770894

Email: paul.kickdrum@tiscali.co.uk

Website: www.sandhollow.co.uk

Map ref: 6 SJ55

Directions: From A41, turn off to Tattenhall, follow
signs to Burwardsley. Continue past post office,
0.25m on right **Rooms:** 3 en suite (1GF) **S** £55-£60
D £76-£90 **Notes:** Wi-fi (free) ⊗ on premises ⚲ under 12yrs **Parking:** 4 **Closed:** annual holiday

Commanding spectacular views of the Cheshire Plain and Welsh hills, this lovely converted farmhouse is set in the sandstone ridge of the Peckforton Hills, on the Sandstone Trail, midway between Frodsham and Whitchurch. It provides an idyllic base for visiting Chester, Liverpool and Manchester, suiting leisure guests, who might be interested in the wealth of attractions the area has to offer, and business travellers alike. Sandhollow Farm is family run by Elise and Paul Stafford, whose carefully renovated bedrooms offer beautiful views, and each has en suite facilities. Expect exceptional comfort from the goosedown pillows and duvets, Egytian cotton bed linens and towels, Molton Brown toiletries and tea- and coffee-making facilities. Home-made treats and chocolates add a welcoming touch. (Elise's complimentary home-made damson or sloe gin is not for the faint hearted.) Public areas are independently accessed, comfortable and inviting, including a lounge with a log fire. Substantial breakfasts, using organic, home-made and local produce, are served in the adjoining dining room with views across the garden. Guests can explore the two acres of well-kept grounds or sit, relax and enjoy the views from the terrace. There are several good local restaurants and pubs for meals. Finalist for AA Landlady of the Year 2007.

Recommended in the area

Beston Castle; Oulton Park; Chester

Lavender Lodge

★★★★ GUEST ACCOMMODATION

Address: 46 Hoole Road, CHESTER, CH2 3NL
Tel: 01244 323204
Fax: 01244 329821
Email: bookings@lavenderlodgechester.co.uk
Website: www.lavenderlodgechester.co.uk
Map ref: 5 SJ46
Directions: 1m NE of city centre on A56, opp All Saints church
Rooms: 5 en suite S £35-£50 D £65-£80
Notes: Wi-fi **Parking:** 7 **Closed:** 24 Dec-2 Jan

Built towards the end of the 20th century, Lavender Lodge is a friendly, family-run establishment occupying a smart Edwardian property. Set back from the road, just off the A56, it is a peaceful place to stay with free on-site parking available. There is a quiet garden that gets the afternoon sun and makes a lovely place to sit and relax. Hoole village is an interesting part of Chester; a self-contained area with a traditional high street and lots of smaller shops. It is a pleasant place to explore, with good places to eat, all just a stroll from the house. The entrance hall at the Lodge leads to a large and impressive staircase sweeping up to the guest bedrooms, which have views over the garden or the grounds of the church opposite. Double, triple and family bedrooms are available, with tea, coffee, herbal and fruit infusions, hot chocolate, mineral water and biscuits provided. Rooms are also equipped with hairdryers, colour televisions and wireless broadband. The en suite bathrooms feature luxury toiletries and plenty of large fluffy towels. A freshly cooked full English breakfast, using local produce where possible, is served at separate tables in the attractive dining room.

Recommended in the area

Blue Planet Aquarium; Chester Zoo; Chester's Roman walls

Oddfellows

★★★★★ ◉ RESTAURANT WITH ROOMS

Address: 20 Lower Bridge Street,
CHESTER, CH1 1RS
Tel: 01244 400001
Email: reception@oddfellows.biz
Website: www.oddfellows.biz
Map ref: 5 SJ46
Rooms: 4 en suite
Notes: Wi-fi ⊗ on premises
Parking: 4

Surrounded by designer shops and only a few minutes' walk from the Chester Rows, this stylish Georgian mansion, formerly Oddfellows Hall, is now a fashionable boutique establishment offering a choice of eating areas. It is a place where old meets new, and the upper ground floor comprises a walled garden with ornamental moat, Arabic tents, a roofed patio, a cocktail bar with an excellent wine selection, a bustling brasserie and an Alice in Wonderland tea room. Good food is skilfully prepared in the formal second-floor restaurant. Celebrity chef Richard Phillips, who oversees as consultant chef, waves the flag for British cuisine, with the emphasis on local, seasonal produce. A sumptuous members' lounge is also available to diners and resident guests, while the Pantry café, located at street level, which continues the hotel's eclectic design with oversized furniture and cake stands, is open for breakfast, morning coffee, lunch, afternoon tea and dinner. For those who wish to enjoy Oddfellows during an overnight stay, the en suite bedrooms all have the wow factor, with super beds and every conceivable extra to enhance the guest experience. Residents' parking is available, and special events can be booked and catered for.

Recommended in the area

Chester Castle; Grosvenor Museum; Chester Zoo

The Farndon

★★★★ INN

Address: High Street, FARNDON, Chester, CH3 6PU
Tel: 01829 270570
Fax: 01829 272060
Email: enquiries@thefarndon.co.uk
Website: www.thefarndon.co.uk
Map ref: 5 SJ45
Directions: Just off A534
Rooms: 5 (4 en suite) (1 pri facs) S £55-£70
D £60-£95 **Notes:** Wi-fi **Parking:** 25

Built in the 16th century and originally known as The Raven, The Farndon sits in a picturesque village, renowned for its strawberry fields, which lies on the Cheshire Plain at the border between England and Wales. Extensive renovation had taken place, and log fires, candles and comfy chairs combine to create a welcoming ambience inside. The luxurious boutique-style bedrooms are well equipped and include plasma-screen TVs and free Wi-fi. There's a bar and restaurant offering a selection of hand-pulled cask ales and fine wines, together with a locally sourced, regularly updated menu.

Recommended in the area

Chester Castle; Grosvenor Museum; Chirk Castle (NT)

The Tollemache Arms

★★★★ INN

Address: Nantwich Road, Alpraham,
TARPORLEY, CW6 9JE
Tel: 01829 261716
Email: enquiries@tollemachearms.co.uk
Website: www.tollemachearms.co.uk
Map ref: 5 SJ56
Directions: On A51 Chester to Crewe road, 2.5m
from Tarporley **Rooms:** 4 en suite S £50-£60
D £55-£60 **Notes:** Wi-fi **Parking:** 38

Located on the main road between Crewe and Chester, in the village of Alpraham, the Tollemache Arms makes a convenient base for business or exploring the many local attractions. An 18th-century inn, it has recently been refurbished to a high standard, while retaining its log fires, oak beams and other interesting features. There is a good choice of food available using local produce, along with fine wines and real ales. The en suite accommodation is attractive and well equipped, with showers, flatscreen TV and tea- and coffee-making facilities. A large beer garden is popular in summer.

Recommended in the area

Oulton Park Circuit; Tatton Park Gardens (NT); Bunbury Locks

Mow Cop Castle

The Bear's Paw

★★★★★ ⇔ INN

Address: School Lane, WARMINGHAM,
Sandbach, CW11 3QN
Tel: 01270 526317
Email: info@thebearspaw.co.uk
Website: www.thebearspaw.co.uk
Map ref: 5 SJ76
Directions: M6 junct 17 A534/A533 for Middlewich/
Northwich. On A533, left onto Mill Ln, left onto
Warmingham Ln. Right onto Plant Ln, left onto Green
Ln Rooms: 14 en suite **S** £75-£115 **D** £90-£130 **Notes:** Wi-fi **Parking:** 75

Located in the heart of Cheshire, this 19th-century gastro inn was totally refurbished in 2009. Today it provides very comfortable and well equipped luxurious boutique-style en suite bedrooms, including family rooms. All feature flatscreen HD televisions and complimentary Wi-fi, along with many thoughtful extras. Imaginative, home-cooked food is served in the friendly open-plan dining room, and a choice of sumptuous lounge areas is available, as well as a traditional yet stylish bar.

Recommended in the area

The Bull Ring; Hack Green Secret Nuclear Bunker; Middlewich

CORNWALL

St Ives

Polperro

Green Pastures Bed & Breakfast

★ ★ ★ BED & BREAKFAST
Address: Longhill, CALLINGTON, PL17 8AU
Tel: 01579 382566
Email: greenpast@aol.com
Website: www.tamarvalleyview.co.uk
Map ref: 1 SX36
Directions: 0.5m E of Callington on A390 to
Tavistock **Rooms:** 3 (2 en suite) (1 pri facs) (3GF)
Notes: ⊗ on premises 🐾 under 18yrs ⊜
Parking: 8

Located on the southern side of Kit Hill, in the old market town of Callington, this friendly, homely
establishment has a panoramic outlook across the Tamar Valley and distant views of Dartmoor.
It makes an ideal spot for touring Devon and Cornwall and the surrounding areas, including many
coastal resorts. Within, the ground-floor bedrooms of this modern bungalow, all with private facilities,
are comfortably furnished and there is a sun lounge. Guests can also enjoy the five acres of land, home
to ducks, geese and chickens. There is extensive off-road parking.
Recommended in the area
Cotehele (NT); Buckland Abbey (NT); Morwellham Quay

Lower Tresmorn Farm

★★★★ 🏠 FARMHOUSE

Address: CRACKINGTON HAVEN, Bude, EX23 0NU
Tel/Fax: 01840 230667
Email: rachel.crocker@talk21.com
Website: www.lowertresmorn.co.uk
Map ref: 1 SX19
Directions: Take Tresmorn turn off coast road 2m N of Crackington Haven
Rooms: 6 (5 en suite) (2GF) S £36-£60 D £60-£76
Notes: ⊗ on premises 🚸 under 8yrs
Parking: 6

Set in the North Cornwall Heritage Coast area, Lower Tresmorn Farm makes a great choice for exploring Devon and Cornwall. It is a bracing walk along the coastal path to Crackington Haven's beach and a short drive from attractions such as Bude and Boscastle. Parts of this charming farmhouse date back to medieval times, and self-catering accommodation is also available, all within the grounds of a working family farm. Anyone who fancies some brisk exercise, as well as learning a little of farming ways, is welcome to accompany owner Chris as he checks the sheep and South Devon cattle on the cliff pastures. Otherwise, guests can simply unwind in this most relaxing location over a reviving cup of tea and a piece of hot buttered saffron cake. The tastefully furnished bedrooms, some with views of the sea and Lundy Island, are located in the main house – reached via a spiral staircase – or in an adjacent converted barn. All provide plenty of home comforts, with individual touches such as a carved French bed in one or full-length French windows in others. Breakfast and the popular candlelit dinners (by prior arrangement) make full use of local or farm produce, served in the oak-beamed dining room.

Recommended in the area

Clovelly; Port Isaac; Bodmin Moor

Cotswold House

★★★★ GUEST HOUSE
Address: 49 Melvill Road, FALMOUTH, TR11 4DF
Tel: 01326 312077
Email: info@cotswoldhousehotel.com
Website: www.cotswoldhousehotel.com
Map ref: 1 SW83
Directions: On A39 near town centre & docks
Rooms: 10 en suite (1GF)
Notes: ⊗ on premises **Parking:** 10 **Closed:** Xmas

With Falmouth's superb sandy Gyllyngvase Beach and the busy estuary, harbour and yachting marina just a short walk away, this small family-run hotel is ideal for both a holiday or a short break. The smart Victorian property is also close to the picturesque, cobbled town centre with its historic buildings and range of specialist shops. All the bedrooms have a bath or shower room en suite and hospitality trays; and many have lovely views of the sea and the River Fal. Well-cooked traditional cuisine is a feature of a stay here, and the friendly owners offer attentive service. The convivial bar is another plus at this relaxed house, and a popular place for socialising in the evening.

Recommended in the area

Falmouth National Maritime Museum; The Eden Project; Trebah and Glendurgan gardens

Tregerrick Farm B & B

★★★★ ⌂ FARMHOUSE
Address: GORRAN, St Austell, PL26 6NF
Tel/Fax: 01726 843418
Email: fandc.thomas@btconnect.com
Website: www.tregerrickfarm.co.uk
Map ref: 1 SW94
Directions: 1m NW of Gorran. B3273 S from St Austell, right after Pentewan Sands campsite to The Lost Gardens of Heligan, continue 3m, farm on left
Rooms: 4 (2 en suite) (2 pri facs) (2GF) S £45

D £70-£90 **Notes:** Wi-fi ⊗ on premises 🍴 under 4yrs ⊛ **Parking:** 4 **Closed:** Nov-Jan

In the heart of the countryside, yet close to The Lost Gardens of Heligan and popular beaches, Tregerrick Farm offers a peaceful rural retreat. All the well-equipped bedrooms are en suite, and have comfortable beds. Guests return regularly appreciating the imaginative breakfasts that use quality, local produce plus the delicious home-made bread and preserves. The Meadowside garden apartment is especially popular with families and couples, and features a microwave and fridge.

Recommended in the area

Lost Gardens of Heligan; South West Coast Path; The Eden Project

Hurdon Farm

★ ★ ★ ★ 🍴 FARMHOUSE
Address: LAUNCESTON, PL15 9LS
Tel: 01566 772955
Map ref: 1 SX38
Directions: A30 onto A388 to Launceston, at rdbt exit for hospital, 2nd right signed Trebullett, premises 1st on right
Rooms: 6 en suite (1GF) **S** £32-£36 **D** £54-£66
Notes: ⊗ on premises 🅿 **Parking:** 10
Closed: Nov-Apr

Situated just south of the historic Cornish capital of Launceston, Hurdon is a 400-acre working farm with cows and pigs, where guests are welcome to wander around and enjoy the countryside. Quietly located at the end of a tree-lined drive, the elegant 18th-century stone and granite farmhouse has retained many original features, especially in the kitchen, with its open granite fireplace, original Dutch oven and collection of old jacks and trivets. Bedrooms, including one ground-floor family room with adjoining children's room, are all en suite and individually furnished. They come with many thoughtful extras such as electric blankets and hot-water bottles, bathrobes, TV, hairdryer, playing cards, magazines and tea and coffee-making facilities. Breakfasts, and delicious dinners by prior arrangement, make use of produce from the farm whenever possible, and the home-made clotted cream is a special treat. Meals are served in the dining room, with its sash windows, original panelled shutters, built-in dressers and tables overlooking the garden, while the lounge features a log stove and has large, comfortable chairs, TV and a selection of books, magazines and games. Hurdon Farm makes an ideal base for exploring Cornwall and its coastlines.

Recommended in the area

The Eden Project; South West Coast Path; Dartmoor and Bodmin Moor

Primrose Cottage

★★★★★ 🛏 BED & BREAKFAST

Address: Lawhitton, LAUNCESTON, PL15 9PE
Tel: 01566 773645
Email: enquiry@primrosecottagesuites.co.uk
Website: www.primrosecottagesuites.co.uk
Map ref: 1 SX38
Directions: Exit A30 Tavistock, follow A388
through Launceston for Plymouth then B3362,
Tavistock 2.5m
Rooms: 3 en suite (1GF) **S** £70-£90 **D** £80-£130
Notes: ⊗ on premises 🐾 under 12yrs **Parking:** 5

Set in 4 acres of gardens and ancient woodland on the banks of the River Tamar, Primrose Cottage is located between Dartmoor and Bodmin Moor, and within easy reach of both the north and south coasts. The three luxury suites – The Stable, Tamar View and The Garden Room all enjoy beautiful views across the Tamar valley, and all have their own private entrance, sitting room and en suite facilities. Furnished with designer fabrics, antiques and thoughtful extra touches, every luxury is provided. A bottle of chilled white wine will be waiting to welcome you on your arrival. Sip your wine admiring the stunning views from your sitting room or choose one of the secluded corners of the garden. Once settled you can stroll down through the woods to the river to watch the salmon jump or wait quietly for a kingfisher to dive. Each season brings its own delights; the woodland is an untouched natural haven where wildlife lives undisturbed. After a day out exploring this beautiful undiscovered part of the South West return to Primrose Cottage and enjoy afternoon tea in the garden or by the log fire on a colder day.

Recommended in the area

Dartmoor; Tavistock; North Coast

The Eden Project

Redgate Smithy

★★★★ 🛏 BED & BREAKFAST

Address: Redgate, St Cleer, LISKEARD, PL14 6RU
Tel: 01579 321578
Email: enquiries@redgatesmithy.co.uk
Website: www.redgatesmithy.co.uk
Map ref: 1 SX26
Directions: 3m NW of Liskeard. Off A30 at
Bolventor/Jamaica Inn onto St Cleer Rd for 7m, B&B
just past x-rds
Rooms: 3 (2 en suite) (1 pri facs) S £45 D £70
Notes: 🧒 under 12yrs ⊛ **Parking:** 3 **Closed:** Xmas & New Year

Redgate Smithy, situated just above Golitha Falls on the southern edge of rugged Bodmin Moor, was
built around 200 years ago and is great for walkers and less energetic holidaymakers alike. Guests
can relax in the comfortable cottage-style bedrooms, which come with digital TV, hairdryer, local food
guide, and tea and coffee-making facilities. A full breakfast using local produce offers a range of
options, including full Cornish, continental and Redgate Eggs Royale. Garden and patio available.
Recommended in the area
Golitha Falls; The Eden Project; Bodmin Moor and The Cheesewring

Barclay House

★ ★ ★ ★ ◉◉ GUEST ACCOMMODATION

Address: St Martin's Road, LOOE, PL13 1LP
Tel: 01503 262929
Fax: 01503 262632
Email: reception@barclayhouse.co.uk
Website: www.barclayhouse.co.uk
Map ref: 1 SX25
Directions: 1st house on left on entering Looe from A38
Rooms: 11 en suite (1GF) S £75-£120 D £89-£160
Notes: Wi-fi ⊗ on premises **Parking:** 25

High on the hill overlooking the fishing village of Looe, but within walking distance of the town, Barclay House has striking views of the river and the ever-changing countryside beyond. The 11-bedroom Victorian villa, set in six acres of grounds, oozes charm and offers a relaxed atmosphere. Newly enhanced, the smart, contemporary bedrooms provide a refuge from today's hectic pace of life. The award-winning restaurant serves a seasonal menu showcasing the best quality produce including fresh 'day boat' fish landed at Looe. The restaurant's French doors open out to the terrace and gardens where visitors can sample a refreshing glass of local wine whilst perhaps watching a beautiful sunset. Also available are eight luxury self-catering one-, two- and three-bedroom cottages which feature a split-level design to include en suite bathrooms with jacuzzi-style baths, as well as a BBQ area and private balcony. Visitors can also take advantage of the heated outdoor swimming pool set in a natural sun-trap and a fully fitted, state-of-the-art gym with a sauna; there's also the opportunity for an enjoyable walk along one of the woodland paths.

Recommended in the area

Lost Gardens of Heligan; The Eden Project; Historic fishing villages of Looe and Polperro

Bay View Farm

★ ★ ★ ★ 🛏 FARMHOUSE

Address: St Martins, LOOE, PL13 1NZ
Tel/Fax: 01503 265922
Email: mike@looebaycaravans.co.uk
Website: www.looedirectory.co.uk/bay-view-farm.
htm
Map ref: 1 SX25
Directions: 2m NE of Looe. Off B3253 for Monkey
Sanctuary, farm signed
Rooms: 3 en suite (3GF) **S** £35-£40 **D** £60-£65
Notes: ⊗ on premises 🛏 under 5yrs **Parking:** 3

A genuine warm Cornish welcome, an air of tranquillity and great food are the hallmarks of Bay View Farm, which is home to a team of prize-winning shire horses. Mrs Elford is a delightful host and it's easy to see why her guests are drawn back to this special place again and again. The renovated and extended bungalow is situated in a truly spectacular spot with ever-changing views across Looe Bay, and is beautifully decorated and furnished throughout to give a light, spacious feel. The three en suite bedrooms each have their own very individual character – one is huge with comfy sofas and a wonderful view, the others smaller but still very inviting. Two of the rooms also have spacious private conservatories. Guests can relax at the end of the day either in the lounge or on the lovely patio and watch the sun set over Looe. Breakfasts at Bay View Farm are substantial and the evening meals feature home-made desserts accompanied by clotted cream. If you do choose to eat out there are numerous restaurants and pubs nearby. The old town of East Looe is a delight of tall buildings, narrow streets and passageways and the fishing industry brings a maritime bustle to the harbour and quayside. West Looe, the smaller settlement, has a lovely outlook across the harbour to East Looe.

Recommended in the area

Lost Gardens of Heligan; The Eden Project; Looe

The Beach House

★★★★★ 🏠 GUEST ACCOMMODATION
Address: Marine Drive, Hannafore, LOOE, PL13 2DH
Tel: 01503 262598
Fax: 01503 262298
Email: enquiries@thebeachhouselooe.co.uk
Website: www.thebeachhouselooe.co.uk
Map ref: 1 SX25
Directions: From Looe W over bridge, left to
Hannafore & Marine Dr, past Tom Sawyer Tavern
Rooms: 5 en suite (4GF) S £75-£120 D £100-£130
Notes: Wi-fi ⊗ on premises 🧒 under 16yrs Parking: 6

This big, white-painted house is on the seafront at Hannafore, with the South West Coastal Path running past the front gate. Huge windows make the most of the stunning views and create a lovely bright interior. The bedrooms are equally light and many enjoy the sea views; the ground-floor rooms have the use of the garden room. All rooms have quality linens, luxury towels and bathrobes, toiletries and TV. Breakfast is served in the balcony dining room. This is a particularly relaxing place to stay.
Recommended in the area
The Eden Project; Lost Gardens of Heligan; walking the South West Coastal Path to Polperro

Bucklawren Farm

★★★★ FARMHOUSE
Address: St Martin-by-Looe, LOOE, PL13 1NZ
Tel: 01503 240738
Fax: 01503 240481
Email: bucklawren@btopenworld.com
Website: www.bucklawren.co.uk
Map ref: 1 SX25
Directions: 2m NE of Looe. Off B3253 to Monkey
Sanctuary, 0.5m right to Bucklawren, farmhouse
0.5m on left
Rooms: 7 (6 en suite) (1 pri facs) (1GF) S £37.50-£50 D £60-£75 Notes: ⊗ on premises 🧒 under 5yrs Parking: 6 Closed: Nov-Feb

Only half a mile from the coastal path, and a mile from the beach, this spacious 19th-century farmhouse, set in 400 acres, is the perfect place for a holiday. Front-facing rooms have amazing sea and coastal views, and all bedrooms are attractively furnished. The Granary Restaurant, in an adjacent converted barn, is the setting for evening meals prepared from fresh local produce. Jean Henly is a charming hostess.
Recommended in the area
The Eden Project; Lost Gardens of Heligan; fishing villages of Looe & Polperro

Polraen Country House

★★★★ 🏠 ☕ GUEST ACCOMMODATION

Address: Sandplace, LOOE, PL13 1PJ
Tel: 01503 263956
Email: enquiries@polraen.co.uk
Website: www.polraen.co.uk
Map ref: 1 SX25
Directions: 2m N of Looe at junct A387 & B3254
Rooms: 5 en suite D £64-£99
Notes: Wi-fi ⊗ on premises
Parking: 20 **Closed:** 25-27 Dec

At this charming, family-run 18th-century country house 2 miles north of Looe and 5 minutes from the sea, guests can combine bed and breakfast with evening dinner in fully licensed premises. Known for its warm hospitality extended to guests of all ages and delectable home-cooked fare, dinner can be enjoyed in the conservatory overlooking the large garden, or relax in the guest lounge and bar. With a large onsite car park, this delightful peaceful retreat nestling in the Looe Valley is a convenient touring base for Devon and Cornwall. Children welcome.

Recommended in the area

Polperro; Lanhydrock (NT); Lost Gardens of Heligan

Trehaven Manor

★★★★ 🏠 ☕ GUEST ACCOMMODATION

Address: Station Road, LOOE, PL13 1HN
Tel: 01503 262028
Fax: 01503 265613
Email: enquiries@trehavenhotel.co.uk
Website: www.trehavenhotel.co.uk
Map ref: 1 SX25
Directions: In East Looe between railway station & bridge. Trehaven's drive adjacent to The Globe PH
Rooms: 7 en suite (1GF)
Notes: ⊗ on premises **Parking:** 8

Neil and Ella Hipkiss, the enthusiastic owners of Trehaven Manor, are committed to providing the best service. Bedrooms provide a high level of comfort and style, with quality furnishings and thoughtful extras such as clocks and hairdryers; most overlook the estuary. Guests are welcomed on arrival with home-made scones and local clotted cream in the lounge. Fresh local produce again features at breakfast. Evening meals are available on request, or Neil and Ella can recommend local restaurants.

Recommended in the area

Polperro; Looe town and beach; St Mellion Golf Course

Tintagel

Colvennor Farmhouse

★★★★ BED & BREAKFAST

Address: Cury, Nr Mullion, HELSTON, TR12 7BJ
Tel: 01326 241208
Email: colvennor@aol.com
Website: www.colvennorfarmhouse.com
Map ref: 1 SW61
Directions: A3083 (Helston-Lizard), over rdbt at end
of airfield, next right to Cury/Poldhu Cove, farm 1.4m
on right at top of hill
Rooms: 3 en suite (1GF) S £40-£45 D £60-£70
Notes: Wi-fi ⊗ on premises ⏵ under 10yrs Parking: 4 Closed: Dec & Jan

This lovingly restored Grade II listed building, dating from the 17th century, is set in an acre of attractive gardens surrounded by open countryside, with glimpses of the sea at Poldhu Cove. Friendly proprietors provide a range of maps and books to help guests plan their days and are happy to give advice. The beamed lounge with a granite fireplace offers the perfect setting for guests to relax at any time. The delightful cottage-style bedrooms are individually furnished with guests' comfort in mind.
Recommended in the area
Kynance Cove; Trevarno; St Ives

The Old Mill House

★★★★ ⌂ GUEST HOUSE

Address: Little Petherick, PADSTOW, PL27 7QT
Tel: 01841 540388
Fax: 01841 540406
Email: enquiries@theoldmillhouse.com
Website: www.theoldmillhouse.com
Map ref: 1 SW97
Directions: 2m S of Padstow. In centre of Little Petherick
on A389
Rooms: 7 en suite S £80-£120 D £80-£120 Notes: ⊗ on
premises ⏵ under 14yrs Parking: 20 Closed: Dec-Feb

You are assured of a warm welcome in this licensed Grade II listed mill house just two miles from the popular village of Padstow. The idyllic converted corn mill and millhouse is next to a pretty stream with ducks and a pair of swans – you may even spot a kingfisher. The seven comfortable bedrooms are individually decorated, well equipped and all have good views. An extensive breakfast menu is served in the original mill room.
Recommended in the area
The Eden Project; Lost Gardens of Heligan; Camel Trail Cycle Path

Camilla House

★★★★★ ⌂ GUEST HOUSE

Address: 12 Regent Terrace,
PENZANCE, TR18 4DW
Tel/Fax: 01736 363771
Email: enquiries@camillahouse.co.uk
Website: www.camillahouse.co.uk
Map ref: 1 SW43
Directions: A30 to Penzance, at rail station follow
road along harbour front onto Promenade Rd. Opp
Jubilee Bathing Pool, Regent Ter 2nd right
Rooms: 8 (7 en suite) (1 pri facs) (1GF) **S** £35-£37.50 **D** £75-£85
Notes: Wi-fi ⊗ on premises **Parking:** 6

The friendly proprietors of this attractive Grade II listed terrace house do their utmost to ensure a comfortable stay. On arrival, guests are served with tea and coffee with 'Thunder and Lightning', a real Cornish treat. Bedrooms and bathrooms are attractively furnished, providing many added extras, such as fluffy towels and bathrobes, refreshment trays with Fairtrade products and Cornish mineral water, flat-screen Freeview TV/DVD, hairdryer, magazines and sweets. Some bedrooms and the dining room also provide delightful sea views over Mount's Bay. Wireless internet connection is available throughout, and there is also access to computers in the stylish, high-ceilinged lounge, which stocks a library of DVDs as well as Cornish Monopoly. A range of breakfast options is on offer in the dining room (home to a well-stocked residents' bar), using home-made or fresh local produce; options include Cornish cheese platters. Evening meals are available by prior arrangement. Camilla House has been registered and inspected by the Green Tourism Business Scheme award since 2006 and is committed to operating in an environmentally responsible fashion.

Recommended in the area

Land's End; Lizard Peninsula; South West Coastal Path

Chy-an-Mor

★★★★ GUEST ACCOMMODATION

Address: 15 Regent Terrace, PENZANCE, TR18 4DW
Tel: 01736 363441
Email: reception@chyanmor.co.uk
Website: www.chyanmor.co.uk
Map ref: 1 SW43
Directions: A30 to Penzance, at rail station, follow along harbour front onto Promenade Rd. Pass Jubilee Pool, right at Stanley Guest House
Rooms: 9 en suite **S** £40-£42 **D** £74-£88
Notes: Wi-fi ⊗ on premises 🚶 under 14yrs **Parking:** 15

This elegant Grade II listed Regency house has an attractive sea-facing location, overlooking Mount's Bay and the promenade. Chy-an-Mor – the name is Cornish for 'house of sea' – has been refurbished to provide high standards throughout. The impressive entrance leads to spacious, high-ceilinged public rooms, and residents can linger over the changing sea views in the stylish lounge with its comfortable sofas and range of board games. Guests are also welcome to soak up the sun in the pretty south-facing garden, which features benches and a patio area, lit up by fairy lights at night. Inside, each of the en suite bedrooms is individually designed and equipped with thoughtful extras, such as flat-screen digital TVs, Fairtrade tea, coffee and hot chocolate, organic cotton wool and shoe-polishing kits, and many of the rooms enjoy spectacular views. Satisfying breakfasts are served in the large, bright dining room, including vegetarian options and home-made preserves and muffins, all served on tables dressed with crisp white tablecloths and linen napkins. Ample off-street parking is available. A range of in-house beauty treatments is also a draw.

Recommended in the area

St Michael's Mount (NT); The Minnack Theatre; Land's End

The Summer House

★★★★★ 🏨 🍽 GUEST ACCOMMODATION

Address: Cornwall Terrace, PENZANCE, TR18 4HL
Tel: 01736 363744
Fax: 01736 360959
Email: reception@summerhouse-cornwall.com
Website: www.summerhouse-cornwall.com
Map ref: 1 SW43
Directions: A30 to Penzance, at rail station follow along harbour onto Promenade Rd, pass Jubilee Pool, right after Queens Hotel. Summer House 30yds on left
Rooms: 5 en suite S £105-£150 D £120-£150 **Notes:** Wi-fi ⊗ on premises 🚼 under 13yrs **Parking:** 6 **Closed:** Nov-Mar

The philosophy of The Summer House is to combine great food and beautiful surroundings with a happy, informal atmosphere, making it the perfect seaside retreat. Close to the seafront and harbour, this stylishly converted, stunning Grade II listed Regency house features bold decor, polished wood, bright colours, and a curving glass-walled tower that fills the building with light. Fresh flowers are among the thoughtful extras provided in the spacious twin and double en suite bedrooms, which are light, airy and individually decorated, and enhanced by interesting family pieces and collectables, as well as a range of home comforts to help you relax, such as TV, radio, DVD player, hairdryer, books and magazines. Fresh local food and regional produce is simply prepared to provide memorable dining from a weekly changing menu, with dishes distinctly Mediterranean in feel, and good wines on hand to accompany them. The rich Cornish puddings are especially hard to resist. The restaurant opens out onto a walled garden with terracotta pots, sub-tropical planting and attractive blue tables and chairs, where in warmer weather evening drinks and dinner may be enjoyed.

Recommended in the area

St Michael's Mount (NT); Land's End; The Minack Theatre

Ednovean Farm

★ ★ ★ ★ ★ 🏠 FARMHOUSE
Address: PERRANUTHNOE, TR20 9LZ
Tel: 01736 711883
Email: info@ednoveanfarm.co.uk
Website: www.ednoveanfarm.co.uk
Map ref: 1 SW52
Directions: Off A394 towards Perranuthnoe at
Dynasty Restaurant, farm drive on left on bend by
post box
Rooms: 3 en suite (3GF) S £90-£105 D £90-£105

Notes: Wi-fi ⊗ on premises 🚭 under 16yrs Parking: 4 Closed: 24-28 Dec & New Year

Spectacular sea views over St Michael's Mount and Mount's Bay are a delightful feature of this converted 17th-century farmhouse which stands high above the village in beautiful grounds. The stylish bedrooms are furnished with comfortable beds and quality pieces, chintz fabrics, and thoughtful extras like flowers, magazines and fruit. Guests can relax in the elegant sitting room, the garden room and on several sunny patios. The coastal footpath and the beach and pub are just three minutes away.

Recommended in the area

St Michael's Mount (NT); Godolphin House; Penlee House Gallery (Newlyn School paintings)

Penryn House

★ ★ ★ GUEST ACCOMMODATION
Address: The Coombes, POLPERRO, PL13 2RQ
Tel: 01503 272157
Fax: 01503 273055
Email: enquiries@penrynhouse.co.uk
Website: www.penrynhouse.co.uk
Map ref: 1 SX25
Directions: A387 to Polperro, at mini-rdbt left
down hill into village (ignore restricted access).
200yds on left

Rooms: 12 en suite S £40-£45 D £70-£100 Notes: Wi-fi Parking: 13

Situated in tranquil surroundings close to the lovely fishing village of Polperro and with easy access to the coastal paths, Penryn House prides itself on having a relaxed and friendly atmosphere. Guests here will be among the few allowed to drive into the village, which has restricted access. Inside, the en suite bedrooms are neatly presented and reflect the character of the building. After a day exploring the area, residents can enjoy a drink at the bar or just relax in the comfortable lounge.

Recommended in the area

The Eden Project; Bodmin Moor; Cotehele medieval house (NT)

Trenake Manor Farm

★ ★ ★ ★ FARMHOUSE

Address: Pelynt, POLPERRO, PL13 2LT
Tel/Fax: 01503 220835
Email: lorraine@cornishfarmhouse.co.uk
Website: www.cornishfarmhouse.co.uk
Map ref: 1 SX25
Directions: 3.5m N of Polperro. A390 onto B3359 for Looe, 5m left at small x-rds
Rooms: 3 en suite D £72-76
Notes: Wi-fi Parking: 10

Situated midway between the historic fishing ports of Looe and Polperro, this welcoming 15th-century farmhouse is surrounded by 300 acres of its own farmland. It has been owned by the same family for five generations and makes a good base for touring Cornwall. En suite bedrooms, including one family room, are spacious and boast elegant Victorian king-sized bedsteads and a number of thoughtful finishing touches. Breakfast is made from local produce and served in the cosy dining room. Guests are welcome to relax on the sunloungers provided in the large, well-kept garden.

Recommended in the area

The Eden Project; Lost Gardens of Heligan; Polperro

The Coach House

★ ★ ★ ★ GUEST ACCOMMODATION

Address: Kuggar, RUAN MINOR, Helston, TR12 7LY
Tel: 01326 291044
Email: mjanmakin@aol.com
Website: www.the-coach-house.net
Map ref: 1 SW71
Directions: 1m N of Ruan Minor in Kuggar
Rooms: 5 en suite (2GF) D £70
Notes: Wi-fi ⊗ on premises ☻ Parking: 10
Closed: Xmas

This 17th-century house, close to Kennack Sands and Goonhilly Downs nature reserve, retains many interesting original features. Its location makes it an ideal base for hikers. The friendly proprietors look after their guests well, and they can relax in the spacious lounge-dining room where a fire burns in colder months and which boasts low beamed ceilings and an inglenook fireplace and old bread oven. The en suite bedrooms, two of which are in a converted stable block, are attractively decorated and offer extras such as hairdryer, tea and coffee-making facilities and Sky television.

Recommended in the area

Lizard Peninsula; The Earth Satellite Station; Flambards Theme Park

Tintagel

Hunter's Moon

★★★★ GUEST HOUSE

Address: Chapel Hill, Polgooth,
ST AUSTELL, PL26 7BU
Tel/Fax: 01726 66445
Email: enquiries@huntersmooncornwall.co.uk
Website: www.huntersmooncornwall.co.uk
Map ref: 1 SX05
Directions: 1.5m SW of town centre. Off B3273 into
Polgooth, pass village shop on left, 1st right
Rooms: 4 en suite S £50-£52 D £70-£74
Notes: ⊗ on premises ⅙ under 14yrs ⊛ **Parking:** 5

A friendly welcome awaits at Hunter's Moon – the perfect location for a peaceful holiday. The en suite guest rooms are decorated and furnished to a high standard, and two rooms have super king-sized beds which can be converted into twin beds. There is plenty of space to sit and enjoy the garden and the countryside views, and with its central location this is an ideal touring base for the whole of Cornwall. The Polgooth Inn is just five minutes' walk away and there are many restaurants nearby.

Recommended in the area

The Eden Project; Lost Gardens of Heligan; Charlestown Harbour

Lower Barn

★★★★★ GUEST ACCOMMODATION

Address: Bosue, St Ewe, ST AUSTELL, PL26 6ET
Tel: 01726 844881
Email: janie@bosue.co.uk
Website: www.bosue.co.uk
Map ref: 1 SX05
Directions: 3.5m SW of St Austell. Off B3273 at
x-rds signed Lost Gardens of Heligan, Lower Barn
signed 1m on right
Rooms: 3 en suite (1GF)
Notes: ⊗ on premises **Parking:** 7 **Closed:** Jan

Tucked away down a meandering country lane yet with easy access to local attractions, this converted barn has huge appeal. The warm colours and decoration create a Mediterranean feel that is complemented by informal and genuine hospitality from proprietors Mike and Janie Cooksley. It is the attention to detail that places Lower Barn a cut above the rest. The three en suite bedrooms are equipped with a host of extras from daily fresh towels and fridges to tea and coffee-making facilities. Breakfast is chosen from an extensive menu and served round a large table or on the patio deck overlooking the garden, which also has a luxurious hot tub. You can even collect your own free-range eggs for breakfast. A candlelit dinner, available most nights of the week, is served in the conservatory or on the terrace – and you can bring your own wine. After exploring the many attractions the area has to offer, including Mevagissey, where a bustling harbour shelters a fishing fleet and the narrow streets are lined with colour-washed old houses, galleries and gift shops, you can unwind with some gorgeous massage and therapy treatments to make your experience at Lower Barn even more memorable.

Recommended in the area

The Eden Project; Lost Gardens of Heligan; Mevagissey; cliff walks; Roseland Peninsula

Penarwyn House

★ ★ ★ ★ ★ 🏛 GUEST ACCOMMODATION

Address: ST BLAZEY, Par, PL24 2DS
Tel/Fax: 01726 814224
Email: stay@penarwyn.co.uk
Website: www.penarwyn.co.uk
Map ref: 1 SX05
Directions: A390 W through St Blazey, left before
2nd speed camera into Doubletrees School,
Penarwyn straight ahead
Rooms: 4 en suite S £55-£75 D £110-£150
Notes: Wi-fi ⊗ on premises 🐕 under 10yrs Parking: 6

True Cornish hospitality and memorable breakfasts complement this spacious Victorian residence which is set in tranquil surroundings, yet close to main routes. The owners Mike and Jan Russell – who have many years' experience successfully running bed and breakfast establishments – have painstakingly restored the house to its original glory. Many of the old features have been faithfully restored alongside luxury en suites, which include a bath by candlelight for romantics. The bedrooms are most impressive – spacious, delightfully appointed and equipped with a host of extras including tea and coffee facilities, hairdryer, flat-screen TV and DVD/CD player. Treffry is a king-size double room, looking out over the front garden, with a large corner bath. Prideaux, the largest room, has large comfy chairs and an en suite with a slipper bath and a separate shower. The De Cressy suite comprises a lounge with two sofas, fridge and desk plus a large bedroom (with adaptable twin or super king-sized bed), a chaise longue and an art deco style bathroom with separate bath and shower. There is a panelled snooker room with a 3/4 size snooker table and Wi-fi access is available.

Recommended in the area
The Eden Project; Lanhydrock (NT); Lost Gardens of Heligan

St Michael's Mount

Edgar's

★★★★ GUEST ACCOMMODATION

Address: Chy-an-Creet, Higher Stennack,
ST IVES, TR26 2HA
Tel/Fax: 01736 796559
Email: stay@edgarshotel.co.uk
Website: www.edgarshotel.co.uk
Map ref: 1 SW54
Directions: 0.5m W of town centre on B3306,
opp Leach Pottery
Rooms: 8 en suite (4GF) S £45-£75 D £59-£105
Notes: Wi-fi ⊗ on premises Parking: 8 Closed: Nov-Feb

Tucked away, surrounded by a border of palms, trees and shrubs and with on-site parking, Edgar's offers an excellent base for exploring picturesque St Ives and farther afield. The well equipped en suite guest rooms are complemented by a spacious breakfast room and comfortable lounge with soft drinks honesty bar. Freshly cooked breakfast includes vegetarian options and fine locally sourced ingredients.
Recommended in the area
Leach Pottery; Penlee House Gallery; Tate St Ives

Giant's Head, The Lost Gardens of Heligan

The Old Count House

★★★★ GUEST HOUSE

Address: 1 Trenwith Square, ST IVES, TR26 1DQ
Tel: 01736 795369
Fax: 01736 799109
Email: counthouse@btconnect.com
Website: www.theoldcounthouse-stives.co.uk
Map ref: 1 SW54
Directions: Follow signs to St Ives, house between leisure centre & school
Rooms: 10 en suite (2GF) S £38-£45 D £72-£90
Notes: ⊗ on premises ⊮ **Parking:** 8 **Closed:** 20-29 Dec

Built in 1825, this granite stone house is situated in a quiet residential area with private parking, yet is just a five-minute walk from town, with its many restaurants. Bedrooms here vary in size and all are comfortably furnished and most enjoy magnificent views over the harbour and bay. One luxurious room has a four-poster bed and whirlpool-style bath. Breakfast offers extensive choices made from fresh local produce, including kippers. Guests are welcome to relax in the conservatory, garden and sauna.

Recommended in the area

Tate St Ives; Porthmeor Beach; St Ives town

The Regent

★★★★ GUEST ACCOMMODATION

Address: Fernlea Terrace, ST IVES, TR26 2BH
Tel: 01736 796195
Fax: 01736 794641
Email: keith@regenthotel.com
Website: www.regenthotel.com
Map ref: 1 SW54
Directions: In town centre, near bus & railway station
Rooms: 10 (8 en suite) **S** £35-£48 **D** £73-£98
Notes: Wi-fi ⊗ on premises 🚸 under 16yrs
Parking: 12

The Regent was established 78 years ago when a local architect purchased Penwyn House from a retired sea captain and converted it to provide an interest for his wife and daughter. In 1972 the late Mr and Mrs SH Varnals bought the property and in due course passed it on to Keith and Sandi Varnals the present proprietors. Sandi, a former lingerie designer, has worked her magic on the interior of the old building, while Keith, an engineer turned chef, has modernised the facilities to appeal to today's modern traveller. Bedrooms are well equipped with colour TV, radio alarm clocks and tea and coffee-making facilities. Eight rooms have facilities en suite, and most benefit from spectacular sea views. The breakfast menu offers a good choice of hot dishes, cooked to order, and an extensive buffet of cereals, yoghurts, pastries, fruit and juice. The oak-smoked fish and bacon is sourced locally. Also on offer are espresso, cappuccino, cafetière coffee, hot chocolate and a choice of teas. There is a lounge and bar for evening relaxation, and parking is provided for all rooms. If you prefer not to drive, the hotel is situated close to the local bus, coach and rail stations. The Regent is ideally located to explore the local area, being just a short stroll from the narrow cobbled streets and harbour in St Ives.

Recommended in the area

South West Coast Path; Tate St Ives; Penzance on Cornwall's south coast

The Rookery

★★★★ GUEST ACCOMMODATION

Address: 8 The Terrace, ST IVES, TR26 2BL
Tel: 01736 799401
Email: therookerystives@hotmail.com
Website: www.rookerystives.com
Map ref: 1 SW54
Directions: A3074 through Carbis Bay,
right fork at Porthminster Hotel, The Rookery
500yds on left
Rooms: 7 en suite (1GF) S £35-£45 D £60-£90
Notes: Wi-fi ⊗ on premises ⋆❢ under 7yrs Parking: 7

Ron and Barbara Rook's friendly establishment stands on an elevated position overlooking the harbour, sandy beaches and St Ives Bay, near the town's train and bus stations, and only a short walk to the town's shops, galleries and restaurants. The rooms are attractively decorated, and are well equipped with considerate extras such as a chiller to keep soft drinks and wines cool. A choice of full English, continental or vegetarian breakfast is served in the dining room.

Recommended in the area

Tate St Ives; Barbara Hepworth Museum; The Minack Theatre

Treliska

★★★★ ≙ GUEST ACCOMMODATION

Address: 3 Bedford Road, ST IVES, TR26 1SP
Tel/Fax: 01736 797678
Email: info@treliska.com
Website: www.treliska.com
Map ref: 1 SW54
Directions: A3074 to St Ives, fork at Porthminster
Hotel into town, at T-junct facing Barclays Bank left
onto Bedford Rd, house on right
Rooms: 5 en suite S £40-£60 D £70-£80
Notes: Wi-fi ⊗ on premises ⋆❢ under 10yrs ▦

This stylish, friendly and relaxed home boasts a great location, close to the seafront, High Street, restaurants and galleries. There is a refreshing approach here and a contemporary feel throughout. Bedrooms, featuring impressive bathrooms with power showers, are designed to maximise comfort, with Egyptian cotton bedding and CD player provided as standard. Enjoyable, freshly cooked breakfasts include organic home-made breads and muesli. Additional facilities include free internet and Wi-fi.

Recommended in the area

Barbara Hepworth Museum; Bernard Leach Pottery; Paradise Park Wildlife Sanctuary, Hayle

The Woodside

★★★★ GUEST ACCOMMODATION

Address: The Belyars, ST IVES, TR26 2DA
Tel: 01736 795681
Email: woodsidehotel@btconnect.com
Website: www.woodside-hotel.co.uk
Map ref: 1 SW54
Directions: A3074 to St Ives, left at Porthminster Hotel onto Talland Rd, 1st left onto Belyars Ln, Woodside 4th on right
Rooms: 10 en suite S £40-£55 D £80-£120
Notes: ⊗ on premises ⱞ under 5yrs **Parking:** 12

Suzanne and Chris Taylor are welcoming hosts who diligently attend to their beautiful property. They promise personal attention, ensuring an enjoyable holiday here. Woodside stands in peaceful grounds above St Ives Bay, with fantastic views from most bedrooms and all of the public rooms. Just a 5-minute walk away are lovely stretches of golden beaches for bathing and surfing, the picturesque harbour with its traditional fishing fleet, and the narrow cobbled streets lined with artists' studios, galleries and craft shops. The comfortable, spacious en suite bedrooms range from single, double and twin to family rooms, and all are well equipped with colour TV, a radio-alarm clock, hairdryer and a hospitality tray. Guests can relax in the comfortable lounge with a TV and games area, enjoy a drink at the bar, or relish the sea views from the attractive gardens or terrace. A heated outdoor swimming pool is open from June to August. Breakfast is another delight, you'll find a hearty choice of full English, continental or vegetarian dishes prepared from fresh local produce where possible. A short-hole golf course and a leisure centre with a superb gym and indoor pool are both within a short distance of Woodside.

Recommended in the area

Tate St Ives; Land's End; The Eden Project

New Inn

★★★★ ⊛ INN

Address: TRESCO, Isles of Scilly, TR24 0QQ
Tel: 01720 422844 & 423006
Fax: 01720 423200
Email: newinn@tresco.co.uk
Website: www.tresco.co.uk
Map ref: 1 SV81
Directions: By New Grimsby Quay
Rooms: 16 (15 en suite) (2GF) S £70-£172
D £140-£230
Notes: Wi-fi ⊗ on premises

Located by the sea, the popular and lively New Inn makes a great base from which to enjoy the diverse local flora and fauna. It is for many the social hub of the island. Inside the inn offers a range of bright, comfortably furnished and well-equipped en suite bedrooms, many with splendid sea views and two of which are on the ground floor. Diners will find a well thought out menu that offers modern and more traditional British dishes at lunch and dinner, including daily specials and afternoon snacks. Quality local ingredients are selected - Tresco reared beef and seafood in particular. There is a choice where to take meals – in the bistro-style Pavilion or the popular bar with its fine collection of nautical memorabilia, which serves a good selection of real ales and often has live music. In fine weather, dining alfresco is always an option. There is also a lounge area where guests can retire to enjoy some peace and quiet. A heated outdoor pool is another draw to the establishment, as are the outdoor boules area and a range of special winter breaks and real ale and cider festivals.

Recommended in the area

The Isles of Scilly; Tresco Abbey Gardens; seal and birdwatching boat trips

CUMBRIA

Aira Force, Ullswater

Kent House

★★★★ GUEST HOUSE

Address: Lake Road, AMBLESIDE, LA22 0AD
Tel: 015394 33279
Email: mail@kent-house.com
Website: www.kent-house.com
Map ref: 5 NY30
Directions: From town centre, pass Post Office on one-way system 300mtrs on left on terrace above main road
Rooms: 5 (4 en suite) (1 pri facs) S £42-£55 D £68-£110
Parking: 3

Kent House, an elegant Victorian guest house, been welcoming guests from all over the world since the mid-1800s. Sandra and Simon continue this tradition, offering spacious, stylishly furnished accommodation combining many original features with the convenience of complimentary Wi-fi access and flat-screen LCD TVs in all bedrooms. Breakfast is prepared to order using fresh locally produced fare. Located in the centre of Ambleside, this establishment is ideally situated for restaurants, hostelries and the cinema.

Recommended in the area

Lake Windermere; Dove Cottage & The Wordsworth Museum; Hill Top (Beatrix Potter's home) (NT)

Wanslea Guest House

★★★★ GUEST HOUSE

Address: Low Fold, Lake Road,
AMBLESIDE, LA22 0DN
Tel/Fax: 015394 33884
Email: information@wanslea.co.uk
Website: www.wanslea.co.uk
Map ref: 5 NY30
Directions: On S side of town, opp garden centre
Rooms: 8 en suite S £35-£50 D £50-£90
Notes: Wi-fi ⊗ 🐾 under 6yrs Closed: 23-26 Dec

Located at the foot of Wansfell, on the quieter south side of Ambleside village, this Victorian house is an ideal base for exploring the Lake District. Guests can relax in the comfortable bedrooms, some of which are individually themed, such as the Arabian Nights Room with its canopied bed and starry ceiling or the Rock and Roll Room, with a retro feel. Rooms are well equipped with colour TV, hairdryer and tea- and coffee-making facilities; and the themed rooms have spa baths and widescreen TV. Comprehensive breakfasts are served in the spacious dining room, and there's a cosy lounge.

Recommended in the area

Hill Top (Beatrix Potter's home) (NT); Lakeside Railway; Dove Cottage & The Wordsworth Museum

Hall Croft

★ ★ ★ ★ 🛏 BED & BREAKFAST

Address: Dufton, APPLEBY-IN-WESTMORLAND,
CA16 6DB
Tel: 017683 52902
Email: r.walker@leaseholdpartnerships.co.uk
Map ref: 6 NY62
Directions: 3m N of Appleby. In Dufton by village
green **Rooms:** 3 (2 en suite) (1 pri facs) **S** fr £35
D fr £60 **Notes:** 🐾 **Parking:** 3 **Closed:** 24-26 Dec

A large Victorian villa situated on the green in the tranquil village of Dufton at the foot of the Pennines with spectacular views in all directions. Owners Frei and Ray Walker extend a warm welcome and do everything to make your stay memorable. Rooms offer high quality facilities with a range of little extras for additional comfort. Substantial cooked breakfasts, including a varied range of home-made produce, are served in the period lounge/dining room; afternoon tea and cakes and packed lunches are also available. Guests can relax in the large gardens and explore the wide network of paths and walks that start from the village.

Recommended in the area

North Pennines (Area of Outstanding Natural Beauty); Northern Lake District; Appleby-in-Westmorland

Number 43

★ ★ ★ ★ ★ 🛏 GUEST ACCOMMODATION

Address: The Promenade, ARNSIDE, LA5 0AA
Tel: 01524 762761
Fax: 01524 761455
Email: lesley@no43.org.uk
Website: www.no43.org.uk
Map ref: 6 SD47
Rooms: 6 en suite **D** £110-£180
Notes: ⊗ on premises

Set in a Victorian townhouse on the promenade at the coastal village of Arnside, the second smallest area of Outstanding Natural Beauty in the country, Number 43 enjoys expansive views across the Kent estuary towards the Lakeland Fells. It has recently been professionally renovated to a high standard, and now offers elegance and comfort throughout. Guests can expect luxurious surroundings and enjoy excellent guest care from Lesley Hornsby and her team during their stay. All suites and superior rooms are contemporary styled. Enjoy award-winning breakfasts and later unwind with a glass of organic wine on the terrace and watch the herons feeding, dramatic sunsets and the Arnside Bore wave.

Recommended in the area

Blackwell, The Arts & Crafts House; Holker Hall; Morecambe Bay

The Wheatsheaf

★ ★ ★ ★ ⊛ INN
Address: BRIGSTEER, Kendal, LA8 8AN
Tel: 015395 68254
Email: wheatsheaf@brigsteer.gb.com
Website: www.thewheatsheafbrigsteer.co.uk
Map ref: 6 SD48
Directions: Off A591 signed Brigsteer, Wheatsheaf
at bottom of hill Rooms: 3 en suite Notes: ⊗ on
premises Parking: 25

The Wheatsheaf, which dates back to 1762, lies in the peaceful hamlet of Brigsteer, to the west of Kendal, just off the A591. Once three cottages and a shoeing room for horses, today it provides good food in the gastro-style pub, and attractive, well-equipped en suite bedrooms, all of which have been refurbished to offer modern comforts. The bar itself is cosy and well stocked, while the spacious, contemporary dining room, with its polished oak and stone floors, delights diners with locally sourced home-cooked fare eaten at hand-crafted oak tables. Specialities include game and fresh fish; a bar menu is also available.

Recommended in the area

Sizergh Castle (NT); Kendal; Scout Scar

Swaledale Watch Farm

★ ★ ★ ★ GUEST ACCOMMODATION
Address: Whelpo, CALDBECK, CA7 8HQ
Tel/Fax: 016974 78409
Email: nan.savage@talk21.com
Website: www.swaledale-watch.co.uk
Map ref: 5 NY34
Directions: 1m SW of Caldbeck on B5299
Rooms: 4 en suite (4GF) S £25-£33 D £50-£56
Parking: 8 Closed: 24-26 Dec

This busy farm is set in idyllic surroundings, with views of the fells and mountains. Just a mile away is the village of Caldbeck, once renowned for its milling and mining, or take a walk through The Howk, a beautiful wooded limestone gorge with waterfalls. Nan and Arnold Savage work hard to make their hospitality seem effortless and to put you at ease. The lounges have TVs, books and games while the bedrooms have bath and shower en suite. Two bedrooms and a lounge are in the converted cowshed, ideal for a group of four. Nan's hearty Cumbrian breakfasts are delicious.

Recommended in the area

Northern Fells; Howk Walk to Caldbeck village; quality village shops and cafés

Crosthwaite House

★★★★ GUEST HOUSE
Address: CROSTHWAITE, Kendal, LA8 8BP
Tel/Fax: 015395 68264
Email: bookings@crosthwaitehouse.co.uk
Website: www.crosthwaitehouse.co.uk
Map ref: 6 SD49
Directions: A590 onto A5074, 4m right to Crosthwaite, 0.5m turn left
Rooms: 6 en suite S £28-£33 D £56-£66
Parking: 8 **Closed:** mid Nov-Mar

A sturdy mid 18th-century house, this establishment is in the village of Crosthwaite, at the northern end of the Lyth Valley, famous for its damson orchards. You can see across the valley from the lounge, and from the dining room where guests can enjoy Aga-cooked breakfasts prepared from local ingredients. The spacious en suite bedrooms offer many thoughtful extras, plus tea and coffee facilities. The owners create a relaxed atmosphere in which it is easy to feel at home.

Recommended in the area

Lake Windermere; Sizergh Castle and Garden (NT); three golf courses within four miles

Moss Grove Organic

★★★★★ 🛏 GUEST ACCOMMODATION
Address: GRASMERE, Ambleside, LA22 9SW
Tel: 015394 35251
Fax: 015394 35306
Email: enquiries@mossgrove.com
Website: www.mossgrove.com
Map ref: 5 NY30
Directions: From S, M6 junct 36 onto A591 signed Keswick, from N M6 junct 40 onto A591 signed Windermere **Rooms:** 11 en suite (2GF) S £125-£250

D £125-£250 **Notes:** Wi-fi 🐾 under 14yrs **Parking:** 11 **Closed:** 24-25 Dec

Located in the centre of Grasmere, this impressive Victorian house has been refurbished using as many natural products as possible, with ongoing dedication to causing minimal environmental impact. The bedrooms are decorated with beautiful wallpaper and natural clay paints, and feature hand-made beds and furnishings. Home entertainment systems, flat-screen TVs and luxury bathrooms add further comfort. Extensive organic Mediterranean breakfasts are taken at the large dining table in the guest lounge.

Recommended in the area

Grasmere Lake; Rydal Water; Dove Cottage & The Wordsworth Museum

Dalegarth House

★★★★ ⊜ GUEST ACCOMMODATION

Address: Portinscale, KESWICK, CA12 5RQ

Tel: 017687 72817

Email: allerdalechef@aol.com

Website: www.dalegarth-house.co.uk

Map ref: 5 NY22

Directions: Off A66 to Portinscale, pass Farmers Arms, 100yds on left

Rooms: 10 en suite (2GF) S £40-£45 D £84-£100

Notes: ⊗ on premises ⛄ under 12yrs

Parking: 14 Closed: Dec-1 Mar

The views from this spacious Edwardian house, in the village of Portinscale, just south of Keswick, are nothing short of stunning. It sits on high ground, with a panoramic vista that takes in Derwent Water (just 400 metres from the door), Skiddaw, Catbells and the expanse of the fells of the northern Lakeland. It would be hard to find a better location for a walking holiday, and the full meal service here is a real bonus for hungry hikers. A full English breakfast starts the day, packed lunches are available on request and guests can return to a daily-changing four-course dinner, prepared by the resident chef-proprietors Pauline and Bruce Jackson. Traditional and contemporary dishes feature, many of which have a regional emphasis, and there's an extensive wine list. Afterwards, guests can stroll in the gardens or relax in the comfortable lounge. The bedrooms at Dalegarth vary, with double, twin, family and single rooms all available. Each has an en suite bathroom, TV radio and tea- and coffee-making facilities. Special rates are available for guests staying on a dinner, bed and breakfast basis. The Jacksons have also embued the house with a charming family atmosphere while providing the most professional of standards.

Recommended in the area

Cars of the Stars, Keswick; Theatre by the Lake, Keswick; Mirehouse

The Grange Country Guest House

★★★★★ GUEST HOUSE

Address: Manor Brow, Ambleside Road,
KESWICK, CA12 4BA
Tel: 017687 72500
Fax: 0707 500 4885
Email: info@grangekeswick.com
Website: www.grangekeswick.com
Map ref: 5 NY22
Directions: M6 junct 40, A66 15m. A591 for 1m,
turn right onto Manor Brow
Rooms: 10 en suite (1GF) **S** £72-£85 **D** £90-£108
Notes: Wi-fi ⊗ on premises ⭧ under 10yrs **Parking:** 10
Closed: Jan

A stylish Victorian residence, this house stands in beautiful gardens on the outskirts of the lovely market town of Keswick. Here you will be assured of a warm welcome from Mark and Sally and their team. The location with its wonderful views, together with the quality of the facilities and the hospitality attracts many returning guests. The bedrooms are spacious and beautifully decorated, each featuring quality bedding and digital, flat-screen TVs, plus complimentary Fairtrade beverage trays, mineral water and super toiletries. Superb, freshly prepared Cumbrian breakfasts are offered along with free Wi-fi, a comfortable lounge, and an outdoor terrace where a nice cold beer or a glass of wine might be enjoyed while watching the sun set behind the fells. Alternatively, guests could settle in the lovely lounge to read or play chess and backgammon. This is the place for a relaxing break in good company - a chance to do lots of walking and sightseeing during the day and to absorb the lovely atmosphere in Keswick in the evenings.

Recommended in the area

Dove Cottage; Theatre by the Lake; Castlerigg Stone Circle

Sunnyside Guest House

★★★★ GUEST HOUSE

Address: 25 Southey Street, KESWICK, CA12 4EF
Tel: 017687 72446
Email: enquiries@sunnysideguesthouse.com
Website: www.sunnysideguesthouse.com
Map ref: 5 NY22
Directions: 200yds E of town centre. Off A5271
Penrith Rd onto Southey St, Sunnyside on left
Rooms: 7 en suite D £62-£78
Notes: ⊗ on premises ⚑ under 12yrs **Parking:** 8

Sunnyside is a stylish Victorian house set in a quiet area close to the town centre. Bedrooms, including a triple room, have all been appointed to a high standard and are equipped with refreshment-making facilities, hairdryer and flat-screen TV. There is a spacious lounge with plenty of books, magazines and board games. A hearty breakfast is served at individual tables in the attractive dining room. Fresh Cumbrian produce provides plenty of variety, including vegetarian options. For special occasions, you can arrange to have chocolates, flowers or champagne in your room on arrival.

Recommended in the area

Derwentwater; Borrowdale; Keswick's Theatre by the Lake

Ees Wyke Country House

★★★★★ ◉ 🍴 GUEST HOUSE

Address: NEAR SAWREY, Ambleside, LA22 0JZ
Tel: 015394 36393
Email: mail@eeswyke.co.uk
Website: www.eeswyke.co.uk
Map ref: 5 SD39
Directions: On B5285 on W side of Hawkshead
Rooms: 8 en suite (1GF) S £50-£82 D £100-£132
Notes: ⊗ on premises ⚑ under 12yrs **Parking:** 12

Visitors to this elegant Georgian country house can enjoy the same views over Esthwaite Water and the surrounding countryside that once drew Beatrix Potter to the area. The thoughtfully equipped en suite bedrooms have all been decorated and furnished with care, and there is a charming lounge with an open fire. In summer, guests can sit on the terrace and spot some of the most well-known fells in the Lake District. Above all, Ees Wyke is renowned for its splendid dining room, where a carefully prepared five-course dinner is served. Breakfasts have a fine reputation due to the skilful use of local produce.

Recommended in the area

Grizedale Forest; Coniston Old Man; Langdale Pikes; Hill Top (Beatrix Potter's Home) (NT)

Lyndhurst Country House

★★★★ 🛏 GUEST HOUSE

Address: NEWBY BRIDGE, Ulverston, LA12 8ND
Tel: 015395 31245
Email: chris@lyndhurstcountryhouse.co.uk
Website: www.lyndhurstcountryhouse.co.uk
Map ref: 5 SD38
Directions: On junct of A590 & A592 at Newby Bridge rdbt
Rooms: 3 en suite D £70-£75
Notes: ⊗ on premises 🚼 under 8yrs **Parking:** 3
Closed: 23-28 Dec

Situated at the southern tip of beautiful Lake Windermere and set in its own lovely gardens, Lyndhurst is well located within easy reach of a host of local amenities, such as hotels, restaurants and country inns. The comfortable bedrooms are well equipped and tastefully decorated. Hearty breakfasts here feature local produce as much as possible and are served in the pleasant dining room, which also has a lounge area that opens out onto the garden.

Recommended in the area

Windermere Lake Cruises; Hill Top (Beatrix Potter's home) (NT); Holker Hall Gardens and Motor Museum

Brandelhow Guest House

★★★★ GUEST HOUSE

Address: 1 Portland Place, PENRITH, CA11 7QN
Tel: 01768 864470
Email: enquiries@brandelhowguesthouse.co.uk
Website: www.brandelhowguesthouse.co.uk
Map ref: 6 NY53
Directions: In town centre on one-way system, left at town hall
Rooms: 5 (4 en suite) (1 pri facs) S £35 D £70-£80
Notes: Wi-fi ⊗ on premises **Closed:** 31 Dec & 1 Jan

Situated in the historic market town of Penrith, on the Coast to Coast Walk, this friendly guest house is within easy walking distance of central amenities and is also ideally located for the Lakes and the M6. Guests are welcomed with a hot or cold drink and a selection of home-made cakes, and can relax in the thoughtfully furnished, comfortable bedrooms. Breakfasts utilise ingredients from some of the best Lakeland producers, and are served in a Cumbria-themed dining room overlooking the courtyard garden. Afternoon and cream teas are available by arrangement, as are packed lunches.

Recommended in the area

Hadrian's Wall; Moot Hall, Keswick; Aira Force (NT)

Lane Head Farm

★★★★ GUEST HOUSE

Address: TROUTBECK, Keswick,
CA11 0SY
Tel: 017687 79220
Email: info@laneheadfarm.co.uk
Website: www.laneheadfarm.co.uk
Map ref: 5 NY32
Directions: On A66 between Penrith & Keswick
Rooms: 7 en suite (1GF) S £45-£90 D £70-£90
Notes: ⊗ on premises ⴱ under 12yrs
Parking: 9

Visitors quickly relax in the tranquil setting of this Lakeland farmhouse, dating from 1750 and set in rolling countryside, which guests can view with pleasure from the colourful garden. Lane Head Farm is just 10 minutes' drive from Keswick and Ullswater, so makes a great base from which to explore the Lake District National Park. The park is only 40 miles long and 33 miles wide so nowhere is too far from the door. Individually designed en suite bedrooms are thoughtfully equipped with televisions, radio-alarm clocks, hairdryers and complimentary toiletries. The attention to detail by the hosts Josette and Mark extends to the provision of Fairtrade coffee, hot chocolate, sugar and ethically sourced tea. Larger, four-poster bedrooms also offer 20-inch flat-screen televisions and iPod docking radio-alarm clocks. Freshly prepared and well cooked breakfasts are served in the spacious dining room, where two- or three-course farmhouse dinners are also available in the evening, prepared from locally sourced produce. Browse the wine list in the lounge over a pre-dinner drink and chat with fellow residents. After dinner teas and coffees are also taken in the lounge, or you may prefer to sample a malt whisky, Cognac, Armagnac or one of the local beers.

Recommended in the area

Keswick Pencil Museum; Ullswater Steamers; Honister Slate Mine

The Coppice

★★★★ 🛏 🍽 GUEST HOUSE

Address: Brook Road, WINDERMERE, LA23 2ED
Tel: 015394 88501
Fax: 015394 42148
Email: chris@thecoppice.co.uk
Website: www.thecoppice.co.uk
Map ref: 6 SD49
Directions: 0.25m S of village centre on A5074
Rooms: 9 en suite (1GF) S £40-£65 D £68-£120
Notes: Wi-fi **Parking:** 10

This traditional Lakeland vicarage retains all its character and charm. Built of local stone, The Coppice sits in an elevated position between the villages of Windermere and Bowness, perfectly placed for touring or walking in the Lake District National Park. Hosts Chris and Barbara promise a memorable experience and can provide extras such as flowers, chocolates and champagne on arrival or the chance to upgrade to a four-poster bed. The en suite bedrooms, some with bath, some with shower, have been individually designed so each has its own distinctive feel. All have TV and complimentary tea and coffee trays. The renowned Lakeland breakfast and dinner are enjoyed in the light and airy dining room and a pre-dinner drink can be taken in the spacious lounge which has an open fire. Dinner is served most evenings and the restaurant has an excellent reputation in the area with locally sourced seasonal ingredients used in the dishes. This includes championship sausages and fine cured bacon, fell-bred beef, pork and lamb and fish from Fleetwood. The dinner menu also features vegetarian options, together with home-made bread and desserts. Additional facilities at The Coppice include a private car park, local leisure club membership and fishing. Dogs are welcome in some of the rooms.

Recommended in the area

Hill Top (Beatrix Potter's home) (NT); Wordsworth's homes – Rydal Mount and Dove Cottage

The Cranleigh

★ ★ ★ ★ ★ GUEST HOUSE

Address: Kendal Road, Bowness, WINDERMERE, LA23 3EW
Tel: 015394 43293
Fax: 015394 47283
Email: enquiries@thecranleigh.com
Website: www.thecranleigh.com
Map ref: 6 SD49
Directions: Lake Rd onto Kendal Rd, 150yds on right
Rooms: 17 en suite (3GF) S £75-£170 D £82-£220
Notes: Wi-fi ⊗ on premises ⋈ under 15yrs Parking: 17

Expect the unexpected in this new concept guest house just
two minutes' walk from Lake Windermere. Owners Stephen
and Louise Hargreaves have established something fresh and exciting here, maintaining a traditionally
friendly and informal atmosphere while creating accommodation with all the cutting-edge style of
an expensive boutique hotel. The guest lounge, with its lovely open fireplace, leather furniture and
mellow decor is in classic style, and is a great place to relax with a glass of wine or one of the local
ales. Hearty breakfasts are served in equally stylish surroundings. Bedrooms are simply stunning and
uncompromisingly contemporary, each having received the attention of a professional interior designer
and each with its own individual style. Rooms vary in size, with the largest having king-sized or super
king-sized beds. All have luxurious goose-down duvets and fine cotton sheets, iPod docking stations,
large-screen LCD TVs, DVD players and free Wi-fi access. The fully tiled bathrooms feature designer
fittings by Villeroy & Boch, heated floors, and bathrobes. Those with air spa baths have a mirrored TV at
the foot of the bath for utter indulgence. As an added bonus, guests have free use of nearby 3 million
pound spa facilities, including a gym, large swimming pool, sauna and access to spa treatments.

Recommended in the area

Windermere; cruises on the lake; Beatrix Potter Museum

Fairfield House and Gardens

★★★★ 🏠 GUEST HOUSE

Address: Brantfell Road, Bowness-on-Windermere,
WINDERMERE, LA23 3AE
Tel: 015394 46565
Fax: 015394 46564
Email: tonyandliz@the-fairfield.co.uk
Website: www.the-fairfield.co.uk
Map ref: 6 SD49
Directions: Into Bowness town centre, turn opp St
Martin's Church & sharp left by Spinnery restaurant,
house 200yds on right

Rooms: 10 en suite (3GF) **S** £65-£110 **D** £70-£160 **Notes:** Wi-fi 🐾 under 10yrs **Parking:** 10

Situated close to Bowness Bay, this establishment is the perfect place to take a tranquil break. Owners Tony and Liz Blaney offer genuine hospitality and high standards of personal service at their 200-year-old home, which is set in half an acre of its own beautifully landscaped gardens. All rooms are en suite and there are twin as well as double rooms; the deluxe rooms feature spa baths. The four-poster room has its own wet room with heated floor for that added touch of luxury – the power shower here is big enough for two, and comes with body jets and massage pebbles on the floor. A roof-space penthouse featured on TV), has a glass shower and spa bath as well as a flat-screen TV and surround-sound. Options are available for guests to have sparkling wine or Belgian chocolates in their room on arrival and, for special occasions, to have rose petals scattered on the bed. Special facilities are available for visitors with mobility requirements. Breakfasts come in hearty or healthy versions, each made with the finest ingredients. There is free internet access via a public terminal or, for those with their own laptops, Wi-fi is available.

Recommended in the area

Blackwell (The Arts & Crafts House); Windermere lake steamers; Wordsworth House (NT)

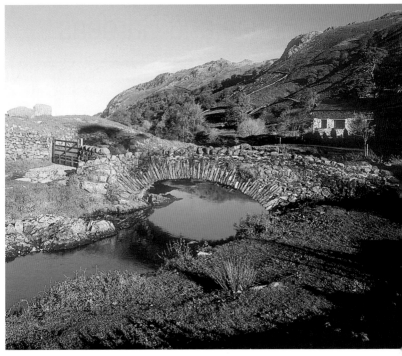

Watendlath Beck, Lake District

St Johns Lodge

★ ★ ★ ⌂ GUEST ACCOMMODATION
Address: Lake Road, WINDERMERE, LA23 2EQ
Tel: 015394 43078
Fax: 015394 88054
Email: mail@st-johns-lodge.co.uk
Website: www.st-johns-lodge.co.uk
Map ref: 6 SD49
Directions: On A5074 between Windermere & lake
Rooms: 12 en suite S £40-£50 D £55-£110
Notes: Wi-fi ⊗ on premises ⱦ under 12yrs
Parking: 3 Closed: Xmas

Adult-only, pet-free, eco-friendly St John's Lodge is just 10 minutes' walk from Windermere and the lake, and restaurants, pubs and shops are all nearby. A choice of bedrooms is offered to suit all pocke from budget to premium. All the rooms have en suite shower rooms, TVs, Fairtrade tea- and coffee-making facilities and hairdryers. An extensive menu offers over 30 cooked breakfasts and more than 1 vegetarian and vegan options. Gluten free options also available. Free internet access and Wi-fi.
Recommended in the area
Lake Windermere; Beatrix Potter Attraction; Blackwell

The Willowsmere

★★★★ 🏠 GUEST HOUSE

Address: Ambleside Road,
WINDERMERE, LA23 1ES
Tel: 015394 43575
Fax: 015394 44962
Email: info@thewillowsmere.com
Website: www.thewillowsmere.com
Map ref: 6 SD49
Directions: On A591, 500yds on left after
Windermere station, towards Ambleside
Rooms: 12 en suite (1GF) **S** £38-£66 **D** £64-£132
Notes: Wi-fi ⊗ on premises 🚼 under 12yrs **Parking:** 15

Wonderful views of Lake Windermere are available only a few minutes' stroll from this luxuriously renovated gentleman's residence dating from 1850. The town centre and the railway station, too, are just an eight-minute walk away, and ample off-road parking is provided on site. Willowsmere is an imposing property, built from Lakeland stone, set in large, landscaped gardens, which have won the titles 'Windermere in Bloom 2008, Winner Best Kept Garden', and 'Cumbria in Bloom 2008, Winner Best Kept Garden B&B/Guest House'. Guests can relax over a drink from the well stocked cellar, either in the secluded gardens during fine weather or in either of the two guest lounges. The large, comfortable bedrooms are all en suite and include single, twin, double and four-poster rooms. Luxury pocket sprung beds and Egyptian cotton duvets ensure a sound night's sleep. A double ground floor room has wheelchair access and a bathroom with facilities for the disabled. No family rooms are available so only children of 12 years or older can be accommodated. English breakfasts, home cooked to order, are served at individual tables in the stylish dining room.

Recommended in the area

Brockhole Lake District Visitor Centre; Townend; The World of Beatrix Potter

DERBYSHIRE

Victoria Prospect Tower, Matlock Bath

Pennine Way

Oaktree Farm

★ ★ ★ BED & BREAKFAST

Address: Matlock Road, Oakerthorpe, Wessington, ALFRETON, DE55 7NA
Tel: 01773 832957 & 07999 876969
Email: katherine770@btinternet.com
Map ref: 8 SK45
Directions: 2m W of Alfreton. A615 W under railway bridge & past cottages, farmhouse on left
Rooms: 3 en suite S £30-£32 D £50-£52 **Notes:** ⊗ on premises ⊛ **Parking:** 10 **Closed:** 24-26 Dec

Oaktree Farm is ideally situated for the glorious Peak District and convenient for Derby, Nottingham and Sheffield, with their exciting retail outlets. The working farm provides off-street parking, a coarse fishing lake free to residents and DIY livery stables, set in 22 acres of Derbyshire countryside complete with a mature flower garden and sizeable patio. The comfortable en suite bedrooms feature satellite television and tea- and coffee-making facilities. The home produce is organic and includes free-range eggs, all served in the attractive cottage-style dining room.

Recommended in the area

Crich Tramway Village; Lea Gardens; Hardwick Hall

Dannah Farm Country House

★ ★ ★ ★ ★ ≘ ⇔ GUEST ACCOMMODATION

Address: Bowmans Lane, Shottle,
BELPER, DE56 2DR
Tel: 01773 550273 & 550630
Fax: 01773 550590
Email: reservations@dannah.co.uk
Website: www.dannah.co.uk
Map ref: 8 SK34
Directions: A517 from Belper towards Ashbourne, 1.5m right into Shottle after Hanging Gate pub on right, over x-rds & right
Rooms: 8 en suite (2GF) **S** £75-£95 **D** £150-£200
Notes: Wi-fi ⊗ on premises **Parking:** 20 **Closed:** 24-26 Dec

Dannah, a Georgian farmhouse on a working farm on the Chatsworth Estate, is home to Joan and Martin Slack and their collection of pigs, hens and cats, and Cracker the very good-natured English Setter. Each bedroom has its own individual character, beautifully furnished with antiques and old pine, and filled with a wealth of thoughtful extras. Some rooms have private sitting rooms, four-poster beds and amazing bathrooms featuring a double spa bath or Japanese-style tubs – the Studio Hideaway suite even has its own private terrace with hot tub. All the bedrooms look out onto green fields and open countryside. The two delightful sitting rooms have open fires on chilly evenings and views over the gardens. The English farmhouse breakfasts are a true delight, served in relaxed and elegant surroundings. Dinner is available by arrangement, alternatively there are excellent pubs and restaurants within easy reach. Footpaths criss-cross the surrounding area in the heart of the Derbyshire Dales, making it an ideal location for walking enthusiasts.

Recommended in the area

Chatsworth; Dovedale; Alton Towers

The Samuel Fox Country Inn

★ ★ ★ ★ ★ ❀ INN

Address: Stretfield Road, BRADWELL,
Hope Valley, S33 9JT
Tel: 01433 621562
Fax: 01433 623770
Email: thesamuelfox@hotmail.co.uk
Website: www.samuelfox.co.uk
Map ref: 7 SK18 **Directions:** M1 junct 29, A617
towards Chesterfield, A619 signed Baslow & Buxton,
2nd rdbt A623 for 7m, take B6049 to Bradwell,
through village on left **Rooms:** 4 en suite **S** £75 **D** £115 **Notes:** ⊗ on premises **Parking:** 15

Now taking its name from Bradwell's most famous son, the industrial magnate who built the steelworks at Stocksbridge, the Samuel Fox has been fully refurbished to provide accommodation that successfully combines modern and stylish touches with rustic charm. Located in the beautiful Peak District National Park, it offers guests a chance to get away from it all, with many picturesque walks within easy reach. Fresh coffee and home-made cookies are served on arrival and service is highly attentive throughout. Guests can relax by the log fires with a local ale, including regular guest ales, or enjoy a fine wine before retiring to the en suite bedrooms, which are both immaculately presented and extensively equipped, with bathrobes, TV, chocolates and mineral water as standard. The rooms benefit from large windows, giving them a bright and airy feel. Diners can take in the restaurant's breathtaking views over Bradwell while enjoying the modern British cuisine. Fresh seafood is delivered daily and features on the ever-changing menus, while home-baked breads, chutneys and preserves all add an extra touch of quality and indulgence. Breakfasts are served on the private patios or in the restaurant. Special interest breaks, such as fly fishing and falconry, are also on offer.

Recommended in the area

Haddon Hall; Chatsworth Estate; Peak District National Park

Tissington village, Peak District National Park

Buxton's Victorian Guest House

★★★★★ GUEST HOUSE
Address: 3A Broad Walk, BUXTON, SK17 6JE
Tel: 01298 78759
Fax: 01298 74732
Email: buxtonvictorian@btconnect.com
Website: www.buxtonvictorian.co.uk
Map ref: 7 SK07
Directions: Signs to Opera House, proceed to Old Hall Hotel, right onto Hartington Rd, car park 100yds on right **Rooms:** 8 en suite (1GF) S £54-£80
D £78-£100 **Notes:** ⊗ on premises ⁇ under 4yrs **Parking:** 8 **Closed:** 22 Dec-12 Jan

Standing in a prime position overlooking the Pavilion Gardens and boating lake, this delightfully furnished house was built in 1860 for the then Duke of Devonshire. It has been extensively refurbished in recent years and today offers high-quality, comfortable accommodation with its own car park. The en suite bedrooms have individual themes and many extras such as TVs, hairdryers and hospitality trays. Some rooms overlook the Gardens. Excellent breakfasts are served in the Oriental breakfast room.
Recommended in the area
Buxton Opera House; Poole's Cavern; Chatsworth House

Roseleigh

★★★★ GUEST HOUSE

Address: 19 Broad Walk, BUXTON, SK17 6JR
Tel/Fax: 01298 24904
Email: enquiries@roseleighhotel.co.uk
Website: www.roseleighhotel.co.uk
Map ref: 7 SK07
Directions: A6 to Safeway rdbt, onto Dale Rd, right at lights, 100yds left by Swan pub, down hill & right onto Hartington Rd
Rooms: 14 (12 en suite) (2 pri facs) (1GF) S £38-£88
D £74-£88 Notes: Wi-fi ⊗ on premises 🚸 under 6yrs
Parking: 9 **Closed:** 16 Dec-16 Jan

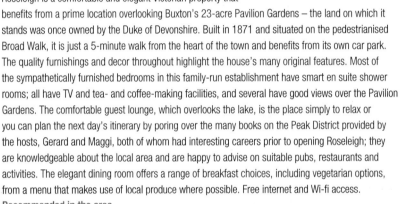

Roseleigh is a comfortable and elegant Victorian property that benefits from a prime location overlooking Buxton's 23-acre Pavilion Gardens – the land on which it stands was once owned by the Duke of Devonshire. Built in 1871 and situated on the pedestrianised Broad Walk, it is just a 5-minute walk from the heart of the town and benefits from its own car park. The quality furnishings and decor throughout highlight the house's many original features. Most of the sympathetically furnished bedrooms in this family-run establishment have smart en suite shower rooms; all have TV and tea- and coffee-making facilities, and several have good views over the Pavilion Gardens. The comfortable guest lounge, which overlooks the lake, is the place simply to relax or you can plan the next day's itinerary by poring over the many books on the Peak District provided by the hosts, Gerard and Maggi, both of whom had interesting careers prior to opening Roseleigh; they are knowledgeable about the local area and are happy to advise on suitable pubs, restaurants and activities. The elegant dining room offers a range of breakfast choices, including vegetarian options, from a menu that makes use of local produce where possible. Free internet and Wi-fi access.

Recommended in the area

Buxton Opera House; Chatsworth; Peak District National Park

Bentley Brook Inn

★ ★ ★ INN

Address: FENNY BENTLEY, Ashbourne, DE6 1LF
Tel: 01335 350278
Fax: 01335 350422
Email: all@bentleybrookinn.co.uk
Website: www.bentleybrookinn.co.uk
Map ref: 7 SK14
Directions: 2m N of Ashbourne at junct of A515
& B5056 Rooms: 11 en suite (2GF) Notes: Wi-fi
Parking: 100

This popular country inn, located within the Peak District National Park, makes a good base for walkers and those visiting Alton Towers. It is a charming building with an attractive terrace, sweeping lawns and play area. The en suite bedrooms are well appointed, with extras such as TVs, hairdryers and hospitality trays. Overlooking the gardens, the comfortable restaurant offers a wide range of dishes available all day in summer (12-3, 6-9 in winter months), from snacks through to main meals, using organic and locally sourced ingredients. A new function suite is now available.

Recommended in the area
Bakewell; Haddon Hall; Drayton Manor Theme Park

Underleigh House

★ ★ ★ ★ ★ 🏠 GUEST ACCOMMODATION

Address: Off Edale Rd, HOPE, Hope Valley, S33 6RF
Tel: 01433 621372
Fax: 01433 621324
Email: info@underleighhouse.co.uk
Website: www.underleighhouse.co.uk
Map ref: 7 SK18
Directions: From village church on A6187 onto Edale
Rd, 1m left onto lane Rooms: 5 en suite (2GF)
S £60-£80 D £80-£100 Notes: Wi-fi 🐾 under 12yrs
Parking: 6 Closed: Xmas, New Year & 4 Jan-4 Feb

Surrounded by glorious scenery, Underleigh House was converted from a barn and cottage that dates from 1873. An ideal base for walkers, Vivienne and Philip Taylor provide thoughtfully furnished bedrooms each with a hairdryer, radio-alarm, and tea and coffee facilities. Some rooms have direct access to the gardens, two have their own lounge. Enjoy a drink on the terrace in summer or by the log fire in the lounge in winter. Memorable breakfasts are served around one large table in the dining room.

Recommended in the area
Castleton Caverns; Chatsworth; Eyam

Yew Tree Cottage

★ ★ ★ ★ ☷ BED & BREAKFAST

Address: The Knoll, Tansley, MATLOCK, DE4 5FP
Tel: 01629 583862 & 07799 541903
Email: enquiries@yewtreecottagebb.co.uk
Website: www.yewtreecottagebb.co.uk
Map ref: 7 SK35
Directions: 1.2m E of Matlock. Off A615 into
Tansley centre
Rooms: 3 en suite **S** £65 **D** £75-£95 **Notes:** Wi-fi ⊗
on premises 🚶 under 12yrs **Parking:** 3

This 18th-century cottage, full of original character and charm and with stunning views, is set in pretty gardens in the village of Tansley. The cottage is a true home away from home, with outstanding service and hospitality, and ideally situated for all the Derbyshire Dales and Peak District. The elegantly furnished and decorated bedrooms have TV/radios, DVD players, bath robes, hairdryers, toiletries and refreshment trays. Breakfast is a memorable feast of home-made and local produce, and light refreshments are served in the sitting room where log fires cheer up the cooler days.

Recommended in the area

Chatsworth; Crich Tramway Village; Heights of Abraham cable cars

The Smithy

★ ★ ★ ★ ★ ☷ GUEST ACCOMMODATION

Address: NEWHAVEN, Biggin, Buxton, SK17 0DT
Tel/Fax: 01298 84548
Email: lynnandgary@thesmithybedandbreakfast.
co.uk
Website: www.thesmithybedandbreakfast.co.uk
Map ref: 7 SK16
Directions: 0.5m S of Newhaven on A515. Next to
Biggin Ln, private driveway opp Ivy House
Rooms: 4 en suite (2GF) **D** £74-£100
Notes: ⊗ on premises 🐾 **Parking:** 8

Welcoming owners Lynn and Gary Jinks have restored this former drovers' inn and blacksmith's shop to a high standard with all modern comforts and a very personal service. The well-decorated good-sized bedrooms are all en suite with hospitality trays and many extras. Flavoursome breakfasts, including free-range eggs and home-made preserves, are served in the forge, which still has its vast open hearth, and is adjacent to a cosy lounge. The pleasant gardens are set within 4 acres of meadowland.

Recommended in the area

Chatsworth; Tissington and High Peak Trails (within walking distance); Peak District National Park

Cable cars over Heights of Abraham

The Old Manor House

★★★★★ BED & BREAKFAST

Address: Coldwell Street, WIRKSWORTH,
Matlock, DE4 4FB
Tel: 01629 822502
Email: sandie@wirkworthmanorhouse.co.uk
Map ref: 7 SK25
Directions: On B5035 Coldwell St off village centre
Rooms: 1 pri facs **S** £50-£60 **D** £80-£85
Notes: ⊗ on premises ☜ under 12yrs ⓐ
Parking: 1 **Closed:** Xmas & New Year

This impressive 17th-century house is located on the edge of the pleasant town of Wirksworth, which is well worth a visit for its period buildings, narrow streets and intricate alleyways. The house and the private bathroom and bedroom, with its four-poster bed and quality furnishings, retains many original features. A full, hearty breakfast is served in the elegant dining room and a spacious drawing room is available to relax in after a day out. There are good restaurants and pubs in the vicinity.

Recommended in the area

Peak District National Park; Chatsworth; Carsington Water

DEVON

Hartland Point lighthouse

Greencott

★ ★ ★ ★ GUEST HOUSE
Address: Landscove, ASHBURTON, TQ13 7LZ
Tel: 01803 762649
Map ref: 2 SX77
Directions: 3m SE of Ashburton. Off A38 at Peartree junct, Landscove signed on slip road, village green 2m on right, opp village hall
Rooms: 2 en suite **Notes:** ⊗ on premises ☻
Parking: 3 **Closed:** 25-26 Dec

Modern facilities in a traditional atmosphere are offered at this renovated house in the village of Landscove, which is just three miles from Ashburton. Greencott stands in a garden with lovely country views. The bedrooms are carefully furnished and well equipped with baths and showers en suite, and tea and coffee amenities. Television, books, maps and local information are provided in the comfortable sitting room, and traditional country cooking is served around the oak dining table. The full English breakfast includes home-made bread, and dinner is available on request. Service is attentive and caring, and many guests return time and time again.

Recommended in the area
Dartington; Buckfast Abbey; riding, fishing and golf nearby

The Rising Sun

★★★★ ☛ INN
Address: Woodland, ASHBURTON, TQ13 7JT
Tel: 01364 652544
Email: admin@therisingsunwoodland.co.uk
Website: www.therisingsunwoodland.co.uk
Map ref: 2 SX77
Directions: A38, exit signed Woodland/Denbury, continue straight on for 1.5m Rising Sun on left
Rooms: 5 en suite (2GF) **Parking:** 30

Mid-way between Exeter and Plymouth, this delightful family-run country inn was taken over in 2007 by its head chef, Paul Cheakley and his wife Louise, ensuring that its reputation as a great place to eat would be maintained. Fresh fish from Brixham, local game in season and other top quality local produce features on the menu, which offers classic pub fare with gourmet touches, a choice of home-made pies and a great selection of West Country cheeses. The bedrooms, which vary in size, have a bright, unfussy decor, en suite bathrooms and television. Families are very welcome here with a play area in the large garden, where you can also eat and drink in the warmer months.

Recommended in the area
Dartmoor National Park; Torquay; Buckfast Abbey

Turtley Corn Mill

★★★★ 🛌 INN

Address: AVONWICK, TQ10 9ES
Tel: 01364 646100
Fax: 01364 646101
Email: mill@avonwick.net
Website: www.avonwick.net
Map ref: 2 SX75
Directions: From A38, S towards Avonwick, 0.5m on left
Rooms: 4 en suite S £89-£110 D £89-£110
Notes: Wi-fi 🚫 on premises
Parking: 90 **Closed:** 25 Dec

Located just off the A38 in an idyllic area, this fine mill is set within six acres of grounds complete with a small lake and its own island and bordered by the River Glazebrook. Once a working corn mill then a chicken hatchery, it became a pub in the 1970s before undergoing a complete renovation in recent years. Today the emphasis is on relaxation, with a light, fresh design and no fruit machines, pool tables or music. The en suite bedrooms, one a family room, are decorated in a contemporary style, all with king-sized beds. There are some thoughtful extras provided, including Egyptian cotton linen, flatscreen Freeview TVs, free Wi-fi and powerful, spacious showers. Guests can even pre-arrange to borrow a fully programmed satnav device, ready for exploring the surrounding area. The food on offer is locally sourced and of a high quality. While breakfast provides a hearty start to the day, other meals are served all day from an ever-changing menu in a variety of relaxed dining areas, or outside in warmer weather, by friendly, efficient staff. Interesting wines and a good range of local beers complete the picture. Ample parking is provided.

Recommended in the area

Dartmoor National Park; Dartmoor Otter Sanctuary; Salcombe Harbour

The Pines at Eastleigh

★★★★ 🏛 GUEST ACCOMMODATION

Address: The Pines, Eastleigh,
BIDEFORD, EX39 4PA
Tel: 01271 860561
Fax: 01271 861689
Email: pirrie@thepinesateastleigh.co.uk
Website: www.thepinesateastleigh.co.uk
Map ref: 2 SS42
Directions: A39 onto A386 signed East-the-Water.
1st left signed Eastleigh, 500yds next left, 1.5m to
village, house on right
Rooms: 6 en suite (4GF) S £39-£45 D £75-£90 Notes: Wi-fi 🐾 under 9yrs Parking: 20

From its magnificent hilltop position overlooking the Torridge estuary and Lundy Island, this Georgian
house, standing in 7 acres of grounds, is perfect for a relaxing break. Most of the comfortable
bedrooms are in converted stables around a charming courtyard. There are two rooms in the main
house. The memorable breakfasts feature local and home-made produce.
Recommended in the area
Instow and Clovelly; cycling and walking on The Tarka Trail; Hartland Heritage Coast

Hansard House

★★★★ GUEST ACCOMMODATION

Address: 3 Northview Road,
BUDLEIGH SALTERTON, EX9 6BY
Tel: 01395 442773
Fax: 01395 442475
Email: enquiries@hansardhotel.co.uk
Website: www.hansardhousehotel.co.uk
Map ref: 2 SY08
Directions: 500yds W of town centre
Rooms: 12 en suite (3GF) S £39-£49 D £84-£91
Notes: Wi-fi Parking: 11

Set in an ideal situation a short walk from central Budleigh Salterton, Hansard House is just five minutes
from the beach and the cliff path of this beautiful part of the East Devon coast. The tastefully decorated
en suite bedrooms have TV, tea- and coffee-making facilities and hairdryers, and most have views
across the town, to the countryside and estuary beyond. The varied and hearty breakfasts are served in
the light and airy dining room. Children and pets are welcome.
Recommended in the area
Otter Estuary Bird Sanctuary; Bicton Park Botanical Gardens

Haytor Rocks, Dartmoor National Park

Easton Court

★★★★ GUEST ACCOMMODATION

Address: Easton Cross, CHAGFORD, TQ13 8JL
Tel: 01647 433469
Email: stay@easton.co.uk
Website: www.easton.co.uk
Map ref: 2 SX78
Directions: 1m E of Chagford at junct A382 & B3206
Rooms: 5 en suite (2GF) S £50-£65 D £65-£80
Notes: Wi-fi ❧ under 10yrs **Parking:** 5

Debra and Paul Witting's impressive thatched Tudor farmhouse stands in acres of gardens and paddocks in the Teign Valley. With its oak beams and thick granite walls, Evelyn Waugh was charmed by the place and wrote *Brideshead Revisited* here, and you too should find it inspiring. An Edwardian extension houses the en suite bedrooms with fabulous views of the countryside – four rooms are superior, and there is a mixture of showers and bathrooms.

Recommended in the area

Castle Drogo (NT); Fingle Bridge; Dartmoor National Park

Tor Cottage

★ ★ ★ ★ ★ 🛎 GUEST ACCOMMODATION

Address: CHILLATON, Tavistock, PL16 0JE
Tel: 01822 860248
Fax: 01822 860126
Email: info@torcottage.co.uk
Website: www.torcottage.co.uk
Map ref: 1 SX48
Directions: A30 Lewdown exit through Chillaton towards Tavistock, 300yds after Post Office right signed 'Bridlepath No Public Vehicular Access' to end
Rooms: 4 en suite (3GF) S £98 D £140-£150
Notes: Wi-fi 🚫 on premises 🚼 under 14yrs **Parking:** 8 **Closed:** mid Dec-beg Feb

This romantic cottage offers tranquillity and seclusion in 28 acres of grounds. Nothing is too much trouble for Maureen Rowlatt, who has equipped the en suite bed-sitting rooms with everything you could wish for. Each one is individually designed, from the warmth and style of the Art Deco Room to the blue and cream elegance of The Craftsman's Room – both converted from an original craftsman's workshop. One room is in the cottage wing and the others are in converted barns – each has a private terrace/garden and a log fire. Laughing Waters, the garden retreat, is nestled in its own private valley. Breakfast is an imaginative range of dishes, and can be taken in the conservatory-style dining room or on the terrace in fine weather. The gardens are a feature in their own right with many private corners, a stream and, in summer, a heated swimming pool. Woodlands cloaking the hillside behind the cottage are home to a variety of wildlife including badgers, pheasants and deer that enjoy the cover of the gorse, while buzzards and the occasional heron can be seen overhead. Autumn and spring breaks are available – 3 nights for the price of 2.

Recommended in the area
Dartmoor; The Eden Project; National Trust houses and gardens

The New Angel Rooms

★ ★ ★ ★ RESTAURANT WITH ROOMS
Address: 51 Victoria Road, DARTMOUTH, TQ6 9RT
Tel: 01803 839425
Fax: 01803 839505
Email: info@thenewangel.co.uk
Website: www.thenewangel.co.uk
Map ref: 2 SX85
Directions: In Dartmouth take one-way system,
1st left at NatWest Bank
Rooms: 6 en suite D £85-£125
Notes: ⊗ on premises **Closed:** Jan

This establishment offers luxurious, stylish accommodation in the heart of Dartmouth's pretty town centre. This is the perfect place to retreat after a day spent exploring the South Hams area, whether to the individually decorated en suite bedrooms or the guest lounge with its fire and reading materials. Each bedroom has a plasma-screen TV and DVD player as well as quality toiletries, soft white towels, a fridge with fresh milk and water, and home-made shortbread and nibbles. One room even has its own private staircase, and weekend guests can also indulge in a complimentary half-bottle of red or white wine. It's then just a short stroll to the picturesque waterfront and the establishment's award-winning three AA Rosette New Angel restaurant, which features an open kitchen and a menu based on local, regional and seasonal produce. The stylishly decorated third-floor cocktail lounge offers great views over the Dart Estuary. Breakfast is served in the restaurant between 9-11am, and residents can choose from specials such as eggs Benedict or scrambled eggs with smoked salmon, served with freshly squeezed orange juice. A specially tailored boat trip can be arranged, from a leisurely cruise to a fishing trip, on the New Angel's fully equipped Sunseeker vessel.

Recommended in the area

Dartmoor National Park; Dartmouth Castle; Bayards Cove Fort

Wheal Betsy Tin Mine, Dartmoor National Park

Nonsuch House

★ ★ ★ ★ ★ 🏠 🍽 GUEST ACCOMMODATION

Address: Church Hill, Kingswear,
DARTMOUTH, TQ6 0BX
Tel: 01803 752829
Fax: 01803 752357
Email: enquiries@nonsuch-house.co.uk
Website: www.nonsuch-house.co.uk
Map ref: 2 SX85
Directions: A3022 onto A379 2m before Brixham.
Fork left onto B3205. Left up Higher Contour Rd,

down Ridley Hill, house on bend on left at top of Church Hill **Rooms:** 4 en suite (2GF) S £80-£115
D £105-£150 **Notes:** Wi-fi ⊗ on premises 👶 under 10yrs **Parking:** 4

Kit and Penny Noble's lovely Edwardian house is set on a south-facing hill in Kingswear, with panoramic
views of both the Dart estuary and the sea. The accommodation is of a very high quality – the spacious
bedrooms are comfortable with lots of little extras. Meals are prepared from fresh, local ingredients
whenever possible, and you can also be assured of a wonderful breakfast.
Recommended in the area
Dartmouth; Brixham; South West Coast Path

Barn

★★★★ 🏨 GUEST ACCOMMODATION

Address: Foxholes Hill, Marine Drive,
EXMOUTH, EX8 2DF
Tel: 01395 224411
Fax: 01395 225445
Email: exmouthbarn@googlemail.com
Website: www.barnhotel.co.uk
Map ref: 2 SY08
Directions: From M5 junct 30 take A376 to
Exmouth, then follow signs to seafront. At rdbt last
exit into Foxholes Hill. Located on right
Rooms: 11 en suite
Notes: Wi-fi **Parking:** 30 **Closed:** 23 Dec-10 Jan

Close to miles of sandy beaches, this Grade II listed establishment is set in an impeccable and stunning 2-acre garden, which is sea facing and with spectacular views of the East Devon Heritage Coast. There is a terrace and a swimming pool for summer. The building is a leading example of the Arts and Crafts movement and was built in the early 1900s by Edward Prior, a contemporary of William Morris. The Barn has been sympathetically modernised and furnished in keeping with its architectural design and creates an atmosphere of country-house style. The public rooms and most of the bedrooms have outstanding sea views. The attractively decorated, en suite bedrooms have TV, hospitality tray, hairdryer and direct-dial telephone. Breakfast, featuring freshly squeezed juices and local produce, is served in the bright, airy dining room. Exmouth is 15 minutes' walk away along the tree-lined and landscaped Madeira Walk. There are also several rural and coastal walks in the area and the estuary of the River Exe offers opportunities for birdwatching, sailing, fishing and windsurfing.

Recommended in the area

Crealy Adventure Park; Exeter; Bicton Park Botanical Gardens

Leworthy Farm House

★ ★ ★ ★ GUEST ACCOMMODATION
Address: Lower Leworthy, Nr Pyworthy,
　　　　 HOLSWORTHY, EX22 6SJ
Tel/Fax: 01409 259469
Email: leworthyfarmhouse@yahoo.co.uk
Website: www.leworthyfarmhouse.co.uk
Map ref: 1 SS30
Directions: From Holsworthy onto Bodmin St towards
North Tamerton, 4th left signed Leworthy/Southdown
Rooms: 7 en suite S £45-£65 D £65
Notes: Wi-fi ⊗ on premises ⊜ Parking: 8

Pat and Phil Jennings' passions for the countryside, collecting books, curios and classical music, and meeting new people come together wonderfully at Leworthy Farm House. Spacious public rooms include a softly lit dining room with an oak parquet floor and colourful displays of old china, a peaceful drawing room with comfortable old sofas and armchairs and more displays of pictures and china, and a warmly decorated conservatory. Bedrooms, some with window seats, are beautifully furnished with pine or antique pieces and thoughtfully equipped with radio alarms, hairdryers, electric blankets, books and magazines. Hospitality trays are set with bone china, fresh milk, a selection of teas, coffees and chocolate, biscuits and fresh flowers. All the rooms are en suite and have ample supplies of soft towels and toiletries. A good choice of dishes is served at breakfast, and picnics are available by arrangement. Evening meals are not served here, but there are plenty of cafés, pubs and restaurants to choose from in the area. Leworthy is an ideal base for exploring Dartmoor and Bodmin Moor and the lovely villages of Clovelly, Tintagel, Boscastle and Padstow. Bude and its wonderful four-mile sweep of golden sand is also within easy driving distance.

Recommended in the area
Rosemoor Gardens; South West Coast Path; Dartington Glass

Courtmoor Farm

★ ★ ★ ★ FARMHOUSE
Address: Upottery, HONITON, EX14 9QA
Tel: 01404 861565
Email: courtmoor.farm@btinternet.com
Website: www.courtmoor.farm.btinternet.co.uk
Map ref: 2 ST10
Directions: 4m NE of Honiton off A30
Rooms: 3 en suite S £38-£40 D £62-£66
Notes: Wi-fi ⊗ on premises **Parking:** 20
Closed: 20 Dec-1 Jan

Rosalind and Bob Buxton welcome you to their spacious farmhouse with marvellous views over the Otter Valley and surrounding countryside. The extensive grounds are home to a flock of sheep, two ponies and Aberdeen Angus cattle. Accommodation is provided in a family room, double room and twin, all equipped with digital TVs, hairdryers, electric blankets, clock radios as well as tea and coffee facilities. There are satisfying full English breakfasts to enjoy, plus special diets can be catered for. A fitness suite and a sauna are available, plus woodland walks and a nature trail.

Recommended in the area

Honiton antiques shops and Lace Museum; Lyme Regis; Forde Abbey and Gardens

Norbury House

★ ★ ★ ★ GUEST HOUSE
Address: Torrs Park, ILFRACOMBE, EX34 8AZ
Tel: 01271 863888
Email: info@norburyhouse.co.uk
Website: www.norburyhouse.co.uk
Map ref: 2 SS54
Directions: From A399 to end of High St/Church St. At mini-rdbt after lights take 1st exit onto Church Rd. Bear left onto Osbourne Rd. At T-junct left onto Torrs Park. House at top of hill on right
Rooms: 6 en suite D £75-£95 **Notes:** Wi-fi ⊗ on premises **Parking:** 6

Norbury House stands in a quiet elevated position with views over the sea and countryside. Adam and Paula have restyled this Victorian property with contemporary twists and boutique touches. The well-equipped bedrooms come in a choice of suites; many have sea views. All are en suite and have flat-screen TVs and DVD players. There's a modern lounge with honesty bar, and breakfast, using mainly local produce, is served in the sunny dining room.

Recommended in the area

Marwood Hill Gardens; Arlington Court (NT); Lundy Island

Watersmeet, Exmoor National Park

Night In Gails

★ ★ ★ ★ GUEST ACCOMMODATION

Address: Kentisbury Mill, KENTISBURY,
Barnstaple, EX31 4NF

Tel: 01271 883545

Email: info@kentisburymill.co.uk

Website: www.kentisburymill.co.uk

Map ref: 2 SS64

Directions: M5 junct 27 onto A361 towards
Barnstaple, A399 to Blackmoor Gate. Left onto A39,
right onto B3229 at Kentisbury Ford, 1m on right

Rooms: 4 en suite S £28-£30 D £60-£65 **Notes:** Wi-fi ⊗ **Parking:** 6 **Closed:** Xmas

Situated in the north Devon hills and bordered to the east by Exmoor National Park, Night In Gails originally consisted of an 18th-century cottage and mill. This relaxing hideaway, set in 2 acres of gardens with a pond and Exmoor stream, has been sympathetically renovated to provide impressive levels of comfort. The en suite bedrooms offer many luxuries and garden views. Breakfast, cooked on the Aga and served in the 1850s dining room, includes eggs from the resident hens, together with local produce.

Recommended in the area

Arlington Court (NT); Valley of the Rocks; Exmoor National Park

Moor View House

★ ★ ★ ★ ★ ⊖ GUEST ACCOMMODATION
Address: Vale Down, LYDFORD, EX20 4BB
Tel/Fax: 01822 820220
Map ref: 2 SX58
Directions: 1m NE of Lydford on A386
Rooms: 4 en suite S fr £50 D £70-£85
Notes: ⊗ on premises ⚹ under 12yrs ⊛
Parking: 15

A Victorian, licensed country guest house situated in 2-acre grounds on the western slopes of Dartmoor, where guests have enjoyed hospitality for more than a hundred years. The house has a very interesting history: in around 1900 it changed hands over a game of cards whilst, in Edwardian times, the writer Eden Phillpotts visited and wrote the famous play *A Farmer's Wife* and the novel *Widecombe Fair*. For the last 20 years David and Wendy Sharples have lovingly restored and upgraded Moor View House and offer first class accommodation, relaxed atmosphere and friendly hospitality. There are four en suite bedrooms, each with TV, radio, hospitality trays and bathrobes amongst other facilities. A large conservatory leads from the drawing room to the garden beyond and offers lovely views. The sunsets are a delight to behold. Guests are offered a choice of English or continental breakfast. Dinner is available by prior arrangement and Wendy's award-winning cooking uses locally-produced meat, fish, game and vegetables. There are also fine, sensibly-priced wines to complement the good food. Moor View House is an ideal base from which to tour Devon and Cornwall's heritage sites, coast and, of course, Dartmoor; after which it is a delight to return and relax in the large moorland garden on warm evenings or, on cooler days, by a blazing log fire in the traditionally-furnished reception rooms.

Recommended in the area

Lydford Gorge (NT); Tavistock; The Eden Project

Rickham Sands, Salcombe

Rock House

★★★★ GUEST ACCOMMODATION
Address: Manor Grounds, LYNMOUTH, EX35 6EN
Tel: 01598 753508
Fax: 0800 7566964
Email: enquiries@rock-house.co.uk
Website: www.rock-house.co.uk
Map ref: 2 SS74
Directions: On A39, at foot of Countisbury Hill right onto drive, pass Manor green/play area to Rock House

Rooms: 8 en suite (1GF) **S** £45 **D** £93-£110 **Notes:** Wi-fi **Parking:** 8 **Closed:** 24-25 Dec

Standing alone by the river at the mouth of the harbour, the 18th-century Rock House has wonderful sea views. The bedrooms, some with four-poster beds, are well appointed and furnished to a high standard with en suite facilities, TV/DVD, Wi-fi, hairdryers, alarm clocks and complimentary tea and coffee. They also have superb views of the Lyn Valley, the river or the sea. A choice of menus is offered in the spacious lounge/bar or the Harbour View Restaurant. The large gardens are popular for cream teas in summer.

Recommended in the area

Combe Martin Wildlife & Dinosaur Park; Lyn & Exmoor Museum; Arlington Court

Sea View Villa

★ ★ ★ ★ ★ 🛏 🍽 GUEST ACCOMMODATION

Address: 6 Summer House Path, LYNMOUTH, EX35 6ES
Tel: 01598 753460
Fax: 01598 753496
Email: seaviewenquiries@aol.com
Website: www.seaviewvilla.co.uk
Map ref: 2 SS74
Directions: A39 from Porlock, 1st left after bridge, Sea View Villa on right 20yds along path opp church
Rooms: 5 (3 en suite) S £35-£40 D £110-£130
Notes: Wi-fi ⊗ on premises 👶 under 14yrs **Closed:** Jan

This charming Grade II listed Georgian villa, built in 1721, has been appointed to a high standard by owners Steve Williams and Chris Bissex, who bought the house after moving from London, where they were both involved in the arts as performers and directors. Walking and surfing are popular local pursuits and there are wonderful walks directly from the door, including the Two Moors Walk and Lynton's Valley of the Rocks. Tucked away from the bustle of the main streets, the house provides elegant and peaceful accommodation. The name says it all, and indeed all of the individually decorated bedrooms enjoy impressive views of the harbour and sea. Many thoughtful extras are provided, including Egyptian cotton linen, luxury toiletries and TV/VCR, with a choice of films available to borrow. The proprietors' genuine hospitality assures a relaxed and comfortable stay. Dinner and breakfast are not to be missed, and home-made bread is a speciality here. For guests planning a day out, picnics, hikers' feasts and ploughman's hampers can all be provided. To top it all off, a range of beauty therapies and holistic treatments is available by prior arrangement.

Recommended in the area

Exmoor National Park; Clovelly; Watersmeet Valley

The Valley of the Rocks

Pine Lodge

★ ★ ★ ★ GUEST HOUSE

Address: Lynway, LYNTON, EX35 6AX
Tel: 01598 753230
Email: info@pinelodgelynton.co.uk
Website: www.pinelodgelynton.co.uk
Map ref: 2 SS74
Directions: 500yds S of town centre off Lynbridge Rd opp Bridge Inn
Rooms: 4 en suite D £60-£75
Notes: ⊗ on premises ⚸ under 12yrs **Parking:** 6

A stunning Victorian guest house located in a sunny, sheltered, traffic-free location, Pine Lodge offers panoramic views over the beautiful West Lyn Valley. A paradise for walkers; Exmoor and a variety of walks start right from the doorstep. The Victorians named Lynton as 'England's Little Switzerland' and from the village and nearby coast, attractions such as the Valley of the Rocks and Watersmeet Estate can be found. Beautiful and spacious en suite rooms have hospitality trays, TV, and sofa or chairs to make your stay relaxing. Home-made bread features at breakfast and there's a conservatory lounge.

Recommended in the area

Exmoor National Park; Cliff Railway between Lynton & Lynmouth; South West Coast Path

Victoria Lodge

★ ★ ★ ★ ★ 🛏 GUEST ACCOMMODATION

Address: 30-31 Lee Road, LYNTON, EX35 6BS
Tel: 01598 753203
Email: info@victorialodge.co.uk
Website: www.victorialodge.co.uk
Map ref: 2 SS74
Directions: Off A39 in village centre opp Post Office
Rooms: 8 en suite **S** £63.75-£119 **D** £75-£140
Notes: Wi-fi ⊗ on premises 🚼 under 11yrs
Parking: 6 **Closed:** Nov-23 Mar

Victoria Lodge is a large, elegant villa, built in the 1880s and located in the heart of Lynton. Full of character and original features, the house offers luxurious accommodation with quality furnishings including some antique pieces. The bedrooms are named after Queen Victoria's daughters and other members of the royal family and reflect the style of the period. They are decorated in rich colours and feature coronet, half-tester and four-poster beds. Guests can relax in the gardens, which include a colourful front terrace overlooking the water garden, ideal for fine weather. Otherwise there are two guest lounges with bay windows, comfortable sofas and shelves of books and magazines for guests to read. A good choice is offered at breakfast, with cooked dishes ranging from pancakes with maple syrup or porridge with (or without) Devon cream, through eggs Benedict and home-made kedgeree to the full Exmoor Works, with egg, sausage, bacon, tomato, mushrooms, hash brown and the Devon delicacy of hogs and black pudding. A meat-free full English breakfast is also offered, with vegetarian sausages, and you can finish off with toast and home-made preserves. Breakfast is served in the sumptuously decorated dining room, with its period fireplace and over mantle.

Recommended in the area

Exmoor National Park; Valley of the Rocks; The Tarks Trail

Mariners

★★★★ 🛏 ☕ GUEST ACCOMMODATION
Address: East Walk Esplanade, SEATON, EX12 2NP
Tel: 01297 20560
Website: www.marinershotelseaton.co.uk
Map ref: 2 SY29
Directions: Off A3052 signed Seaton,
Mariners on seafront
Rooms: 10 en suite (2GF) S £37-£45 D £66-£72
Notes: ⊗ on premises 🧒 under 5yrs **Parking:** 10

Situated in a commanding position just yards from the beach, Mariners combines comfortable, modern accommodation with a friendly and relaxed atmosphere. The en suite bedrooms – most with sea views – have all been renovated and offer crisp white linen, digital radios, flatscreen TVs, DVD players and many other thoughtful extras. A private apartment with a balcony from which to enjoy panoramic views is also available. Served in the modern dining room, breakfasts at Mariners have an enviable reputation due to the skilful cooking of owner/chef Nigel. Afternoon tea can be taken on the seafront terrace, and guests may relax in the light, airy public rooms.

Recommended in the area

Beer Pecorama; Seaton Tramway; Jurassic Coast World Heritage Site

Strete Barton House

★★★★★ GUEST HOUSE
Address: Totnes Rd, STRETE, Dartmouth, TQ6 0RU
Tel: 01803 770364
Fax: 01803 771182
Email: info@stretebarton.co.uk
Website: www.stretebarton.co.uk
Map ref: 2 SX85
Directions: Off A379 into village centre, just below
church **Rooms:** 6 (5 en suite) (1 pri facs) (1GF)
D £80-£120 **Notes:** Wi-fi 🧒 under 8yrs **Parking:** 4

This beautiful 16th-century manor has panoramic sea views and a large garden. Just 200yds from the coastal path, Blackpool Sands and Slapton Sands are only a mile away. The contemporary interior offers spacious double bedrooms with king-size beds (one with a super-king, four poster) and twin-bedded rooms. All bedrooms feature flat-screen TVs, DVD/CD players, Wi-fi access, extensive beverage trays, Egyptian cotton sheets, fluffy towels and luxury toiletries. In addition there is a luxury cottage suite with living room and inglenook log-burning stove. The full English breakfasts use local produce.

Recommended in the area

Greenway (NT); Blackpool Sands; Dartmouth

Thomas Luny House

★★★★★ ≘ GUEST ACCOMMODATION

Address: Teign Street, TEIGNMOUTH, TQ14 8EG
Tel: 01626 772976
Email: alisonandjohn@thomas-luny-house.co.uk
Website: www.thomas-luny-house.co.uk
Map ref: 2 SX97
Directions: A381 to Teignmouth, at 3rd lights turn right to quay, 50yds turn left onto Teign St, after 60yds turn right through white archway
Rooms: 4 en suite **S** £62-£70 **D** £75-£98
Notes: Wi-fi ⊗ on premises ⍦ under 12yrs **Parking:** 8

This delightful late 18th-century house is run by John and Alison Allan whose relaxed yet attentive approach is much appreciated by their guests. The large drawing room and dining room are beautifully furnished and have French doors opening onto a walled garden with a terraced sitting area. The bedrooms are well equipped and very comfortable. Home-made dishes and a full cooked breakfast are a speciality.

Recommended in the area

Tuckers Maltings; Powderham Castle; Cockington Village

The Colindale

★★★★ ≘ GUEST ACCOMMODATION

Address: 20 Rathmore Road, Chelston, TORQUAY, TQ2 6NY
Tel: 01803 293947
Fax: 01803 231050
Email: rathmore@blueyonder.co.uk
Website: www.colindalehotel.co.uk
Map ref: 2 SX96
Directions: From Torquay station 200yds on left in Rathmore Rd **Rooms:** 7 (6 en suite) (1 pri facs)

£40-£45 **D** £60-£75 **Notes:** Wi-fi ⊗ on premises ⍦ under 12yrs **Parking:** 6 **Closed:** 20 Dec-3 Jan

The Colindale is set in a quiet road overlooking Torre Abbey and close to the seafront and railway station. This elegant establishment, with its antiques and artworks and a library of books, offers attractively co-ordinated en suite bedrooms, some with views over Torbay, and lots of extra touches such as digital TVs, towelling robes and mineral water. Memorable breakfasts are enjoyed in the smart dining room, using local eggs, organic bacon and sausages, and home-made breads and preserves.

Recommended in the area

Paignton Zoo Environmental Park; Babbacombe Model Village; Cockington Village

Headland View

★★★★ 🛏 GUEST HOUSE

Address: 37 Babbacombe Downs, Babbacombe,
           TORQUAY, TQ1 3LN
Tel: 01803 312612
Email: reception@headlandview.com
Website: www.headlandview.com
Map ref: 2 SX96
Directions: A379 S to Babbacombe, off Babbacombe
Rd left onto Portland Rd & Babbacombe Downs Rd
& seafront Rooms: 6 (4 en suite) (2 pri facs) S fr £45
D fr £68 Notes: Wi-fi ⊗ on premises ♥️ under 5yrs ⊜ Parking: 4 Closed: Nov-Mar

Every comfort is thought of in this delightful little guest house by the sea. There are spectacular views over the World Heritage Coast of Lyme Bay from the sun lounge and most of the bedrooms have balconies. Those without sea views have four poster beds. Colin and Sue Jezard will ensure a memorable stay. The excellent breakfast includes kedgeree, fresh fruit pancakes, home-made yoghurt and bread. Lovely beaches, and a good choice of pubs and restaurants, are nearby.

Recommended in the area

Dartmoor; South-West Coastal Path; Oddicombe beach

Millbrook House

★★★★ GUEST ACCOMMODATION

Address: 1 Old Mill Road, Chelston,
           TORQUAY, TQ2 6AP
Tel: 01803 297394
Email: marksj@sky.com
Website: www.millbrook-house-hotel.co.uk
Map ref: 2 SX96
Rooms: 10 en suite (2GF) S £30 D £50-£60
Notes: ⊗ on premises Parking: 8 Closed: Nov-Feb

The delightful, personally run Millbrook House is within easy walking distance of Torquay's many attractions and has a friendly and relaxed atmosphere. The well-maintained en suite bedrooms provide many useful facilities; a king-size bed and a four-poster room are available and there is a family room, thoughtfully divided by a partition wall. One room features a sunken bath. There is a cosy bar on the lower ground floor with pool and darts, and the vibrant garden has a summer house for guests to relax in on hotter days. The freshly cooked breakfasts here include local produce as much as possible.

Recommended in the area

Torquay's beaches; Paignton; Brixham

The Durant Arms

★ ★ ★ ★ ⬳ INN

Address: Ashprington, TOTNES, TQ9 7UP
Tel: 01803 732240
Email: info@durantarms.co.uk
Website: www.durantarms.co.uk
Map ref: 2 SX86
Directions: A381 from Totnes for Kingsbridge, 1m left for Ashprington
Rooms: 8 en suite (2GF)
Parking: 8
Closed: 25-26 Dec evenings only

This beautifully kept inn with well-tended shrubs and plants is a focal point in the picturesque village of Ashprington, deep in the heart of Devon's South Hams district. Owners Eileen and Graham Ellis proudly offer their own brand of hospitality and provide attractive accommodation in either the main building or the Old Coach House. The bedrooms are individually designed to a very high standard, using stylish furnishings, and include a host of thoughtful touches to help ensure a memorable stay. Each room has a luxurious well-appointed en suite bathroom that adds additional comfort. The inn is renowned locally for its delicious food. A blackboard menu of home-cooked food is available in the character bar or the smart dining room, both furnished in rich red velvets. All dishes are freshly cooked to order, offering fresh vegetables and a wide variety of meat and fish; seasonal local produce is used whenever possible. Packed lunches are also available. To complement your meal there is a good choice of real ales, beers and wines, some from the local Sharpham Vineyard, just a 15-minute walk away and open to the public for visiting and wine tasting. There are stunning views of the River Dart too, making The Durant Arms the perfect place to stay.

Recommended in the area

Historic Totnes; The Eden Project; Sharpham Vineyard

Culloden House

★ ★ ★ GUEST HOUSE
Address: Fosketh Hill, WESTWARD HO!, EX39 1UL
Tel: 01237 479421
Email: theaa@culloden-house.co.uk
Website: www.culloden-house.co.uk
Map ref: 1 SS42
Directions: S of town centre. Off B3236 Stanwell Hill onto Fosketh Hill
Rooms: 7 en suite (1GF) S £52 D £65-£75
Parking: 4 Closed: Xmas & New Year

Set in a commanding position on a wooded hillside, overlooking Westward Ho! beach and Bideford Bay, Culloden House was built in 1865 as a Victorian gentleman's residence. It is now a family-run guest house with large, elegant rooms retaining many original features. Westward Ho! is the perfect place for a short break or family holiday, only five minutes' drive from the A39 'Atlantic Highway' with one of the safest and most beautiful Blue Flag beaches in the West Country, two miles long and perfect for surfing. It is in the middle of the North Devon Area of Outstanding Natural Beauty, the first UNESCO biosphere reserve in Europe, and a Site of Special Scientific Interest. Guests are favoured with reduced rates at the Royal North Devon Golf Club, the oldest golf course in England. All of the guest bedrooms are en suite, offering a choice of king-size, double or twin beds, with Freeview television and a hospitality tray. Children are welcome and many rooms are suitable for families. Well-behaved pets can also be accommodated with prior notice. A traditional English breakfast is served in the large dining room with its splendid views over the whole of Golden Bay.

Recommended in the area

Burton Art Gallery; RHS Garden Rosemoor; Milky Way Adventure Park

The River Dart at Dartmeet, Dartmoor National Park

Harrabeer Country House

★ ★ ★ ★ GUEST ACCOMMODATION

Address: Harrowbeer Lane, YELVERTON, PL20 6EA
Tel: 01822 853302
Email: reception@harrabeer.co.uk
Website: www.harrabeer.co.uk
Map ref: 3 SX56
Directions: In village. Off A386 Tavistock Rd onto Grange Rd, right onto Harrowbeer Ln
Rooms: 6 (5 en suite) (1 pri facs) (1GF)
S £55-£80 D £69.50-£95
Notes: Wi-fi Parking: 10 Closed: 3rd wk Dec, 2nd wk Jan

This lovely Devon longhouse on the edge of Dartmoor has a relaxing lounge, a bar for a convivial evening drink and well-equipped comfortable bedrooms. Breakfast is a leisurely affair served in the dining room which overlooks the garden, and dinner can be served by arrangement. The Harrabeer provides an excellent base for exploring the beautiful surrounding countryside. Two self-catering units are available.

Recommended in the area

The Garden House; The Eden Project; Dartmoor National Park

DORSET

Mupe Bay

The beach and pier, Bournemouth

Westcotes House

★★★★ GUEST HOUSE

Address: 9 Southbourne Overcliff Drive,
Southbourne, BOURNEMOUTH, BH6 3TE
Tel/Fax: 01202 428512
Website: www.westcoteshousehotel.co.uk
Map ref: 3 SZ09
Directions: 2m E of town centre. A35 onto B3059,
into Grand Av, continue to end, right, house on right
Rooms: 6 en suite (1GF) **S** £45-£80 **D** £70-£80
Notes: ⊗ on premises ⚼ under 10yrs ♿ **Parking:** 6

Situated on the quiet side of the town, on the cliff top at Southbourne, this small, elegantly designed establishment enjoys spectacular views over Poole Bay. The conservatory lounge leads directly onto a sunny, sea-facing terrace, and a zigzag path and cliff lift give easy access to the promenade and sandy beach below. All of the en suite bedrooms are well equipped with tea and coffee-making facilities, bathrobes, tissues and toiletries. There is also a well-presented dining room, where enjoyable home-cooked dinners are served by arrangement. Private parking is available.

Recommended in the area
Poole Harbour; Hengistbury Head; Christchurch

The Lord Bute & Restaurant

★ ★ ★ ★ ★ ◉◉ GUEST ACCOMMODATION

Address: 179-181 Lymington Road, Highcliffe on
Sea, CHRISTCHURCH, BH23 4JS
Tel: 01425 278884
Fax: 01425 279258
Email: mail@lordbute.co.uk
Website: www.lordbute.co.uk
Map ref: 3 SZ19
Directions: A337 towards Highcliffe
Rooms: 13 en suite (6GF) S fr £98 D £98-£225
Parking: 40

The elegant Lord Bute stands directly behind the original entrance lodges of Highcliffe Castle, close
to the beach and the historic town of Christchurch. It was once home to Lord Bute, British Prime
Minister from 1762 to 1763. Comfort and impeccable standards are key here. The luxurious and
very stylish en suite bedrooms, including some family rooms and some on the ground floor, have all
been finished to a very high standard, with many thoughtful extras including direct-dial telephones,
trouser press, air-conditioning and well-stocked tea- and coffee-making facilities. Self-contained suites,
some with their own private landscaped garden areas and including a bridal suite, are available in
what were once the gatehouses to the castle. Elsewhere, guests can relax in the warm and welcoming
lounge, or peruse the menu in the tranquil conservatory-styled orangery. The excellent food makes
dining here memorable. Served in the smart, classically furnished restaurant with a friendly ambience,
breakfast, lunch and dinner are all available, prepared by award-winning chefs. Special events include
cabaret evenings and a jazz diary. Conferences and weddings are also catered for, and a conference
suite is available.

Recommended in the area

The New Forest; Hengistbury Head; Christchurch Priory

Mill Stream House

★ ★ ★ ★ BED & BREAKFAST

Address: 6 Ducking Stool Walk, Off Ducking Stool Lane, CHRISTCHURCH, BH23 1GA
Tel: 01202 480114 & 07733 477023
Email: hjewitt@btinternet.com
Website: www.christchurchbedandbreakfast.co.uk
Map ref: 3 SZ19
Directions: Follow signs to High St, left onto Millhams St then Ducking Stool Ln. Turn right just past tea rooms
Rooms: 2 en suite) (1GF) S £30-£60 D £60-£90
Notes: ⊗ on premises ☼ Parking: 2

Located in the centre of historic Christchurch, this house is ideally placed for the many restaurants, walks and historic sites in the area. It is also just a few minutes' drive from many fine sandy beaches and from the New Forest, famous for its wild ponies. The 900-year-old Priory Church and Christchurch Harbour are within strolling distance and the railway station is just 10 minutes' walk away, yet this is a quiet spot in which to enjoy a tranquil break. The property itself, which takes its name from the mill stream flowing at the rear of the property, provides attractive boutique-style, en suite bedrooms with large, sumptuous beds, flat-screen Freeview TVs and free Wi-fi, hairdryers, bottled water and generous hospitality trays; one room is on the ground floor. Delicious home-cooked breakfasts are made from locally sourced produce and organic free-range eggs, and include dishes such as smoked haddock and smoked salmon with poached eggs as well as traditional English breakfasts and freshly brewed coffee. All are served in the open-plan kitchen/dining room at a communal table. Parking is gated and secure, and The Kings Hotel, which offers evening dining, is within the same complex.

Recommended in the area

Beaulieu Motor Museum; Highcliffe Castle; Brownsea Island (NT)

Baytree House Dorchester

★★★★ BED & BREAKFAST

Address: 4 Athelstan Road, DORCHESTER, DT1 1NR
Tel: 01305 263696
Email: info@baytreedorchester.com
Website: www.bandbdorchester.co.uk
Map ref: 2 SY69
Directions: 0.5m SE of town centre
Rooms: 3 en suite S fr £35 D fr £65
Notes: ⊗ on premises 🚗 **Parking:** 3

In 2006 owners Nicola and Gary Cutler completely refurbished Baytree House, creating a stylish place to stay, with spacious and light rooms, contemporary decor and luxurious fittings. Although it is set in a quiet residential area, it's just a 10-minute stroll to the historic centre of Dorchester and a short drive to many of rural Dorset's attractions. The bedrooms offer either en suite shower room or a private bathroom, which has shower and bath. The Cutlers also own the Walnut Grove Restaurant and Coffee Shop in the town centre, and employ the same high standards of cooking at Baytree House. Guests are offered a 15 percent discount on meals at the Walnut Grove.

Recommended in the area

Thomas Hardy's Cottage; Monkey World; Dorset's Jurassic coastline

Beggars Knap

★★★★ GUEST ACCOMMODATION

Address: 2 Weymouth Avenue,
DORCHESTER, DT1 1QS
Tel: 01305 268191 & 07768 690691
Email: beggarsknap@hotmail.co.uk
Website: www.beggarsknap.co.uk
Map ref: 2 SY69
Rooms: 3 en suite S £45-£59 D £60-£90
Notes: 🚗 **Parking:** 3

Despite its name, Beggars Knap is far from impoverished. A detached Victorian property with links to the local brewery and Thomas Hardy, it sits in the heart of the lovely market town of Dorchester, and offers guests stylish, spacious accommodation. Furnishings are opulent and hark back to the Victorian era, with high ceilings, bay windows, chandeliers and brocade in evidence. The en suite bedrooms feature fine cottons and two offer a French sleigh bed or a four-poster. Freshly cooked breakfasts are served round one large table in a room with towering plants and a huge harp. Off-street parking is available.

Recommended in the area

Maiden Castle; Roman Town House; Maumbury Rings

Rocky coastline of Mupe Bay

Little Court

★★★★★ ≙ GUEST ACCOMMODATION

Address: 5 Westleaze, Charminster, DORCHESTER, DT2 9PZ
Tel: 01305 261576
Fax: 01305 261359
Email: info@littlecourt.net
Website: www.littlecourt.net
Map ref: 2 SY69
Directions: A37 from Dorchester, 0.25m right at Loders Garage, Little Court 0.5m on right **Rooms:** 8 en suite **S** £69-£79 **D** £79-£89 **Notes:** Wi-fi ⊗ on premises **Parking:** 10 **Closed:** Xmas & New Year

A picture-postcard Edwardian house, Little Court nestles in 4 acres of beautiful grounds and gardens. The property has been refurbished to a very high standard and the proprietors are on hand to ensure you have an excellent stay. Bedrooms have a bath and shower en suite, and come with extras such as an umbrella. A delicious breakfast, including home-grown produce, is served in the dining room which adjoins a restful lounge with open fires. A pub nearby serves good food.

Recommended in the area
Jurassic World Heritage Coast; Dorchester; Weymouth

The Acorn Inn

★★★★ ⍟ INN

Address: EVERSHOT, Dorchester, DT2 0JW
Tel: 01935 83228
Fax: 01935 83707
Email: stay@acorn-inn.co.uk
Website: www.acorn-inn.co.uk
Map ref: 2 ST50
Directions: 0.5m off A37 between Yeovil &
Dorchester, signed Evershot & Holywell
Rooms: 10 en suite S £60-£75
Notes: Wi-fi Parking: 40

This 16th-century coaching inn was immortalised as the Sow and Acorn in Thomas Hardy's *Tess of the D'Urbervilles*. It stands at the heart of the village of Evershot, in an Area of Outstanding Natural Beauty, with walking, fishing, shooting and riding all nearby. Inside are two oak-panelled bars – one flagstoned, one tiled – with logs blazing in carved hamstone fireplaces, and a cosy restaurant. There's also a skittle alley in what was once the stables, and it's rumoured that the residents' sitting room was once used by Hanging Judge Jeffreys as a court room. The en suite bedrooms are all individually styled, and each named after a character from Hardy's novel – several feature interesting four-poster beds. All of the rooms, including two family rooms, have a TV, free Wi-fi, a beverage tray and hairdryers. Irons are available on request. Fresh, local produce is included on the varied and interesting menu, with most of the food sourced from within a 15-mile radius, including local fish and game, and bolstered by blackboard specials. Bar snacks and lighter meals are also available, accompanied by a selection of real ales and a comprehensive wine list. Plenty of parking spaces are available.

Recommended in the area

Evershot village; Forde Abbey; Lyme Regis

Ruins of Corfe Castle

Farnham Farm House

★★★★★ GUEST ACCOMMODATION

Address:	FARNHAM, Blandford Forum, DT11 8DG
Tel:	01725 516254
Fax:	01725 516306
Email:	info@farnhamfarmhouse.co.uk
Website:	www.farnhamfarmhouse.co.uk
Map ref:	2 ST91

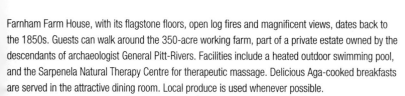

Directions: Off A354 Thickthorn x-rds into Farnham, continue NW from village centre T-junct, 1m bear right at sign

Rooms: 3 en suite **S** £60-£70 **D** £80 **Notes:** ⊗ on premises **Parking:** 7 **Closed:** 25-26 Dec

Farnham Farm House, with its flagstone floors, open log fires and magnificent views, dates back to the 1850s. Guests can walk around the 350-acre working farm, part of a private estate owned by the descendants of archaeologist General Pitt-Rivers. Facilities include a heated outdoor swimming pool, and the Sarpenela Natural Therapy Centre for therapeutic massage. Delicious Aga-cooked breakfasts are served in the attractive dining room. Local produce is used whenever possible.

Recommended in the area

Cranborne Chase; Kingston Lacey (NT); Larmer Tree Gardens

Longpuddle

★ ★ ★ ★ BED & BREAKFAST

Address: 4 High Street, PIDDLEHINTON, DT2 7TD
Tel: 01300 348532
Email: ann@longpuddle.co.uk
Website: www.longpuddle.co.uk
Map ref: 2 SY79
Directions: From Dorchester (A35) take B3143, after entering village 1st thatched house on left after village cross
Rooms: 2 en suite S £50-£80 D £90-£110
Notes: Wi-fi ✆ **Parking:** 3

Set in the Piddle Valley, midway between the abbey town of Sherborne and the county town of Dorchester, Longpuddle is well placed for exploring Thomas Hardy's Dorset and the Jurassic Coast. The 400-year-old thatched cottage overlooks the embryo River Piddle, which runs between the large garden and paddocks, and off-road parking is available. Guest accommodation comprises two spacious, tastefully decorated rooms ideal for an extended stay; one double and one twin, both with en suite facilities. A third bed can be made available if required for a child. Guests have the use of a spacious, comfortable drawing room with a TV and views over the garden and paddocks. Breakfast consists of local produce personally cooked by the proprietor, including homemade marmalade. Individual tastes and vegetarians are catered for. The name Longpuddle was used by Thomas Hardy, collectively, for the villages of the Piddle Valley, where there are several pubs serving local food and the excellent Abbots Tea Room. For a special meal there are some superior restaurants within a 40-minute drive. Ann (the proprietor) and Sassy (the resident Golden Retriever) look forward to meeting you and helping you enjoy this delightful county. Well-behaved pets are welcome by prior arrangement.

Recommended in the area

Cerne Abbas Giant; Maiden Castle; Sherborne

Swanage

Avalon Townhouse

★ ★ ★ ★ BED & BREAKFAST

Address: South Street, SHERBORNE, DT9 3LZ
Tel: 01935 814748
Email: enquiries@avalontownhouse.co.uk
Website: www.avalontownhouse.co.uk
Map ref: 2 ST61
Directions: A30 from Shaftesbury, towards Sherborne town centre, left onto South St
Rooms: 3 en suite S £70-£80 D £80-£90
Notes: Wi-fi ⊗ on premises ⚲ under 18yrs

Avalon is a spacious and comfortable Edwardian townhouse in the heart of historic Sherborne, close to the railway station. The building, recently refurbished to a high standard, retains many original features, such as the open fire in the lounge, and the small garden has been redesigned to create a feeling of space. All of the en suite bedrooms have Freeview flat-screen TVs, free Wi-fi, power showers and luxurious towels and toiletries. A freshly prepared breakfast starts the day around a large oak table in the farmhouse-style kitchen, and there is a real commitment to using locally sourced ingredients.

Recommended in the area

Sherborne Abbey; Sherborne Castle; Jerram Gallery

The Kings Arms

★★★★★ ⊜ INN

Address: Charlton Horethorne,
SHERBORNE, DT9 4NL
Tel: 01963 220281
Fax: 01963 220496
Email: admin@thekingsarms.co.uk
Website: www.thekingsarms.co.uk
Map ref: 2 ST61
Directions: From A303 follow signs for
Templecombe & Sherborne onto B3145 to Charlton
Horethorne Rooms: 10 en suite D £95 Notes: Wi-fi Parking: 30

Situated in the heart of the pretty village of Charlton Horethorne, the Kings Arms has benefited from a total refurbishment, resulting in impressive standards throughout. Behind the imposing Edwardian façade, the atmosphere remains that of a traditional English country pub, but with all modern facilities and conveniences. Indeed, the experienced owners have created something for everyone with a convivial bar, snug and choice of dining environments, including the garden terrace with lovely countryside views. There's also a croquet lawn beside the terrace. All of the bedrooms possess individuality, quality and style, with marble bathrooms, robes and powerful showers, as well as Wi-fi and flatscreen TVs and DVD players. Some of the rooms are in the newly built part of the house, while others are found in the older part of the building. All have lift as well as stair access, and one room is specially adapted for wheelchair users. The food, which has won an AA Dinner Award, is taken seriously here, with assured cooking from a menu majoring on good English ingredients and showcasing the best of local produce. Much is cooked and prepared on the premises – from the fresh-baked bread to the home-made ice cream and pasta.

Recommended in the area

Fleet Air Arm Museum; Sherborne Old Castle; Haynes International Motor Museum; Stourhead House & Gardens

Swanage Haven

★★★★ GUEST HOUSE

Address: 3 Victoria Road, SWANAGE,
BH19 1LY
Tel: 01929 423088
Fax: 01929 421912
Email: info@swanagehaven.com
Website: www.swanagehaven.com
Map ref: 3 SZ07
Rooms: 8 en suite S £40-£45 D £60-£70
Notes: ⊗ on premises 🐾
Parking: 8

Set in the seaside town of Swanage, the gateway to the Jurassic Coast, and just 200 yards from its Blue Flag Beach, this boutique-style guest house is a haven of peace and tranquillity. Catering exclusively for adults, and with the emphasis on attention to detail and relaxation, the accommodation is fresh and modern. The many extras provided in the en suite bedrooms include flat-screen TVs, fluffy robes, slippers, a selection of Fairtrade beverages and luxury chocolates. Some of the rooms also enjoy views over the beautiful Ballard Down. The hands-on owners combine excellent hospitality with relaxed and friendly service. As well as a large guest lounge with roaring open fires in winter and a licensed bar containing a wealth of books on the local area, there's a hot tub in the landscaped gardens and a treatment room offering holistic treatments to help relieve the stresses of the day. Breakfasts are superb here; there's a wide choice of top-quality organic and local produce from an extensive menu that includes a Dorset cooked breakfast or smoked salmon and eggs, as well as vegetarian and vegan options. Ample off-road parking is available, as is Wi-fi.

Recommended in the area

Durlston Country Park; Monkey World; Tynham, Dorset's Lost Village

The Esplanade

★★★★ GUEST ACCOMMODATION
Address: 141 The Esplanade,
 WEYMOUTH, DT4 7NJ
Tel/Fax: 01305 783129
Email: stay@theesplanadehotel.co.uk
Website: www.theesplanadehotel.co.uk
Map ref: 2 SY67
Directions: On seafront, between Jubilee Clock
& pier bandstand
Rooms: 11 en suite (2GF) S £45-£60 D £70-£110
Notes: Wi-fi ⊗ on premises Parking: 9 Closed: Nov-Feb

With a warm welcome assured from owners Rob and Terri Cole, The Esplanade is a Grade II listed Georgian property, built in 1835, and located in a prime seafront location. Ideally situated for all local attractions and amenities, it is just yards from the beach and promenade. The front-facing rooms have stunning seaside views and a panorama of the beautiful golden sands of Weymouth beach. Set against the unforgettable backdrop of Weymouth Bay and the famous World Heritage Coastline, The Esplanade is a haven for those wanting peace and relaxation beside the sea, as well as those seeking a more activity-based seaside experience. The town centre, railway station, bus station and ferry terminal are all within easy walking distance. All bedrooms offer en suite facilities with baths and showers, 100% Egyptian cotton linen with a high degree of luxury and comfort. With an extensive breakfast menu supplied from the highest quality locally sourced produce wherever possible, delicious breakfasts are served overlooking the sea. With a guest lounge and bar on the first floor, the balcony is the perfect place to sip a cool drink and watch the boats sail past. Off-road parking is available.

Recommended in the area

Dorset Beaches; Portland Bill; South West Coastal Path; Monkey World; Sea Life Centre; Abbotsbury Swannery and Subtropical Gardens; Sea fishing and sailing

Portland lighthouse, Portland Bill

Les Bouviers Restaurant with Rooms

★★★★★ ◎◎ RESTAURANT WITH ROOMS

Address: Arrowsmith Road, Canford Magna,
WIMBORNE MINSTER, BH21 3BD

Tel: 01202 889555

Fax: 01202 639428

Email: info@lesbouviers.co.uk

Website: www.lesbouviers.co.uk

Map ref: 2 SZ09

Directions: A31 onto A349. In 0.6m turn left. In approx 1m right onto Arrowsmith Rd. Establishment approx 100yds on right **Rooms:** 6 en suite **S** £90 **D** £100-£180 **Notes:** Wi-fi **Parking:** 50

Ideally located in over five acres of peaceful, landscaped grounds, this house gives the feeling of being deep in the country yet is close to Wimborne, Poole and Bournemouth. Each of the en suite bedrooms has been individually designed with many little luxuries and home comforts such as supremely comfortable beds, in-room coffee systems and Wi-fi. Impressive food, accompanied by wines from an extensive cellar, is a highlight of any stay here, as is the friendly, attentive service.

Recommended in the area

Wimborne Model Town; Purbeck Hills; Poole Harbour

ESSEX

Audley End House near Saffron Walden

The Old Manse

★★★★ GUEST ACCOMMODATION

Address: 15 Roman Road, COLCHESTER, CO1 1UR
Tel: 01206 545154
Fax: 01206 545153
Email: wendyanderson15@hotmail.com
Website: www.theoldmanse.uk.com
Map ref: 4 TL92
Directions: In town centre, 250yds E of castle. Off High St-East Hill onto Roman Rd
Rooms: 3 (2 en suite) (1 pri facs) S £45-£60 D £65-£75 **Notes:** Wi-fi ⊗ on premises ⚡ under 8yrs ⊜ **Parking:** 1 **Closed:** 23-31 Dec

This elegant and spacious Victorian house is in a quiet location, yet just a short walk from the castle and the town centre. The bedrooms here are carefully decorated with coordinated soft furnishings, and equipped with many thoughtful touches. Breakfast is served at a large communal table in the attractive dining room and there is a comfortable lounge. The Old Manse is famous for its warm welcome and friendly atmosphere, and Wendy Anderson was a finalist for AA Friendliest Landlady of the Year 2007.
Recommended in the area
Colchester Castle; Colchester Zoo; Beth Chatto Gardens

Warner's Farm

★★★★ BED & BREAKFAST

Address: Top Road, Wimbish Green, SAFFRON WALDEN, CB10 2XJ
Tel: 01799 599525
Email: info@warnersfarm.co.uk
Website: www.warnersfarm.co.uk
Map ref: 4 TL53
Directions: 4m SE of Saffron Walden. Off B184 to Wimbish Green **Rooms:** 4 en suite S £35-£50 D £60-£80 **Notes:** Wi-fi ⊗ on premises ⚡ by arrangement ⊜ **Parking:** 15 **Closed:** 22 Dec-4 Jan

Dating back to 1430, this delightful property is set in five acres of grounds surrounded by open countryside. The comfortable bedrooms have a wealth of character; each has Freeview TV, refreshment tray, hairdryer, toiletries and bathrobes. There are now two ground-floor Garden Rooms suitable for families or for less able guests. Breakfast is taken in the smart dining room and guests have the use of a drawing room with a blazing fire in winter. Outside there is a heated swimming pool and a sun patio.
Recommended in the area
Audley End House; Duxford Imperial War Museum; Cambridge

Bourton-on-the-Hill

The River Colne, Cassey Compton

The Old Passage Inn

★★★★ ◉◉ 🛏 RESTAURANT WITH ROOMS

Address: Passage Road, ARLINGHAM, GL2 7JR
Tel: 01452 740547
Fax: 01452 741871
Email: oldpassage@ukonline.co.uk
Website: www.theoldpassage.com
Map ref: 2 SO71
Directions: A38 onto B4071 through Arlingham.
House by river
Rooms: 3 en suite **S** £70-£130 **D** £90-£130
Notes: Wi-fi **Parking:** 30 **Closed:** 25-26 Dec

This restaurant with rooms is delightfully located on the very edge of the River Severn. The en suite bedrooms are decorated in contemporary style and welcoming extra includes air conditioning, mini bars and tea and coffee making equipment. In the restaurant the fresh water crayfish is local, and pride is taken in using sustainably sourced fish and shellfish, with lobster fresh from the tanks, and freshly shucked oysters and fruits de mers as house specialities.

Recommended in the area

Dean Heritage Centre; Lydney Park Gardens; Edward Jenner Museum

Cleeve Hill House

★★★★★ GUEST ACCOMMODATION

Address: Cleeve Hill, CHELTENHAM, GL52 3PR
Tel: 01242 672052
Fax: 01242 679969
Email: info@cleevehill-hotel.co.uk
Website: www.cleevehill-hotel.co.uk
Map ref: 2 SO92
Directions: 3m N of Cheltenham on B4632
Rooms: 10 en suite (1GF) S £50-£65 D £85-£110
Notes: Wi-fi ⊗ on premises 🐾 under 8yrs
Parking: 11

This large detached property, which sits near the top of Cleeve Hill, the highest point of the Cotswolds, and backs onto Cleeve Common, makes an ideal base for walking and exploring the area. Now run by experienced hoteliers, it was built in Edwardian times and both the lounge and many of the bedrooms have spectacular views across to the Malvern Hills. The en suite bedrooms vary in shape and size, but all are comfortably furnished with many welcome extras such as plasma-screen TVs with DVD players, tea- and coffee-making facilities and complimentary Wi-fi (laptops can be provided on request); some rooms have four-poster beds and one suite has a private lounge area. Family accommodation can be provided, and one of the rooms is on the ground floor. In addition to the relaxing guest lounge, an honesty bar is in place 24 hours a day, and drinks can be taken in the lounge or back to the bedrooms. Breakfast, served in the light, airy conservatory, which enjoys fine views of the local countryside, offers a good selection of carefully presented hot and cold choices, including vegetarian options and locally produced free-range eggs. Cleeve Hill House has its own private car park.

Recommended in the area

Cheltenham Spa; Snowshill Manor (NT); Stratford-upon-Avon

Lypiatt House

★★★★★ GUEST ACCOMMODATION

Address: Lypiatt Road, CHELTENHAM, GL50 2QW
Tel: 01242 224994
Fax: 01242 224996
Email: stay@lypiatt.co.uk
Website: www.lypiatt.co.uk
Map ref: 2 SO92
Directions: M5 junct 11 to town centre. At Texaco petrol station mini-rdbt take exit signed Stroud. Fork right, pass shops, turn sharp left onto Lypiatt Rd
Rooms: 10 en suite (2GF) **S** £75-£90 **D** £90-£120
Notes: Wi-fi ⊗ on premises 👶 under 10yrs **Parking:** 10

Close to Cheltenham's exclusive and fashionable Montpellier area, Lypiatt House is within walking distance of the main shopping area, restaurants and theatres, as well as being well located for the many festivals that take place in the town. A very fine house, built in typical Victorian style, it is set in its own grounds and provides ample residents' parking. Inside, the atmosphere is intimate and tranquil, with contemporary decor enhancing the building's traditional features. Guests are welcome to relax in the spacious and elegant drawing room or in the conservatory, with the latter featuring an honesty bar. The bedrooms and bathrooms, all en suite, come in a range of shapes and sizes, but all of the rooms are decorated and maintained to a high standard and include a range of welcome extras, such as TVs, beverage trays, direct-dial telephones and free Wi-fi; two of the rooms are on the ground floor. Full English breakfasts are served, and a laundry service is available. All in all, this makes a relaxing base for a stay in Cheltenham, whether travelling on business or for pleasure.

Recommended in the area

Pittville Pump Room; Gloucester Cathedral; Gloucestershire Warwickshire Steam Railway

Chipping Campden

The Moda House

★★★★ GUEST ACCOMMODATION

Address: 1 High Street, CHIPPING SODBURY,
BS37 6BA
Tel: 01454 312135
Fax: 01454 850090
Email: enquiries@modahouse.co.uk
Website: www.modahouse.co.uk
Map ref: 2 ST78
Directions: In town centre
Rooms: 10 en suite (3GF) **S** £65 **D** £82-£95 **Notes:** Wi-fi

Over 300 years old, this house is a fine property and large B&B
that retains a very homely feel. An impressive Grade II listed
building, it has with wonderful views of the town and countryside beyond. Duncan and Jo are widely
travelled and have filled the house with pictures and artefacts from all over the world. Bedrooms differ,
but all are cosy and well decorated with lovely fabrics and colours, and have pocket-sprung mattresses,
bathrobes and thick, fluffy towels. The Aga-cooked breakfast is truly a feast of local produce.

Recommended in the area

Bath; Westonbirt Arboretum; Dyrham Park (NT)

Hare & Hounds

★★★★ ❀ INN

Address: Fosse-Cross, Chedworth,
CIRENCESTER, GL54 4NN
Tel: 01285 720288
Email: stay@hareandhoundsinn.com
Website: www.hareandhoundsinn.com
Map ref: 3 SP00
Directions: 4.50m NE of Cirencester. On A429 by
speed camera
Rooms: 10 en suite (8 GF) **S** £60–£70 **D** £90–£125
Notes: ⊗ on premises **Parking:** 40

This country inn is close to the historic Fosse Way and perfectly situated for visiting nearby Cirencester and the Cotswolds. The smart bedrooms surround a peaceful courtyard and have full disabled access. Guests can dine outside on warm summer days, in the orangerie, or in one of the three elegant dining areas in the main pub. The delicious home-cooked food is highly regarded; chef Gerry Ragosa, an advocate of Cotswold produce, creates superb results using local ingredients where possible.

Recommended in the area

Chedworth Roman Villa (NT); Cheltenham; Cotswold Wildlife Park

The Plough Inn

★★★★ INN

Address: FORD, Temple Guiting, GL54 5RU
Tel: 01386 584215
Fax: 01386 584042
Email: info@theploughinnatford.co.uk
Website: www.theploughinnatford.co.uk
Map ref: 3 SP02
Directions: On B4077 in village
Rooms: 3 en suite
Notes: ⊗ on premises **Parking:** 50

The Plough Inn, popular with locals and the racing fraternity, is a charming 16th-century inn, well located for visiting the Cotswolds. Inside it retains many original features including Cotswold stone walls, open fires and beamed ceilings, while the en suite bedrooms are located across a courtyard in a quaint cobble-stoned building – once a hayloft with stabling, it has now been restored to provide comfortable, modern accommodation. Home-cooked food featuring local produce is a highlight here, as are the well-kept Donnington ales, which can be enjoyed in the delightful beer garden.

Recommended in the area

Cheltenham Racecourse; Bourton-on-the-Water; Chipping Campden

Guiting Guest House

★ ★ ★ ★ GUEST HOUSE

Address: Post Office Lane, GUITING POWER,
Cheltenham, GL54 5TZ

Tel: 01451 850470

Email: info@guitingguesthouse.com

Website: www.guitingguesthouse.com

Map ref: 3 SP02

Directions: In village centre

Rooms: 6 (5 en suite) (1 pri facs) (2GF)

S fr £45 D fr £85 Notes: Wi-fi Parking: 2

Guiting Guest House is an engaging family home at one with its surroundings in a beautiful Cotswold village. Bedrooms are individually decorated and full of charm. Most have en suite facilities, some have four-poster beds, and all of them are equipped with hairdryers, bathrobes, quality toiletries, and hospitality trays, fresh fruit and flowers. Exposed beams, inglenook fireplaces and solid elm floorboards provide character in the inviting public rooms. Breakfast and evening meals, based on fresh local produce, are served in the dining room. Please give at least 48 hours' notice for a dinner booking.

Recommended in the area

Cotswold Farm Park; Sudeley Castle; Blenheim Palace

Cambrai Lodge

★ ★ ★ ★ GUEST ACCOMMODATION

Address: Oak Street, LECHLADE-ON-THAMES,
GL7 3AY

Tel: 01367 253173 & 07860 150467

Email: info@cambrailodgeguesthouse.co.uk

Website: www.cambrailodgeguesthouse.co.uk

Map ref: 3 SU29

Directions: In town centre, off High St onto
A361 Oak St

Rooms: 3 en suite (2GF) S £45-£65 D £60-£75

Parking: 12

This attractive house, on the edge of the market town of Lechlade, is only a stroll from a number of recommended pubs serving food. The bedrooms are all carefully decorated and furnished. Some rooms are in a pretty cottage across the garden and include a king-sized bed and corner bath, and there are two ground-floor bedrooms. All the rooms are en suite, have tea and coffee facilities. Hearty breakfasts are served in the conservatory overlooking the large gardens.

Recommended in the area

Cirencester; Oxford; the Cotswolds

Heavens Above

★★★★ ◎◎ RESTAURANT WITH ROOMS

Address: 3 Cossack Square, NAILSWORTH, GL6 0DB
Tel: 01453 832615
Email: info@wild-garlic.co.uk
Website: www.heavensabove-rooms.co.uk
Map ref: 2 ST89
Directions: M4 junct 18. A46 towards Stroud. In town, left at rdbt and then immediate left. Restaurant opposite Britannia Pub **Rooms:** 3 (1 en suite)
S £65-£85 D £65-£85 **Notes:** Wi-fi ⊗ on premises

Heavens Above is situated over the Wild Garlic Restaurant in the picture postcard Cossack Square of a town renowned for its wonderful craft shops and award-winning farmers market. It provides a tranquil base from which to explore the Cotswolds, with its wealth of cultural attractions, and just a short walk from the bustling town centre. Meals can be taken in the restaurant below, where everything is hand made on the premises, from the fresh pasta, ice creams and sorbets to the daily baked bread, but bookings are essential so don't forget to reserve your table when booking your room.

Recommended in the area

Chavenage; Owlpen Manor; Woodchester Mansion

Northfield Guest House

★★★★ GUEST ACCOMMODATION

Address: Cirencester Road,
NORTHLEACH, GL54 3JL
Tel/Fax: 01451 860427
Email: p.loving@sky.com
Website: www.northfieldbandb.co.uk
Map ref: 3 SP11
Directions: Signed off A429 (Northleach-Cirencester road), 1m from Northleach lights
Rooms: 3 en suite (3GF) D £65-£75
Notes: ⊗ on premises **Parking:** 10 **Closed:** Dec-Feb

Animals graze in the fields around this Cotswold stone house set in immaculate gardens. Indoors there is a clear commitment to presentation and the bedrooms are a pleasure to stay in – two rooms have direct access to the gardens. The relaxing atmosphere extends to the lounge. The friendly dining room is the scene of delicious country breakfasts including eggs from the resident hens. Northleach is convenient for Cirencester and Gloucester.

Recommended in the area

Chedworth Roman Villa (NT); Keith Harding's Musical Museum; Cheltenham; Stow-on-the-Wold

16th-century Church of St Andrew, Naunton

Aston House

★★★★ BED & BREAKFAST

Address: Broadwell, STOW-ON-THE-WOLD,
GL56 0TJ
Tel: 01451 830475
Email: fja@astonhouse.net
Website: www.astonhouse.net
Map ref: 3 SP12
Directions: A429 from Stow-on-the-Wold towards
Moreton-in-Marsh, 1m right at x-rds to Broadwell,
Aston House 0.5m on left **Rooms:** 3 (2 en suite)

(1 pri facs) (1GF) **D** £68-£75 **Notes:** ⊗ on premises ⚄ under 10yrs **Parking:** 3 **Closed:** Nov-Feb

The enthusiastic owner ensures that the accommodation has every comfort, with armchairs in all the rooms, electric blankets and fans. Other amenities include quality toiletries in the en suite bathrooms, televisions, radios and hairdryers, tea-making facilities and bedtime drinks and biscuits. Although rooms are not suitable for wheelchair-bound visitors, the stair lift is a boon for those with limited mobility. A full English breakfast is served and there is a good pub within walking distance.

Recommended in the area

Cotswolds villages; Blenheim Palace; Hidcote Manor Gardens; Warwick Castle

Kings Head Inn & Restaurant

★★★★ ❀ INN

Address: The Green, Bledington,
STOW-ON-THE-WOLD, OX7 6XQ
Tel: 01608 658365
Fax: 01608 658902
Email: kingshead@orr-ewing.com
Website: www.kingsheadinn.net
Map ref: 3 SP12
Directions: 4m SE off B4450
Rooms: 12 en suite (3GF)
Notes: Wi-fi ⊗ on premises **Parking:** 24 **Closed:** 25-26 Dec

Located next to the picturesque village green with a brook running past, this classic English country pub is well worth seeking out. In the 16th century it was used as a cider house, and its timeless interior, full of charm and character, has low ceilings, beams, exposed stone walls and open fires. Nicola Orr-Ewing was once a milliner in London, and she has used her creative talents to transform the accommodation. Husband Archie, born in the next village, helps to maintain a relaxed but efficient atmosphere. The stylish bedrooms are individually decorated and each has a modern bathroom. Some rooms are above the inn (these are full of character and have standard double beds), while others are in a quiet courtyard annexe set well back from the pub. These annexe rooms have king-size beds and are more spacious than those in the main building. All rooms have wireless internet access and televisions. Excellent meals, using locally sourced and organic produce where possible, are served in the smart restaurant. The Aberdeen Angus beef comes from the family's own farm in a neighbouring village and the vegetables from the Vale of Evesham. The interesting breakfast menu offers a choice of delicious and sustaining dishes.

Recommended in the area

Blenheim Palace; Cotswold Farm Park; Cheltenham Races

Westonbirt Arboretum

1 Woodchester Lodge

★ ★ ★ ★ BED & BREAKFAST

Address: Southfield Road, North Woodchester,
STROUD, GL5 5PA
Tel: 01453 872586
Email: anne@woodchesterlodge.co.uk
Website: www.woodchesterlodge.co.uk
Map ref: 2 SO80
Directions: A46 onto Selsley Rd, take 2nd left,
200yds on left **Rooms:** 3 (1 en suite) (2 pri facs)
S £40-£45 D £60-£65 **Notes:** Wi-fi ⊗ on premises
Parking: 4 **Closed:** Xmas & Etr

This large, late Victorian house is situated in the peaceful village of North Woodchester. Spacious bedrooms offer king-size beds, TVs, hospitality trays and comfortable chairs. The colourful gardens are well tended, and guests can enjoy the patio in warmer weather; otherwise, the comfortable lounge/ dining room offers an open fire, books, magazines and games. Excellent breakfasts and meals, prepared by a qualified chef, using fruit and vegetables from the garden and freshly laid eggs.
Recommended in the area
Woodchester Mansion and grounds; WWT Slimbridge; Westonbirt Arboretum

Antony Gormley's 'Sound II', Winchester Cathedral

The Woolpack Inn

★ ★ ★ ★ ❀ INN

Address: Totford, ALRESFORD, SO24 9TJ
Tel: 01962 734184
Fax: 0845 293 8055
Email: info@thewoolpackinn.co.uk
Website: www.thewoolpackinn.co.uk
Map ref: 3 SU53
Directions: M3 take A339 towards Alton, turn right onto A3046. In Totford village on left (B3046)
Rooms: 7 en suite (4GF) S £75-£135 D £75-£135
Notes: Wi-fi Parking: 20

Located in a tranquil village setting, yet within easy reach of the main transport routes, this traditional listed establishment has benefited from an extensive refurbishment. Throughout, it skilfully balances contemporary styling with traditional features, and the en suite bedrooms include many extras, such as plasma-screen TV with DVD, and mini-bar. The award-winning dining room showcases local produce, while breakfast features options such as kippers and home-made muesli, as well as full English.

Recommended in the area

Winchester Cathedral; Watercress Line Steam Railway; Alresford

The Cottage Lodge

★ ★ ★ ★ ★ GUEST ACCOMMODATION

Address: Sway Road, BROCKENHURST, SO42 7SH
Tel: 01590 622296
Fax: 01590 623014
Email: enquiries@cottagelodge.co.uk
Website: www.cottagelodge.co.uk
Map ref: 3 SU30
Directions: Off A337 opp Careys Manor Hotel onto Grigg Ln, 0.25m over x-rds, cottage next to war memorial

Rooms: 12 en suite (6GF) S £50-£136 D £55-£170
Notes: Wi-fi 🐾 under 10yrs Parking: 14 Closed: Xmas & New Year

Owners David and Christina welcome guests to their cosy, award-winning 17th-century B&B with tea or coffee, served in front of the roaring fire. Brockenhurst is one of the few New Forest settlements where grazing ponies and cattle still have right of way. Conveniently close to the high street and the open forest. The individually furnished bedrooms are en suite and a local New Forest breakfast is served.

Recommended in the area

National Motor Museum, Beaulieu; Exbury Gardens; walking, cycling and horse riding

Wisteria House

★ ★ ★ ★ BED & BREAKFAST

Address: 14 Mays Lane, Stubbington,
FAREHAM, PO14 2EP
Tel: 01329 511940
Email: info@wisteria-house.co.uk
Website: www.wisteria-house.co.uk
Map ref: 3 SU50
Directions: M27 junct 9, take A27 to Fareham.
Right onto B3334, at rdbt left onto Mays Ln
Rooms: 2 en suite (2GF) **S** £48 **D** £63
Notes: Wi-fi ⊗ on premises ✦ under 8yrs **Parking:** 2

Wisteria House, a comfortable and tastefully decorated guest house, is just a short walk from local amenities and a mile from the beach at Lee-on-the-Solent, with its stunning panoramic views of the Isle of Wight. The charming and comfortable bedrooms, both on the ground floor, are packed with thoughtful touches such as king-size bed, Freeview TV, radio alarm, hairdryer and well-stocked hospitality tray. A full English breakfast is served in the pretty dining room.

Recommended in the area

Portsmouth Historic Dockyard; The New Forest; Winchester

Ravensdale

★ ★ ★ ★ BED & BREAKFAST

Address: 19 St Catherines Road,
HAYLING ISLAND, PO11 0HF
Tel: 023 9246 3203 & 07802 188259
Fax: 023 9246 3203
Email: phil.taylor@tayloredprint.co.uk
Website: www.ravensdale-hayling.co.uk
Map ref: 3 SU70
Directions: A3023 at Langstone, cross Hayling
Bridge, 3m to mini rdbt, right into Manor Rd 1m.
Right by Barley Mow into Station Rd, 3rd left into St Catherines Rd **Rooms:** 3 (2 en suite) (1 pri facs)
S £40-£42 **D** £66-£68 **Notes:** ⊗ on premises ✦ under 8yrs ⊛ **Parking:** 4 **Closed:** last 2wks Dec

A warm welcome awaits at Ravensdale, where Phil and Jane will make you feel at home in a relaxed and friendly environment. Situated in a quiet, tree-lined road close to the beach and golf course, the house offers tastefully decorated, comfortable accommodation, attractive bedrooms, home cooking and evening meals on request.

Recommended in the area

Chichester Cathedral; Portsmouth Historic Dockyard; walking on the South Downs

West Wind Guest House

★★★★ GUEST ACCOMMODATION

Address: 197 Portsmouth Road,
LEE-ON-THE-SOLENT, Gosport, PO13 9AA
Tel: 023 9255 2550
Email: info@west-wind.co.uk
Website: www.west-wind.co.uk
Map ref: 3 SU50
Directions: M27 junct 11, A32, then B3385 for
Lee-on-the-Solent, left at beach, 800mtrs on left
Rooms: 6 en suite (1GF) Notes: Wi-fi ⊗ on premises
🐾 under 10yrs Parking: 6 Closed: Xmas & New Year

Now under new ownership, this family-run guest house is just 50 metres from the beach. The white painted, double-fronted house makes an ideal base for visiting the cities of Portsmouth, Southampton and Winchester as well as the beautiful New Forest. Bedrooms are individually decorated to a high standard and equipped to offer en suite facilities, TVs, hairdryers and well-stocked hospitality trays, plus Wi-fi access. The freshly cooked breakfasts include locally made sausages.

Recommended in the area

Portsmouth Historic Dockyard; Winchester Cathedral; Southampton Maritime Museum

---

The Rufus House

★★★★ GUEST ACCOMMODATION

Address: Southampton Road, LYNDHURST, SO43 7BQ
Tel: 023 8028 2930
Email: stay@rufushouse.co.uk
Website: www.rufushouse.co.uk
Map ref: 3 SU30
Directions: From Lyndhurst centre onto A35
(Southampton Rd), 300yds on left
Rooms: 11 en suite (2GF) S £35-£50 D £50-£120
Notes: ⊗ on premises 🐾 under 5yrs Parking: 12

A welcoming, peaceful haven in the heart of the New Forest National Park, this grand Victorian house is ideally located at its centre. Within ten minutes' walk, you will be spoilt with the choice of restaurants, tea houses and pubs. Golf courses, equestrian centres, cycle hire and swimming are all within a short distance. A 'stress relief short break' with yoga, meditation and a healthy natural food experience is on offer, as well as counselling services. There is use of a nearby spa at an extra cost. Suitable for business travellers with free Wi-fi. A self-catering cottage is on site.

Recommended in the area

National Motor Museum and Palace House, Beaulieu; Exbury Gardens; New Forest Otter & Wildlife Park

Temple Lodge

★ ★ ★ ★ 🛏 GUEST ACCOMMODATION

Address: 2 Queens Road, LYNDHURST, SO43 7BR
Tel: 023 8028 2392
Fax: 023 8028 4910
Email: templelodge@btinternet.com
Website: www.templelodge-guesthouse.com
Map ref: 3 SU30
Directions: M27 junct 2/3 onto A35 to Ashurst/
Lyndhurst, Temple Lodge on 2nd corner on right,
opposite forest

Rooms: 6 en suite D £60-£110 **Notes:** Wi-fi ⊗ on premises ⚓ under 12yrs **Parking:** 6

Temple Lodge is a beautiful Victorian residence, lovingly restored by its present owners and retaining many original features, such as the large entrance hall with its grand wooden staircase and beautiful stained-glass windows. The six spacious bedrooms, including a family suite and a family room, all have en suite facilities, generous hospitality trays, TVs/DVDs and mini fridges. The attractive guest lounge has a good selection of books and magazines and comfortable leather sofas. There is a wide choice of breakfasts, ranging from continental to full English breakfasts which are freshly prepared, using local ingredients, and served in the elegant dining room, which overlooks the well-stocked gardens. This is an ideal place for a relaxing stay, just a few minutes' level walk from the village of Lyndhurst with its numerous pubs and restaurants, and directly opposite the New Forest National Park. It makes a superb base for walking, cycling and exploring the surrounding countryside and nearby coastal areas. The owners, Mike and Teresa, are always pleased to be of service and make every effort to ensure their guests have a truly memorable stay. Free Wi-fi, good off-road parking and cycle storage are available on site.

Recommended in the area

National Motor Museum, Beaulieu; Exbury Gardens; Buckler's Hard; Lymington; Bournemouth; Christchurch

Hurst Castle

Alma Mater

★★★★ BED & BREAKFAST

Address: 4 Knowland Drive, MILFORD ON SEA,
Lymington, SO41 0RH
Tel: 01590 642811
Email: almamaterguesthouse@googlemail.com
Website: www.almamaternewforest.co.uk
Map ref: 3 SZ29
Directions: A337 at Everton onto B3058 to Milford
on Sea. Pass South Lawn Hotel, right onto Manor Rd,
1st left onto Knowland Dr, 3rd bungalow on right

Rooms: 3 en suite (1GF) S £40-£50 D £70-£80 **Notes:** ⊗ on premises ⚬ under 15yrs **Parking:** 4

Eileen and John Haywood enjoy welcoming guests to their beautifully kept home overlooking
landscaped gardens in a quiet residential area. It is a good base for exploring the New Forest and
coast, the yachting centre of Lymington is close by and the village and the beach are just a walk away.
A full four-course or continental breakfast is served in the dining room. The bedrooms have extras such
as radios, tea and coffee provisions, toiletries and bathrobes.

Recommended in the area

Hurst Castle; Exbury Gardens; National Motor Museum, Beaulieu

Butser Hill

Highcliffe Castle and gardens

The Festing Grove Guest House

★ ★ ★ GUEST ACCOMMODATION

Address: 8 Festing Grove, Southsea, PORTSMOUTH, PO4 9QA
Tel: 023 9273 5239
Email: thefestinggrove@ntlworld.com
Map ref: 3 SU60
Directions: E along seafront to South Parade Pier,
after pier sharp left, around lake, 3rd left & 2nd right
Rooms: 6 (1 en suite) **Notes:** ⊗ on premises

Situated in one of the quieter areas of the seaside resort of
Southsea and within three minutes' walk of the seafront and
pier, this long-established and well-presented property makes
an ideal base for visiting Portsmouth's maritime attractions,
shopping and restaurants at Gunwharf Quay. A continual programme of upgrading ensures that the
bedrooms, two of which are family rooms, enjoy a high standard of decor and comfort. Breakfast is
served in the homely dining room, and there is a well-appointed lounge for guests' use. On street
parking is available and bus routes to all parts of the city pass close to the front door.
Recommended in the area
Isle of Wight; Portsmouth Historic Dockyard; Royal Marines Museum, Southsea

Moortown Lodge

★ ★ ★ ★ GUEST ACCOMMODATION

Address: 244 Christchurch Road, RINGWOOD,
BH24 3AS
Tel: 01425 471404
Fax: 01425 476527
Email: enquiries@moortownlodge.co.uk
Website: www.moortownlodge.co.uk
Map ref: 3 SU10
Directions: 1m S of Ringwood. Off A31 at Ringwood
onto B3347, signs to Sopley, Lodge next to David
Lloyd Leisure Club
Rooms: 7 en suite (2GF) **D** £84-£94 **Notes:** Wi-fi **Parking:** 9

Moortown Lodge is a charming, family-run Georgian property in the attractive market town of Ringwood, the western gateway to the New Forest, where there is a wide range of unusual shops, traditional pubs and lovely restaurants. It offers guests a warm welcome and luxury grade B&B accommodation with many of the features found in a good class hotel. The seven elegantly furnished en suite rooms include one with a romantic four-poster bed and two easy access ground-floor rooms. All suites have digital TV and DVD, free broadband connection and free national direct-dial phones. Generous traditional breakfasts are cooked to order with lighter and vegetarian breakfast options available. Wherever possible fresh New Forest produce is used in the cooking. The peace and tranquillity of the open forest as well as the unspoilt water meadows of the River Avon are only minutes away. Moortown Lodge is the ideal stopover for business people as well as an excellent base for touring and leisure visitors. There are special arrangements for guests wishing to use the bar, restaurant and outstanding recreational facilities at the adjacent private David Lloyd Leisure Club.

Recommended in the area

Bournemouth; New Forest National Park; Stonehenge

Eyeworth Pond, Fritham

Greenvale Farm

★ ★ ★ ★ BED & BREAKFAST

Address: Melchet Park, Sherfield English,
ROMSEY, SO51 6FS
Tel: 01794 884858
Email: suebrown@greenvalefarm.com
Website: www.greenvalefarm.com
Map ref: 3 SU32
Directions: 5m W of Romsey. On S side of A27
through red-brick archway for Melchet Court,
Greenvale Farm 150yds on left, left at slatted barn

Rooms: 1 en suite (1GF) **Notes:** Wi-fi ⊗ on premises 🚼 under 14yrs ⊗ **Parking:** 10

Greenvale Farm in Melchet Park is located on the Hampshire/Wiltshire border, just four miles from the New Forest, near the historic market town of Romsey. The cathedral cities of Salisbury and Winchester are also within easy reach for days out. Greenvale Farm offers spacious, self-contained, ground floor accommodation with a twin or double room, en suite facilities, television and Wi-fi access. A hearty breakfast is served to set you up for the day and, if you're lucky, you can have freshly-laid eggs.

Recommended in the area

The Hillier Arboretum; Mottisfont Abbey and Gardens; Florence Nightingale's Grave

White Star Tavern, Dining and Rooms

★★★★ ⊕ INN

Address: 28 Oxford Street,
SOUTHAMPTON, SO14 3DJ
Tel: 023 8082 1990
Fax: 023 8090 4982
Email: reservations@whitestartavern.co.uk
Website: www.whitestartavern.co.uk
Map ref: 3 SU41
Directions: M3 junct 14 onto A33, towards Ocean Village
Rooms: 13 en suite S £89-£179 D £99-£179
Notes: Wi-fi ⊗ on premises

This award-winning bar, restaurant and boutique establishment is set in the historic maritime district of Southampton in cosmopolitan Oxford Street. Seriously comfortable beds are made up with soft Egyptian linen, and the bathrooms feature roll top baths and oversized showers. Rooms are equipped with the latest technology and entertainment facilities, such as broadband Wi-fi and 20-inch Freeview flat-screen TVs. The ground floor restaurant and bar attract a lively mix of drinkers and diners. Open for hearty and healthy breakfast, lunch and dinner everyday, the seasonal menus make superb use of great local ingredients. To accompany there's a great wine list, award-winning ales and an extensive list of cocktails. In warmer months guests can enjoy alfresco dining, soaking up the vibrant atmosphere.

Recommended in the area

Hall of Aviation; Maritime Museum; Southampton Art Gallery

Highclere Castle

The Cricketers Inn

★ ★ ★ INN

Address: 1 Church Road, STEEP,
Petersfield, GU32 2DW
Tel/Fax: 01730 261035
Email: thecricketerssteep@btconnect.com
Map ref: 3 SU72
Directions: A3 junct with A272, follow signs to
Petersfield. At next rdbt, 1st exit signed Steep,
1.5m on right **Rooms:** 6 en suite (2GF) **S** £69 **D** £79
Notes: Wi-fi **Parking:** 32

Refurbished and finished to a high standard, the Cricketers Inn offers well appointed, en suite
accommodation in the village of Steep, close to Petersfield. Inside this popular village inn, the
comfortable bedrooms are equipped with many thoughtful extras such as TV, alarm clock and
hospitality tray. Free Wi-fi is available on request. One room is mobility friendly, with a spacious wet-
room shower, and some bedrooms are secluded from the pub, which ensures a peaceful stay. The
comfortable, traditional bar and restaurant area offers a Spanish tapas menu.
Recommended in the area
South Downs; Flora Twort Gallery; Petersfield Heath

Giffard House

★★★★★ GUEST HOUSE

Address: 50 Christchurch Road,
WINCHESTER, SO23 9SU
Tel: 01962 852628
Fax: 01962 856722
Email: giffardhotel@aol.com
Website: www.giffardhotel.co.uk
Map ref: 3 SU42

Directions: M3 junct 11, at rdbt 3rd exit onto A333
St Cross road for 1m. Pass BP garage on right, take
next left then 2nd right. 150mtrs on left
Rooms: 13 en suite (4GF) S £69 D £89-£125
Notes: Wi-fi ⊗ on premises **Parking:** 13 **Closed:** 24 Dec-2 Jan

Visitors to this stunning 19th-century Victorian house, located a ten-minute walk from Winchester town centre, with its many amenities and points of interest, will find the recently refurbished establishment maintained to a high standard. Conference facilities are available, making it a good choice for business as well as leisure travellers. Inside, it combines elegance with comfort, and the well-equipped en suite bedrooms come with crisp white bed linen, luxurious bathrooms, beverage trays, direct-dial telephones and TV and radio facilities as standard. A family room and ground-floor rooms are available – one room is large enough for wheelchair users and grab rails can be provided – and for special occasions there is a suite. Guests are welcome to make use of Giffard House's garden, as well as the fully licensed bar, which is set in the elegant conservatory. Traditional breakfasts are served in the dining room and a self-service continental option is also on offer. Special diets can be catered for by arrangement. Wi-fi access is available, and there is ample free parking in the car park.

Recommended in the area

Winchester Castle; Dean Garnier Garden; Winchester City Mill (NT)

River Wye, Ross-on-Wye

Half timbered building, Ledbury

Little Hegdon Farm House

★★★★ BED & BREAKFAST

Address: Hegdon Hill, Pencombe,
BROMYARD, HR7 4SL
Tel: 01885 400263 & 07779 595445
Email: howardcolegrave@hotmail.com
Website: www.littlehegdonfarmhouse.co.uk
Map ref: 2 SO65
Directions: 4m SW of Bromyard. From Bromyard to
Pencombe, 1.5m towards Risbury, at top of Hegdon
Hill down farm lane for 500yds

Rooms: 2 en suite **S** £35 **D** £60 **Notes:** ☻ **Parking:** 4

A 17th-century former farmhouse, Little Hegdon lies in the heart of Herefordshire with clear views over farmland, cider orchards and hop yards to the Malvern and Cotswold hills. Restored to provide high standards of comfort, the period character of the house survives in the open fires and plenty of exposed oak beams. Facilities include a drawing room and attractive garden. There is one double and one twin room with hairdryers and tea and coffee facilities. Children and pets are welcome.

Recommended in the area

Lower Brockhampton Estate (NT); historic towns of Hereford and Ledbury; Worcester

Somerville House

★★★★★ GUEST ACCOMMODATION

Address: 12 Bodenham Road, HEREFORD, HR1 2TS
Tel: 01432 273991
Fax: 01432 268719
Email: enquiries@somervillehouse.net
Website: www.somervillehouse.net
Map ref: 2 SO53
Directions: A465, at Aylestone Hill rdbt towards city centre, left at Southbank Rd, leading to Bodenham Rd
Rooms: 12 en suite (1GF) S £50-£55 D £65-£99
Notes: Wi-fi ⊗ on premises **Parking:** 10

An imposing Victorian villa set in a quiet tree-lined road, Somerville House is run by Bill and Rosie, who provide modern boutique-style accommodation. The house is just a short walk from the railway station, bus station and Hereford city centre shops, restaurants and main attractions, and off-street parking is available within the grounds. To relax after a busy day, guests can sit with a drink on the terrace or in the lovely lounge with its open fire and later, perhaps, take a stroll around the garden. A mixture of large, luxury and smaller character bedrooms all have high quality en suite bathrooms, Wi-fi access, flat-screen Freeview televisions, ironing equipment, hairdryers, hospitality trays and mini bars. Luxury rooms are more spacious and have large beds, CD and DVD players. Flavours of Herefordshire are supported in-house, so enjoy locally produced drinks and snacks, such as Lulham Court wine and Tyrrell's crisps. The dining room has contemporary appeal, and here the full English breakfast is a speciality, using quality, locally sourced, organic produce with vegetarian options. There are also delicious local organic yoghurts, fruit juices, cereals, muesli and fresh fruit. Continental breakfast and healthy options are also offered. Fun breaks available.

Recommended in the area

Hereford Cathedral, Mappa Mundi & Chained Library; Hereford Museum; beautiful country walks

Church Farm

★★★★ FARMHOUSE

Address: Coddington, LEDBURY, HR8 1JJ
Tel: 01531 640271
Website: www.dexta.co.uk
Map ref: 2 SO73
Rooms: 3 en suite (1 pri facs) S £40-£45
D £72-£76 per room
Notes: ⊕ Closed: 17 Dec-17 Jan

Guests at Church Farm, in the quiet hamlet of
Coddington, are guaranteed a relaxing time and rural views during their stay at this small working
farm. There is much to explore in the area, with numerous activities including golf, canoeing, cycling
and various walks through farmland and peaceful country lanes, with the Malvern Hills only five miles
away. Inside, this 16th-century timber-framed farmhouse provides comfortable accommodation and
Aga-cooked breakfasts, with home-made preserves, served round the shared kitchen table or in the
separate dining room. There is also a comfortable lounge with an inglenook fireplace and log fires in
chilly weather.

Recommended in the area

Eastnor Castle; Hereford Cathedral; Malvern Hills; Ledbury and Hampton Court Gardens

Cwm Craig Farm

★★★★ FARMHOUSE

Address: LITTLE DEWCHURCH, HR2 6PS
Tel: 01432 840250
Fax: 01432 840250
Email: leead@btconnect.com
Map ref: 2 SO53 Directions: Off A49 into Little
Dewchurch, turn right in village, Cwm Craig 1st farm
on left Rooms: 3 en suite S £30-£36 D £54-£64
Notes: ⊗ on premises Parking: 6

Cwm Craig Farm is midway between Hereford and Ross-on-Wye and stands on the edge of a village
surrounded by superb countryside. The Georgian property retains many original features and offers
spacious accommodation furnished with fine period pieces. The bedrooms are all en suite and include
two doubles and a family room. Guests have access to their rooms all day, and hospitality trays are
provided. Home-cooked breakfasts are served in the dining room and morning room around large
tables, and you can relax in the sitting room or the games room with its three-quarter-size snooker/pool
table and dartboard. Pets cannot be accommodated.

Recommended in the area

Hereford Cathedral and city; Forest of Dean; Wye Valley

Orles Barn

★★★★ ☕ RESTAURANT WITH ROOMS

Address: Wilton, ROSS-ON-WYE, HR9 6AE
Tel: 01989 562155
Fax: 01989 768470
Email: reservations@orles-barn.co.uk
Website: www.orles-barn.co.uk
Map ref: 2 SO52
Directions: A49/A40 rdbt outside Ross-on-Wye, take slip road between petrol station & A40 to Monmouth. 100yds on left
Rooms: 8 (7 en suite) (1 pri facs) (1GF) **S** £49-£75 **D** £59-£105
Notes: Wi-fi **Parking:** 20

Orles Barn is a characterful Herefordshire property with a lovely south-facing garden. Older sections of the establishment date back to the 14th and 17th centuries, when it was a farmhouse with a barn. Today, it offers guests comfortable accommodation and good food. The bedrooms, most en suite and one a family room, are all named after traditional varieties of apples, such as Orange Pippin, Molly Delicious and Pixie Apple. They provide comfortable beds, TVs, hairdryers, tea- and coffee-making facilities, bottled water and free Wi-fi. As well as a smart, cosy lounge, there is a bar and a spacious restaurant. The food here is of a high standard, and has won an AA Dinner Award. Dinner and Sunday lunch are offered from a balanced and regularly changing menu of fresh local and seasonal dishes, and the sourcing of top quality ingredients is taken seriously. Themed events, such as an Italian night and gala dinners, are an excuse to push the boat out. Breakfast is also based on quality local produce and makes a good start to the day. The Orles Barn Cookery School provides a hands-on opportunity for guests to develop their culinary skills. There are many interesting areas to visit in this locality.

Recommended in the area

Wye Valley; Forest of Dean; Clearwell Caves

Eastnor Castle, Ledbury

HERTFORDSHIRE

St Mary's Church, Clothall

Knebworth House

Farmhouse B&B

★★★★★ BED & BREAKFAST

Address: Hawkins Grange Farm, Hawkins Hall Lane,
DATCHWORTH, Knebworth, SG3 6TF
Tel/Fax: 01438 813369
Email: mail@hawkinsgrangefarm.com
Website: www.hawkinsgrangefarm.com
Map ref: 3 TL21
Directions: A1(M) junct 7 onto A602 (Hertford). From Bragbury
End onto Bragbury Ln, 2m on left after phone box
Rooms: 3 (2 en suite) (1 pri facs) S £35-£45 D £70
Notes: Wi-fi ⊗ on premises **Parking:** 8

This extensively refurbished house is set amid beautiful
countryside, yet is within easy reach of Hertford, Stevenage and Welwyn Garden City. The tastefully
designed bedrooms are comfortably furnished and come with an abundance of thoughtful accessories. All
have good views over the open countryside. Jane's locally sourced organic breakfasts offer Full English,
vegetarian (vegan) and continental choices, including 'Braughing' sausages and Datchworth honey.
Recommended in the area
Hertford; Datchworth Museum; Welwyn

155

KENT

Saxon Shore Way path, Dover

House of Agnes

★★★★ GUEST ACCOMMODATION

Address: 71 Saint Dunstans Street, CANTERBURY, CT2 8BN
Tel: 01227 472185 **Fax:** 01227 470478
Email: info@houseofagnes.co.uk
Website: www.houseofagnes.co.uk
Map ref: 4 TR15
Directions: On A290 between London Rd & Orchard St
Rooms: 8 en suite S £40-£85 D £70-£130 **Notes:** Wi-fi ⊗ on premises ⋈ under 5yrs **Parking:** 20 **Closed:** 24-25 Dec

The original character of this 14th-century property, just a short stroll from the city centre, remains after a refurbishment that created luxury accommodation with an abundance of charm and quirkiness. Each of the individually themed rooms benefits from high-quality bed linen, flat-screen TV and DVD player and free Wi-fi. MP3 docking stations and a DVD library are also available. A heritage garden adds to the appeal of this historically significant property, which features in Charles Dickens's novel *David Copperfield*. The famous Astrolabe Quadrant was recently discovered within its walls.
Recommended in the area
Canterbury Cathedral; Whitstable; Herne Bay

Magnolia House

★★★★★ GUEST ACCOMMODATION

Address: 36 St Dunstan's Terrace,
CANTERBURY, CT2 8AX
Tel: 01227 765121 & 07776 236459
Fax: 01227 765121
Email: info@magnoliahousecanterbury.co.uk
Website: www.magnoliahousecanterbury.co.uk
Map ref: 4 TR15
Directions: A2 E onto A2050 for city centre, 1st rdbt left signed University of Kent. St Dunstan's Ter 3rd right **Rooms:** 7 en suite (1GF) S £55-£65 D £95-£125 **Notes:** Wi-fi ⊗ ⋈ under 12yrs **Parking:** 5

This charming late Georgian property, set in a quiet residential street just 10 minutes' stroll from Canterbury town centre, provides superbly appointed en suite bedrooms. Each is equipped with digital TV and Wi-fi, as well as a fridge containing complimentary wine, mineral water and fresh milk. Generous breakfasts based on fresh local produce are served in the dining room overlooking the attractive walled garden. Guests may relax in the sitting room or garden.
Recommended in the area
Wingham Wildlife Park; Herne Bay; Canterbury Castle

Rochester Cathedral

Yorke Lodge

★★★★★ GUEST ACCOMMODATION
Address: 50 London Road, CANTERBURY, CT2 8LF
Tel: 01227 451243
Fax: 01227 462006
Email: info@yorkelodge.com
Website: www.yorkelodge.com
Map ref: 4 TR15
Directions: From London M2/A2, 1st exit signed
Canterbury. At 1st rdbt left onto London Rd
Rooms: 8 en suite S £50-£55 D £90-£120
Notes: Wi-fi (free) **Parking:** 5

Decked on the outside with colourful window boxes and canopies, this Victorian villa is just a 10-minute walk from the town centre. The interior exudes style and elegance, with light, contemporary furniture and co-ordinated fabrics. The bedrooms are individually styled and the superior rooms have four-posters. All rooms have a TV, radio/alarm and beverage-making facilities. Traditional English breakfasts are served in the spacious dining room or light and airy conservatory which leads to the outside terrace.

Recommended in the area

Canterbury Cathedral; North Downs Way; Howletts Wild Animal Park, Bekesbourne

The Marquis at Alkham

★ ★ ★ ★ ★ ◎◎ RESTAURANT WITH ROOMS

Address: Alkham Valley Road, Alkham,
DOVER, CT15 7DF
Tel: 01304 873410
Fax: 01304 873418
Email: info@themarquisatalkham.co.uk
Website: www.themarquisatalkham.co.uk
Map ref: 4 TR34
Directions: From Dover take A256, at rdbt 1st exit onto London Rd, then left onto Alkham Rd, then Alkham Valley Rd. 1.5m after sharp bend **Rooms:** 5 en suite **S** £65-£185 **D** £75-£195
Notes: Wi-fi ⊗ on premises **Parking:** 22

Located between Dover and Folkestone, in a genteel English village, what was once the old village pub is now a modern, contemporary restaurant-with-rooms offering luxury accommodation with modern comforts. The chic, individually themed, boutique-style bedrooms are just the place to wind down after a fantastic meal at the award-winning restaurant. As well as views of the Alkham Valley, an Area of Outstanding Natural Beauty, the rooms come with sumptuous furnishings and fabrics, pocket-sprung mattresses, flat-screen TV and Wi-fi, with power showers and bathrobes in the en suite bathrooms. The restaurant, a real draw to the Marquis, is open for lunch and dinner, as well as for light bites, under the helm of accomplished chef Charles Lakin. The well-balanced menu, which changes regularly and offers fine modern British cuisine, majors on flavour-packed seasonal Kentish produce, such as Canterbury cheese. There's also a top-notch drinks list that includes wines from Kent vineyards and local real ales and ciders, all served in the sophisticated dining room. A choice of continental and cooked breakfasts are available.

Recommended in the area

Dover Castle; Canterbury Cathedral; Kent Downs

Court Lodge B&B

★ ★ ★ ★ GUEST ACCOMMODATION
Address: Court Lodge, Church Road, Oare,
FAVERSHAM, ME13 0QB
Tel/Fax: 01795 591543
Email: d.wheeldon@btconnect.com
Website: www.faversham.org/courtlodge
Map ref: 4 TR06
Directions: A2 onto B2045, left onto The Street,
right onto Church Rd, 0.25m on left **Rooms:** 2 (1 en
suite) (1 pri facs) **S** £50 **D** £70 **Notes:** Wi-fi 🖳

This sympathetically restored 16th-century listed farmhouse stands in 1.5 acres of gardens amid arable farmland – the perfect place to relax. The spacious rooms have private bathrooms, TV, and tea- and coffee-making facilities. Breakfast is served in the farmhouse kitchen, using the best of local produce including fish and home-made preserves. Court Lodge is ideal for those visiting Oare Creek or walking the Saxon Shore Way. Several pubs and restaurants are only a short distance away. Ample parking is available.

Recommended in the area
Faversham; Canterbury; Whitstable

The Relish

★ ★ ★ ★ ★ GUEST ACCOMMODATION
Address: 4 Augusta Gardens,
FOLKESTONE, CT20 2RR
Tel: 01303 850952
Fax: 01303 850958
Email: reservations@hotelrelish.co.uk
Website: www.hotelrelish.co.uk
Map ref: 4 TR23
Directions: Off A2033 (Sandgate Rd)
Rooms: 10 en suite **S** fr £65 **D** £90-£140
Notes: Wi-fi 😣 on premises **Closed:** 22 Dec-2 Jan

You will get a warm welcome at this stylish Victorian property overlooking Augusta Gardens in the fashionable West End of town. On arrival you will be greeted with a complimentary glass of wine or beer and fresh coffee, tea and home-made cakes are available throughout your stay. The bedrooms feature lovely coordinated fabrics, great showers and all have DVD players. Public rooms include a modern lounge-dining room and a terrace where breakfast is served during summer.

Recommended in the area
Dover Castle; Romney, Hythe and Dymchurch Railway; Canterbury

Seabrook House

★★★★ GUEST ACCOMMODATION
Address: 81 Seabrook Road, HYTHE, CT21 5QW
Tel: 01303 269282
Fax: 01303 237822
Email: seabrookhouse@hotmail.co.uk
Website: www.seabrook-house.co.uk
Map ref: 4 TR13
Directions: 0.9m E of Hythe on A259
Rooms: 13 en suite (4GF) S £35-£45 D £65-£75
Notes: ⊗ on premises **Parking:** 13

This striking Victorian property, easily recognised by the heavily timber-framed frontage and pretty gardens, is conveniently located for the M20 and Eurotunnel. Many of the art-deco style bedrooms have lovely sea views. These spacious en suite rooms, with their attractive decor and furnishings, also have hospitality trays, TV and hairdryers. A memorable full English breakfast sets you up for the ferries from Folkestone or Dover or for sightseeing in the local area, and there are plenty of comfortable places for relaxation, including a sunny conservatory and an elegant lounge.

Recommended in the area

Romney, Hythe and Dymchurch Railway; Dover Castle; Port Lympne Animal Park; Royal Military Canal

Olde Moat House

★★★★★ ⌂ GUEST ACCOMMODATION
Address: IVYCHURCH, TN29 0AZ
Tel: 01797 344700
Fax: 01797 343919
Email: oldemoathouse@hotmail.com
Website: www.oldemoathouse.co.uk
Map ref: 4 TR02
Directions: Off junct A2070 & A259 into Ivychurch, left & 0.75m on left **Rooms:** 3 en suite **Notes:** ⊗ on premises ⊷ under 16yrs **Parking:** 10

This beautiful medieval moated property is set amidst a tranquil location, surrounded by its own moat and 3.5 acres of stunning grounds. Luxurious en suite bedrooms with top quality furnishings and fittings are available, together with many thoughtful additions. The house has a charming elegance from the white-washed walls and pitched roof to the beamed ceilings and canopied beds. From the moment you enter the driveway you will experience peace and extreme comfort down to the last detail – an ideal retreat from the stresses of modern life.

Recommended in the area

Rye; Winchelsea; Kent & East Sussex Heritage Railway

Dover Castle

Danehurst House

★★★★★ BED & BREAKFAST

Address: 41 Lower Green Road, Rusthall,
TUNBRIDGE WELLS, TN4 8TW

Tel: 01892 527739

Fax: 01892 514804

Email: info@danehurst.net

Website: www.danehurst.net

Map ref: 4 TQ53

Directions: 1.5m W of Tunbridge Wells in Rusthall.
Off A264 onto Coach Rd & Lower Green Rd

Rooms: 4 en suite S £69.50-£89.50 D £89.50-£119.50 (Family suite £125-£145)

Notes: ⊗ on premises ✚ under 8yrs **Parking:** 6 **Closed:** Xmas & 1st 2wks Feb

Angela and Michael Godbold's spacious Victorian home stands just west of the historic spa town of Tunbridge Wells. There is a comfortable, relaxing drawing room, and the Victorian-style conservatory is a delightful setting for breakfast, whether full English, fish, cold meats or continental. The four cosy bedrooms are en suite, and have a wealth of thoughtful extras and notably comfortable beds. No pets.

Recommended in the area

Groombridge Place; Hever Castle; Chartwell (NT)

ast house, Bethersden

LANCASHIRE

Forest of Bowland at Whitewell

The Steamtown Museum, Carnforth

Whitestake Farm

★ ★ ★ ★ ★ BED & BREAKFAST

Address: Pope Lane, Whitestake, PRESTON, PR4 4JR
Tel: 01772 619392
Fax: 01772 611146
Email: enquiries@gardenofedenspa.co.uk
Website: www.gardenofedenspa.co.uk
Map ref: 6 SD52
Directions: M6 junct 29, A582 Lytham St Annes, Penwortham Way, left onto Chain House Ln, right onto Pope Ln. Whitestake Farm on right

Rooms: 2 en suite S fr £75 D fr £120 **Notes:** Wi-fi ⊗ on premises **Parking:** 6

This attractive white farmhouse is peacefully located just minutes from Preston and is within easy reach of Southport and Lytham. Inside, the beautifully appointed bedrooms and en suite bathrooms are spacious and thoughtfully equipped, and there is a guest lounge for relaxing. Carefully prepared, substantial breakfasts are taken around a huge table in the elegant dining room. Guests can also make use of the indoor swimming pool and two treatment rooms for added luxury.

Recommended in the area

The National Football Museum; Beacon Fell Country Park; The Ribble Steam Museum

Old John Tower folly, Bradgate Country Park

War Memorial, Bradgate Country Park

The Swan Inn

★★★★ INN

Address: 10 Loughborough Road,
MOUNTSORREL, LE12 7AT

Tel: 0116 230 2340

Fax: 0116 237 6115

Email: office@swaninn.eu

Website: www.the-swan-inn.eu

Map ref: 3 SK51

Directions: In village centre

Rooms: 1 en suite S £110 D £120

Notes: Wi-fi **Parking:** 12

This is a traditional 17th-century inn, a Grade II listed building located on the banks of the River Soar. The accommodation consists of one luxury suite with everything you could want – a large en suite bedroom, a fully equipped office with PC and Wi-fi, a bathroom with shower and antique roll-top cast-ion bath, a fitted kitchen and a private lounge. Meals are served inside or, weather permitting, in the secluded riverside garden. A continental breakfast is served in the suite.

Recommended in the area

Beacon Hill Country Park; Charnwood Museum; Great Central Railway

LINCOLNSHIRE

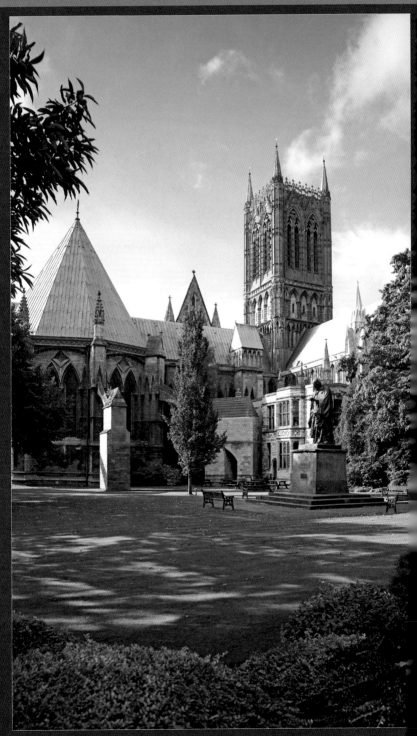

Lincoln Cathedral

Lincolnshire

Greenfield Farm

★★★★ FARMHOUSE
Address: Mill Lane/Cow Lane, Minting, HORNCASTLE, LN9 5PJ
Tel: 01507 578457 & 07768 368829
Email: greenfieldfarm@farming.co.uk
Website: www.greenfieldfarm.net
Map ref: 8 TF26
Directions: A158 NW from Horncastle. 5m left at The New Midge pub, farm 1m on right **Rooms:** 3 en suite S £39 D £58-£64 **Notes:** Wi-fi ⊗ on premises ✪ under 10yrs ⊛ **Parking:** 6 **Closed:** Xmas & New Year

This beautifully appointed, spacious farmhouse is located just one mile from the A158, within easy reach of many attractions. Its stunning grounds ensure a peaceful stay, especially as it also borders a nature reserve. Inside, the comfortable bedrooms provide TVs, radios and modern en suite shower rooms. The hearty Lincolnshire breakfast includes dry-cured bacon, local sausages and free-range eggs, along with home-made marmalade and local honey. There is also a lovely sitting room.
Recommended in the area
Lincolnshire Wolds; Lincolnshire Aviation Heritage Centre; Cadwell Park; Lincoln

The Brownlow Arms

★★★★★ ⊛ INN
Address: High Road, HOUGH-ON-THE-HILL, Grantham, NG32 2AZ
Tel: 01400 250234
Fax: 01400 271193
Email: paulandlorraine@thebrownlowarms.com
Website: www.thebrownlowarms.com
Map ref: 8 SK94 **Rooms:** 4 en suite S fr £65 D fr £96 **Notes:** ⊗ ✪ under 12yrs **Parking:** 20 **Closed:** 25-27 Dec & 31 Dec-20 Jan

This 17th-century country inn enjoys a peaceful location in the heart of a picturesque village. Once owned by Lord Brownlow, today it offers tranquillity and relaxation alongside exceptional modern comforts and country hospitality. It is tastefully decorated throughout, and all the comfortable bedrooms are en suite with LCD flat-screen TVs and power/drench showers. The friendly bar serves real ales, and Chef Paul Vidic works with premium produce to create imaginative dishes from a traditional menu with modern influences. There's also a luxurious lounge and a landscaped terrace.
Recommended in the area
Belton House; Lincoln Castle; Lincoln Cathedral

Minster Lodge

★★★★★ GUEST ACCOMMODATION
Address: 3 Church Lane, LINCOLN,
LN2 1QJ
Tel/Fax: 01522 513220
Email: info@minsterlodge.co.uk
Website: www.minsterlodge.co.uk
Map ref: 8 SK97
Directions: 400yds N of cathedral
Rooms: 6 en suite S £65-£120 D £75-£120
Notes: Wi-fi Parking: 10

Minster Lodge offers high quality facilities and successfully maintains the original character of the building while providing guests with modern comforts and conveniences. The accommodation enjoys an excellent location, just a few steps away from Lincoln's famous Bailgate, in view of Lincoln Cathedral and close to the castle. Although it allows guests easy access to the city centre, with its many shops, restaurants and historic buildings, Minster Lodge remains a peaceful place to stay thanks to the fact that it is set back from the road. Inside, the bright and spacious en suite bedrooms are enhanced by refurbished bathrooms and are full of thoughtful extras. Two family rooms are available, and one offers interconnecting rooms, perfect for those travelling with older children. Residents are welcome to relax in the large comfortable sitting room, with its lovely deep sofas and a TV, and all areas of the house are Wi-fi enabled. A traditional Aga-cooked or continental breakfast is served at individual tables in the attractive dining room, and features produce from the best local suppliers. Ample parking is available.

Recommended in the area

Lincoln Cathedral; Lincoln Victorian Arboretum; Museum of Lincolnshire Life

The Old Bakery

★★★★ ◉◎ RESTAURANT WITH ROOMS
Address: 26/28 Burton Road, LINCOLN, LN1 3LB
Tel: 01522 576057
Email: enquiries@theold-bakery.co.uk
Website: www.theold-bakery.co.uk
Map ref: 8 SK97
Directions: Exit A46 at Lincoln North follow signs for cathedral.
3rd exit at 1st rdbt, 1st exit at next rdbt
Rooms: 4 (2 en suite) (2 pri facs) **S** fr £50 **D** £53-£63
Notes: Wi-fi ⊗ on premises

Situated close to the castle in the Uphill area at the top of the town, this converted bakery is close to Lincoln Cathedral and the castle. It was originally built in 1837 and operated as a bakery until 1954.

In 1994 the property was restored and many of the original bakery features remain. Today it offers well-equipped bedrooms and a delightful and informal dining operation. The pretty bedrooms come with en suite or private facilities, and all benefit from digital colour TV with Freeview, broadband wireless internet access, radio alarm clock, hairdryer and tea- and coffee-making facilities. Ironing facilities are available on request. The restaurant here is popular, and the characterful dining room at the Old Bakery has been created in the location of the original ovens. A superb room has recently been created and described as a 'Garden under Glass' which extends the restaurant from 45 to 85 covers and is fully climate controlled for all year use. The cooking is Modern British with an Italian accent and has a dedication toward the use of local produce – the Old Bakery even has its own garden allotment that provides many of the vegetables served in the restaurant. Expect good friendly service from a dedicated staff at all times.

Recommended in the area

Lincoln Cathedral; Viking Way walking route; The Museum of Lincolnshire Life

Lincoln Cathedral

La Casita

★★★★★ ≙ BED & BREAKFAST

Address: Frith House, Main Street, NORMANTON,
Grantham, NG32 3BH
Tel: 01400 250302 & 07836 695282
Fax: 01400 250302
Email: jackiegonzalez@btinternet.com
Website: www.lacasitabandb.co.uk
Map ref: 8 SK94
Directions: In village centre on A607
Rooms: 1 en suite (1GF) S £95 D £125
Notes: Wi-fi ⊗ on premises **Parking:** 2

Set independently in the grounds of the owner's house, this converted stable offers considerable luxury. The suite provides complete privacy in sumptuous, spacious open-plan accommodation with its own entrance and terrace. There is a living room with kitchen area and log fire, and the slate-tiled bathroom is pure 'state of the art' complete with luxury toiletries and bathrobes. Extras include two flat-screen TVs, DVD, CD and broadband. Excellent rates for three or more nights' stay.

Recommended in the area

Lincoln; Nottingham; Grantham

Winteringham Fields

★ ★ ★ ★ ★ ◉◉ RESTAURANT WITH ROOMS

Address: WINTERINGHAM, DN15 9ND
Tel: 01724 733096
Fax: 01724 733898
Email: wintfields@aol.com
Website: www.winteringhamfields.com
Map ref: 8 SE92
Directions: In village centre at x-rds
Rooms: 11 en suite (3GF)
Parking: 14 **Closed:** 25 Dec for 2 wks, last wk Oct, 2 wks Aug

This highly regarded restaurant-with-rooms is housed in a 16th-century manor house with a cellar that dates back to the 1300s. Its location, deep in the countryside in a quiet village, gives it a real feeling of seclusion, yet it is just six miles west of the Humber Bridge, which can be seen from the pretty, rambling grounds. Here, guests can enjoy a peaceful aperitif or afternoon tea. The public rooms and bedrooms, some housed in renovated barns and cottages, are delightfully cosseting and styled with real flair and individuality. The features vary from room to room, with some enjoying walk-in wardrobes, beamed ceilings, rolltop or aromatherapy baths, four-posters and fully fitted kitchens. The pièce de résistance, chef-patron Colin McGurran's award-winning food, is modern European in style and artfully presented. Served in the lavish, richly decorated restaurant, which has a stained-glass dome in the ceiling and smart, well-spaced tables, it emphasises the sourcing of fresh, local produce: fish is delivered daily from local 'day fishing' boats, game in season comes from nearby shoots, and herbs and vegetables grown in the restaurant's own garden. As well as a six-course 'Menu Surprise', there is an ever-changing carte menu.

Recommended in the area

The Deep, Hull; Humber Bridge Country Park; Sewerby Hall & Gardens

LONDON

Trafalgar Square

MIC Conferences and Accommodation

★★★★ ➾ GUEST ACCOMMODATION

Address: 81-103 Euston Street, LONDON, NW1 2EZ
Tel: 020 7380 0001
Fax: 020 7387 5300
Email: sales@micentre.com
Website: www.micentre.com
Map ref: 3 TQ38

Directions: Euston Rd left at lights onto Melton St, 1st left onto Euston St, MIC 100yds on left
Rooms: 28 en suite S £93-£150 D £105.50-£150 **Notes:** Wi-fi ⊗ on premises

The top floor of the MIC building was completely overhauled in 2004 and has been designed to offer the highest standards and value for money. Staffed around the clock, a safe environment is assured. The stylish, air-conditioned bedrooms are en suite and come with LCD TVs and radios, room safes, a desk space with internet access, complimentary hospitality trays and mineral water. The spacious and airy Atrium Bar and Restaurant is perfect for an informal meeting, drink or meal. For breakfast, a traditional English buffet features eight hot items with eggs cooked to order, pancakes and waffles served with maple syrup or sauces, fruit juices, a good selection of cereals, a fruit and yoghurt bar, plus assorted teas and fresh coffee. The centre also offers a range of meeting rooms and private dining rooms for special events, which can be catered for. There are special weekend discount rates. The building is located in a quiet street close to Euston, which has a mainline station, an underground and local bus connections.

Recommended in the area

West End theatres; The BA London Eye; Madame Tussauds; British Museum; near St Pancras Eurostar Terminal

The New Inn

★ ★ ★ INN

Address: 2 Allitsen Road, St Johns Wood,
LONDON, NW8 6LA
Tel: 020 7722 0726
Fax: 020 7722 0653
Email: thenewinn@gmail.com
Website: www.newinnlondon.co.uk
Map ref: 3 TQ38
Directions: Off A41 by St Johns Wood tube station
onto Acacia Rd, last right, to end on corner
Rooms: 5 en suite **S** £80 **D** £80 **Notes:** Wi-fi ⊗

Built in 1810, this traditional inn is located in a leafy suburb just a stroll from Regents Park, and close to many central London places of interest. The en suite bedrooms are appointed to a high standard and are popular with business and leisure guests alike. Rooms are equipped with TVs, free Wi-fi, hairdryers and tea- and coffee-making facilities. A good choice of English ales, continental beers, wines and spirits is served alongside Thai and English cuisine in the bar lounge. Live music is played at weekends.
Recommended in the area
Madame Tussaud's; London Zoo; Lord's Cricket Ground

San Domenico House

★ ★ ★ ★ ★ GUEST ACCOMMODATION
Address: 29-31 Draycott Place, LONDON, SW3 2SH
Tel: 020 7581 5757
Fax: 020 7584 1348
Email: info@sandomenicohouse.com
Website: www.sandomenicohouse.com
Map ref: 3 TQ38
Rooms: 15 en suite **S** £210-£360 **D** £235-£360
Notes: ⊗ on premises

This newly extended and redesigned property, located in the heart of fashionable Chelsea, just a short walk from Sloane Square underground, offers luxurious accommodation and friendly, personalised service. The individually styled bedrooms and suites, all with antique and period pieces and rich soft furnishings, feature well-appointed marble en suites complete with Italian toiletries and bathrobes. An extensive room-service menu is available, and there is a sumptuous drawing room where guests can relax and enjoy works of art. Breakfast is served either in guests' bedrooms or in the elegant lower ground-floor dining room.
Recommended in the area
Shopping in Sloane Street; King's Road; Royal Hospital Chelsea

The Gainsborough

★★★★ GUEST ACCOMMODATION

Address: 7-11 Queensberry Place, South
Kensington, LONDON, SW7 2DL
Tel: 020 7957 0000
Fax: 020 7970 1805
Email: reservations@eeh.co.uk
Website: www.eeh.co.uk
Map ref: 3 TQ38
Directions: Off A4 opp Natural History Museum
Rooms: 48 en suite **Notes:** Wi-fi ⊗ on premises

This smart Georgian house is in a quiet street near South Kensington's museums and makes an excellent base for exploring this popular area. Inside, the feel is of an English country house, and the en suite bedrooms, which provide extras such as satellite TV, hairdryers and hospitality trays, are individually designed with fine fabrics and good-quality furnishings. Family rooms are available and there are also two-room suites with sitting areas. A choice of breakfasts is offered in the attractive dining room. There is also a delightful lobby lounge, and 24-hour room service is available.

Recommended in the area

Natural History Museum; Victoria and Albert Museum; Science Museum

The Gallery

★★★★ GUEST ACCOMMODATION

Address: 8-10 Queensberry Place, South
Kensington, LONDON, SW7 2EA
Tel: 020 7915 0000
Fax: 020 7970 1805
Email: reservations@eeh.co.uk
Website: www.eeh.co.uk
Map ref: 3 TQ38
Directions: Off A4 Cromwell Rd opp Natural History
Museum, near South Kensington tube station
Rooms: 36 en suite **S** £120-£141 **D** £141-£211.50 **Notes:** Wi-fi ⊗ on premises

This boutique establishment is a tribute to the art of the Victorian era. Everything from the Oriental porcelain in the lobby to the furniture and decor of the aptly named Morris Room has been selected with care. William Morris, Lord Leighton and Dante Gabriel Rossetti would surely feel at home here. The Gallery offers attentive service and sumptuously furnished en suite bedrooms, some with a private terrace. Public areas include a choice of lounges and an elegant bar. 24-hour room service is available.

Recommended in the area

Kensington Gardens; Hyde Park; Science & Natural History Museums

The Cottage

★★★★ GUEST ACCOMMODATION

Address: 150-152 High Street, CRANFORD, Hounslow, TW5 9WB
Tel: 020 8897 1815
Email: info@the-cottage.eu
Website: www.the-cottage.eu
Map ref: 3 TQ17
Directions: M4 junct 3, A312 towards Feltham, left at lights, left after 1st pub on left
Rooms: 20 en suite (12GF) S £75 D £85-£95
Notes: Wi-fi ⊗ on premises Parking: 20 Closed: 24-26 Dec & 31 Dec-1 Jan

This lovely 19th-century family-run property is just a few minutes' drive from Heathrow Airport, yet it benefits from a peaceful location. Guests here can rely on a friendly atmosphere combined with spacious and comfortable accommodation. The en suite bedrooms are tastefully decorated in a country style, using neutral colours and wooden furniture, and all come with a range of home comforts such as hospitality tray, TV, free Wi-fi, alarm clock and hairdryer. Some of the rooms in the main house, which include family rooms, are on the ground floor. There are now six newer bedrooms located at the rear of the landscaped garden, where guests will find fruit trees, shrubs and flowerbeds. These rooms are connected to the main building by a covered walkway overlooking the stunning courtyard, and all have views over the lovely area, as well as beamed ceilings, fridges, ironing facilities and luxury bathrooms with power showers. Breakfast, cooked or continental, is served in a stylishly decorated dining room, which opens on to a conservatory overlooking the garden. Fully secure CCTV-covered parking in the large car park is free for those in residence, and can also be provided by arrangement while guests are away on holiday. Please phone The Cottage and mention the AA for a good discount.

Recommended in the area

Hampton Court Palace; Legoland, Windsor; Kew Gardens

NORFOLK

Hunstanton

Bon Vista

★★★★ GUEST ACCOMMODATION

Address: 12 Alfred Road, CROMER, NR27 9AN
Tel: 01263 511818
Email: jim@bonvista-cromer.co.uk
Website: www.bonvista-cromer.co.uk
Map ref: 4 TG24
Directions: From pier onto A148 (coast road), in 400yds left onto Alfred Rd
Rooms: 5 en suite D £60-£72
Notes: ⊗ on premises ⊚ **Parking:** 2

One might consider this the epitome of the traditional seaside guest house, a sturdy, three-storey Victorian home, peacefully set in a residential area near the town and beach, which, along with its neighbours, sums up much of the character of this charming east-coast resort. Jim and Margaret have renovated the house to a very high standard, while retaining many of its 100-year-old features and have dedicated more than a decade to endowing it with a warm and friendly atmosphere. The first-floor lounge, with its original fireplace and big bay window, makes the most of the sea views and is a cosy place to relax in the evening. The dining room is on the ground floor and it's here that the traditional English breakfasts can be enjoyed, bathed in the light of the morning sun. The five bedrooms, each with an en suite bathroom, are very prettily decorated with cottagey wallpapers and colour-coordinated fabrics. Some still have their original fireplaces, and the climb up to the front room on the first floor is rewarded with a sea view. The other first-floor bedroom can accommodate a family, with bunk beds for the children. Each room has a TV, and Sky channels are available in the lounge. Another plus point here is the off-street parking, but it is limited so early arrival is recommended.

Recommended in the area

Cromer Pier Pavilion Theatre; North Norfolk Railway; Sheringham Park (NT)

Shrublands Farm

★ ★ ★ ★ FARMHOUSE

Address: Church Street, Northrepps,
CROMER, NR27 0AA

Tel/Fax: 01263 579297

Email: youngman@farming.co.uk

Website: www.shrublandsfarm.com

Map ref: 4 TG24

Directions: Off A149 to Northrepps, through village,
past Foundry Arms, cream house 50yds on left

Rooms: 3 (1 en suite) (2 pri facs) S £43-£47

D £66-£74 Notes: ⊗ on premises ⋫ under 12yrs Parking: 5

Shrublands is a working farm set in mature gardens amid 300 acres of arable farmland, an ideal base for exploring the coast and countryside of rural north Norfolk. Traditional hospitality is a distinguishing feature at the 18th-century farmhouse, with good cooking using home-grown and fresh local produce. Breakfast is served at a large table in the dining room, and there is also a cosy lounge, with a log fire, books and a television. The bedrooms have TVs, radio alarms and tea and coffee facilities. No pets.

Recommended in the area

Blickling Hall and Felbrigg Hall (NT); Sandy beaches at Cromer and Overstrand; Blakeney Point

3 Norfolk Square

★ ★ ★ ★ GUEST HOUSE

Address: 3 Norfolk Square,
GREAT YARMOUTH, NR30 1EE

Tel: 01493 843042

Fax: 01493 857276

Email: info@3norfolksquare.co.uk

Website: www.3norfolksquare.co.uk

Map ref: 4 TG50

Directions: From Britannia Pier, 200yds N along
seafront, left onto Albemarle Rd Rooms: 8 en suite

(2GF) S £30-£50 D £40-£100 Notes: Wi-fi ⊗ on premises ⋫ under 18yrs Parking: 3

This elegant, award-winning guest house, exclusively for adults, is situated in the superbly quiet location of Norfolk Square, but is still close to all the amenities of the town. Following a recent and total refurbishment the original features of the house have been enhanced. All the bedrooms are en suite and individually designed; seven have sea views and two have balconies. The facilities here will ensure a luxurious stay. The house has a few parking spaces and there is unlimited free parking opposite.

Recommended in the area

Great Yarmouth Racecourse; Greyhound racing; Norfolk Broads

White House Farm

★★★★★ GUEST ACCOMMODATION
Address: Knapton, NORTH WALSHAM, NR28 0RX
Tel:　　 01263 721344 & 07879 475220
Email:　 info@whitehousefarmnorfolk.co.uk
Website: www.whitehousefarmnorfolk.co.uk
Map ref: 4 TG23
Rooms: 3 en suite S £50 D £55-£65
Notes: Wi-fi ⊗ on premises 🐾 under 12yrs
Parking: 6

A delightful Grade II listed, 18th-century flint cottage that is close to sandy beaches of Norfolk's Heritage Coastline. Surrounded by open farmland it has been carefully restored to ensure the modern decor blends beautifully with historic features. The three large bedrooms have luxury en suite bathrooms and are equipped with many thoughtful touches. The Pulford Room has a four-poster bed and far-reaching views, while the Orton Room, also with a four-poster, has an additional single bedroom that can be used to provide twin accommodation if preferred. The traditional full English breakfast features home-made and local produce. Two self-catering cottages available.

Recommended in the area

Sandringham; Blickling Hall and Felbrigg Hall (NT); Norfolk Broads

Edmar Lodge

★★★ GUEST ACCOMMODATION
Address: 64 Earlham Road, NORWICH, NR2 3DF
Tel:　　 01603 615599
Fax:　　 01603 495599
Email:　 mail@edmarlodge.co.uk
Website: www.edmarlodge.co.uk
Map ref: 4 TG20
Directions: Off A47 S bypass onto B1108 Earlham Rd, follow university and hospital signs Rooms: 5 en suite S £38-£43 D £45-£50 Notes: Wi-fi Parking: 6

Located just a ten-minute walk from the city centre, this friendly, family-run guest house boasts a convenient location and ample private parking. The individually decorated en suite bedrooms, including one family room, are smartly appointed and well equipped, and there are DVD players and a collection of films that guests may borrow. Freshly prepared breakfasts, include many options and are served in the cosy dining room: a microwave and refrigerator along with plates and utensils are thoughtfully provided for those who wish to bring in food later. Guests are also welcome to enjoy the pretty garden.

Recommended in the area

Norwich Cathedral; Norfolk Broads; Norwich Castle

Gothic House Bed & Breakfast

★★★★ GUEST ACCOMMODATION

Address: King's Head Yard, Magdalen Street, NORWICH,
NR3 1JE
Tel: 01603 631879
Email: charvey649@aol.com
Website: www.gothic-house-norwich.com
Map ref: 4 TG20
Directions: Follow signs for A147, turn off at rdbt past flyover
into Whitefriars. Right again onto Fishergate, at end, right onto
Magdalen St **Rooms:** 2 pri facs **S** fr £65 **D** fr £95 **Notes:** Wi-fi
⊗ on premises ⬥ under 18yrs ⊛ **Parking:** 2 **Closed:** Feb

Set in a quiet courtyard in the heart of the most historic part
of Norwich, Gothic House is a Grade II listed building barely five minutes' walk from the cathedral.
The area has a wealth of gracious Georgian and earlier architecture. Gothic House has been lovingly
restored and retains much of its original character. With Wi-fi access available, the bedrooms are
spacious, individually decorated and stylishly presented. Breakfast is served in the elegant dining room.
Recommended in the area
Norwich Castle; Norwich Aviation Museum; Norwich Gallery

Old Thorn Barn

★★★★ GUEST ACCOMMODATION

Address: Corporation Farm, Wymondham Road,
Hethel, NORWICH, NR14 8EU
Tel: 01953 607785 & 07726 961530
Fax: 01953 601909
Email: enquires@oldthornbarn.co.uk
Website: www.oldthornbarn.co.uk
Map ref: 4 TG20
Directions: 6m SW of Norwich. Follow signs for
Lotus Cars from A11or B1113, on Wymondham Rd

Rooms: 7 en suite (7GF) **S** £34-£40 **D** £56-£60 **Notes:** Wi-fi ⊗ on premises **Parking:** 12

Reconstruction of a group of derelict buildings has resulted in this delightful conversion. The substantial
17th-century barns and stables feature a stylish open-plan dining room, where you can linger over
breakfast around individual oak tables. At the other end of the room there is a cosy lounge area with a
wood-burning stove. Antique pine furniture and smart en suites are a feature of the spacious bedrooms
which have tea and coffee trays, trouser presses and hairdryers.
Recommended in the area
Fairhaven Woodland and Water Garden; Pettitts Animal Adventure Park; Wolterton Park

Holkham Bay

Holly Lodge

★★★★★ ⇔ BED & BREAKFAST

Address: The Street, THURSFORD, NR21 0AS
Tel/Fax: 01328 878465
Email: info@hollylodgeguesthouse.co.uk
Website: www.hollylodgeguesthouse.co.uk
Map ref: 4 TF93
Directions: Off A148 into Thursford
Rooms: 3 en suite (3GF) **S** £60-£90 **D** £80-£110
Notes: Wi-fi ⊗ on premises ⚩ under 14yrs
Parking: 5 **Closed:** Jan

This 18th-century property is situated in a picturesque location surrounded by open farmland. The lovely landscaped gardens include a large sundeck, which overlooks the lake and water gardens, providing a great place to relax. The lodge and its guest cottages have been transformed into a splendid guest house, with stylish ground-floor bedrooms that are individually decorated and beautifully furnished. En suite bathrooms, TVs and lots of thoughtful extras make for a pleasant stay. The attractive public areas are full of character, with flagstone floors, oak beams and open fireplaces.

Recommended in the area

North Norfolk Coast; Thursford Museum; Walsingham

Stracey Arms Mill

NORTHAMPTONSHIRE

Holdenby House

Hunt House Quarters

★ ★ ★ ★ GUEST ACCOMMODATION

Address: Main Road, KILSBY, Rugby, CV23 8XR
Tel: 01788 823282
Email: luluharris@hunthouse.fsbusiness.co.uk
Website: www.hunthousekilsby.com
Map ref: 3 SP57
Directions: On B3048 in village
Rooms: 4 en suite (4GF) **S** £59.95-£75 **D** £75-£85
Notes: Wi-fi ⊗ on premises **Parking:** 8

Hunt House Quarters in Kilsby is set in a beautiful peaceful courtyard and forms one part of a magnificently restored 1656 thatched hunting lodge and covered stables. Steeped in history, the lodge was originally used for deer hunting. The property is ideally placed as a touring base for visiting Stratford-upon-Avon, the Cotswolds and Warwick. Nearby there are stately homes, castles and gardens to visit as well as opportunities for some excellent walking. The spacious en suite bedrooms have their own character and are named the Manger, the Smithy, the Saddlery and the Tack Room. Set around a large courtyard, they retain features such as oak beams and old glass but are furnished in a modern, contemporary style. All rooms are equipped to a high standard and have internet broadband connection, colour TV, tea- and coffee-making facilities and hairdryer. Breakfast is served in the restaurant where guests are offered the choice of full English, continental or vegetarian breakfast. All breakfasts are freshly cooked and prepared to order at times convenient to the guests. For other meals, there are two village pubs serving food seven days per week, and a selection of Indian, Chinese, Italian, Mexican, English, and Thai restaurants only 5–10 minutes away. The gardens surrounding Hunt House Quarters are a peaceful haven in which to relax and take a stroll.

Recommended in the area

Rugby School; Crick Boat Show; National Exhibition Centre

The rocky coastline of Inner Farne

Simonside Hills

Market Cross Guest House

★★★★★ 🏛 GUEST ACCOMMODATION

Address: 1 Church Street, BELFORD, NE70 7LS
Tel: 01668 213013
Email: info@marketcross.net
Website: www.marketcross.net
Map ref: 10 NU13
Directions: Off A1 into village, opp church
Rooms: 3 en suite D £70-£120
Notes: Wi-fi Parking: 3

Set in the heart of the charming village of Belford, just off the Great North Road, this Grade II listed building is well placed for visiting the Northumbrian coast. The northern hospitality here is matched by the high quality of the accommodation, with bedrooms large enough for easy chairs and sofas. Each has a flat-screen TV, a fridge with fresh milk for the complimentary beverages, fruit and fresh flowers. The breakfasts, which may include kedgeree, smoked salmon, scrambled eggs, pancakes and griddle scones, have an AA Breakfast Award. Many ingredients are sourced locally and there are vegetarian options. Runner-up in the AA's Friendliest Landlady of the Year Award 2008–9.

Recommended in the area

Lindisfarne (Holy Island); Alnwick Castle and gardens; the Farne Islands; Northumberland National Park

Lindisfarne Inn

★★★ INN
Address: Beal, BERWICK UPON TWEED, TD15 2PD
Tel/Fax: 01289 381223
Email: enquiries@lindisfarneinn.co.uk
Website: www.lindisfarneinn.co.uk
Map ref: 10 NT95
Directions: On A1, turn off for Holy Island
Rooms: 21 en suite (10GF) S £55 D £75
Parking: 25

There could hardly be a more convenient location for anyone wanting to visit Lindisfarne, but this inn has much more to offer than simply being in the right place. Its modernised rustic style presents an appealing setting, and the high standard of the food and accommodation make this a destination in itself. It's also a very convenient stop-over for travellers pounding the A1. The bedrooms, each with an en suite bathroom, occupy the ground and first floors of the adjacent lodge-style wing, and are comfortable, unfussy and well equipped, with digital television and refreshment trays. The bar is warm and welcoming, with its deep red ceiling, wooden floor and exposed stone wall, and a full range of cask ales, fine wines, liqueurs and spirits. Food is available all day, cooked to order by the head chef and his team, and ranges from snacks and sandwiches to full meals. The choice is exceptional, with as many as 10 daily specials and a long menu of British and international dishes, featuring ingredients from Northumberland producers and locally caught fish. There are vegetarian choices and a children's menu alongside classics such as steak and ale pie and 21-day hung Aberdeen Angus steaks.

Recommended in the area

Holy Island and Lindisfarne Castle (NT); Bamburgh Castle; Farne Islands (NT)

Hadrian's Wall, Highshield Crags

West Coates

★★★★★ 🛏 🍽 BED & BREAKFAST

Address: 30 Castle Terrace,
BERWICK-UPON-TWEED, TD15 1NZ
Tel/Fax: 01289 309666
Email: karenbrownwestcoates@yahoo.com
Website: www.westcoates.co.uk
Map ref: 10 NT95
Directions: A6105 into Berwick-upon-Tweed onto
Castle Terrace, half-way down on left
Rooms: 3 (2 en suite) (1 pri facs) **S** £60-£70

D £90-£120 **Notes:** Wi-fi ⊗ on premises 🐾 **Parking:** 3 **Closed:** Xmas & New Year

This beautiful Victorian family house is set in 2.5 acres of interesting, mature gardens. Facilities include a pool house with a 12m heated pool and hot tub, making it a perfect place to relax after a day exploring wonderful Northumberland. With Karen's immaculate attention to detail, the spacious bedrooms are beautifully furnished and come with many thoughtful extras to make your stay all the more memorable. Award-winning breakfast and dinner are prepared using the finest local produce.
Recommended in the area
Alnwick Castle and Gardens; Holy Island; Cragside (NT)

Ivy Cottage

★★★★★ 🛎 GUEST ACCOMMODATION
Address: 1 Croft Gardens, Crookham,
CORNHILL-ON-TWEED, TD12 4ST
Tel/Fax: 01890 820667
Email: ajoh540455@aol.com
Website: www.ivycottagecrookham.co.uk
Map ref: 10 NT83 **Directions:** 4m E of Cornhill.
Off A697 onto B6353 into Crookham
Rooms: 3 (1 en suite) (2 pri facs) (1GF) D £70-£88
Notes: 🐾 under 8yrs ☺ **Parking:** 8

This pristine stone-built modern cottage is testament to the many years spent in the hospitality industry by owner Doreen Johnson, and guests soon feel the benefit of her experience and dedication. Set in delightful gardens, the summerhouse provides a welcome spot in which to take tea on fine afternoons. Inside, everything is bright and spotless, and the three spacious bedrooms offer a choice of furnishings – the downstairs room is smart and modern, one room upstairs is beautifully done out in antique pine, and the new Premier Room has a spacious layout with a huge bed. Each room has fresh flowers, crisp embroidered bedding, home-baked biscuits and tea-making facilities, plus its own private bathroom with a deep tub, Crabtree & Evelyn toiletries, huge terry towels and bathrobes. Breakfasts, served in the formal dining room or in the farmhouse-style kitchen, with its Aga cooking range, are splendid. Whichever room is used, the feast always includes local free-range eggs, organic produce where possible, home-made preserves, freshly squeezed orange juice and home-baked bread made from stone-ground flour from nearby Heatherslaw Mill. The sumptuous guests' sitting room has a log burning stove in the winter. Ivy Cottage is perfectly located for exploring the Northumberland coast and the Cheviot Hills.

Recommended in the area

Holy Island; Alnwick Castle & Gardens; Flodden Battlefield

Pheasant Inn

★★★★ INN

Address: Stannersburn, HEXHAM, NE48 1DD
Tel/Fax: 01434 240382
Email: enquiries@thepheasantinn.com
Website: www.thepheasantinn.com
Map ref: 6 NY78
Directions: 1m S of Falstone. Off B6320 to Kielder Water, via Bellingham or via Hexham A69 onto B6320 via Wall-Wark-Bellingham
Rooms: 8 en suite (5GF) **S** £50-£55 **D** £85-£90
Parking: 40 **Closed:** Xmas

Set close to the magnificent Kielder Water, this classic country inn, built in 1624, has exposed stone walls, original beams, low ceilings, open fires and a display of old farm implements in the bar. Run by the welcoming Kershaw family since 1985, the inn was originally a farmhouse and has been refurbished to a very high standard. The bright, modern en suite bedrooms, some with their own entrances, are all contained in stone buildings adjoining the inn and are set round a pretty courtyard. All the rooms, including one family room, are spotless, well equipped, and have tea and coffee facilities, hairdryer, colour TV and radio-alarm clock; all enjoy delightful country views. Delicious home-cooked breakfasts and evening meals are served in the bar or in the attractive dining room, or may be taken in the pretty garden courtyard if the weather permits. Irene and her son Robin are responsible for the traditional home cooking using local produce and featuring delights such as game pie and roast Northumbrian lamb, as well as imaginative vegetarian choices. Drying and laundry facilities are available and, for energetic guests, cycle hire can be arranged.

Recommended in the area

Hadrian's Wall; Scottish Borders region; Northumberland's castles and stately homes

Vallum Lodge

★★★★ GUEST HOUSE
Address: Military Road, Twice Brewed,
HALTWHISTLE, NE47 7AN
Tel: 01434 344248
Fax: 01434 344488
Email: stay@vallum-lodge.co.uk
Website: www.vallum-lodge.co.uk
Map ref: 6 NY76
Directions: On B6318, 400yds W of Once Brewed
National Park visitors' centre
Rooms: 6 en suite (6GF) **S** £50-£65 **D** £75-£84
Notes: Wi-fi ⊗ on premises **Parking:** 15

Vallum Lodge, situated within an acre of grounds in the heart of the Northumberland National Park, is just over half a mile from a particularly beautiful section of Hadrian's Wall and is on the Pennine Way. It is ideally located for walking and cycling and for visiting all of the nearby Roman sites. Its name comes from the 'vallum', or ditch, built 2,000 years ago as part of the wall's fortifications and which runs through the lodge's back garden. A real home-from-home atmosphere is found at this well-equipped licensed roadside guest house. The stylishly decorated, comfortable en suite bedrooms, all on the ground floor and including one family room, feature open country views and flat-screen Freeview TVs, Wi-fi, hospitality tray, mini-bar, and fluffy robes. A substantial breakfast is cooked to order while guests help themselves to a cold buffet of juices, fresh fruit, cereals and yoghurt, all served in the bright, smart dining room. There is also a cosy residents' lounge, which contains a selection of games, books, magazines, travel guides and a TV/DVD. Drying and laundry facilities are available and there is ample parking in the large private car park.

Recommended in the area
Steel Rigg (Hadrian's Wall); Kielder Forest; Hexham Abbey

Peth Head Cottage

★ ★ ★ ★ BED & BREAKFAST

Address: Juniper, HEXHAM, NE47 0LA
Tel: 01434 673286
Fax: 01434 673038
Email: peth_head@btopenworld.com
Website: www.peth-head-cottage.co.uk
Map ref: 7 NY96
Directions: B6306 S from Hexham, 200yds fork right, next left. Continue 3.5m, house 400yds on right after Juniper sign
Rooms: 2 en suite **S** £29 **D** £58
Notes: ⊗ on premises **Parking:** 2

This lovingly maintained rose-covered cottage dates back to 1825 and is popular for its warm welcome, idyllic setting, and home comforts. Tea and hand-made biscuits are offered on arrival, and the delicious home cooking is enjoyed at breakfast too, along with freshly baked bread and delicious homemade preserves. The inviting sandstone cottage is set in peaceful, well-kept gardens. There are two bright, south-facing bedrooms, both overlooking the garden, with shower rooms en suite, a hairdryer, TV, radio alarm and hospitality trays. The relaxing lounge is heavily beamed and furnished with comfortable chairs. Peth Head Cottage is ideally situated for visiting Durham and Newcastle as well as nearby Roman sites, and there are plenty of opportunities for walking and cycling in the area. A wide range of tourist information and maps are on hand for visitors to browse through and plan the day. The owner, Joan Liddle, is an excellent host who knows how to ensure her guests have an enjoyable stay. There is private off-road parking. Sorry, no pets can be accommodated.

Recommended in the area

Beamish Open Air Museum; Hadrian's Wall; the Northumberland coast; Durham Cathedral; Finchale Priory; Lanercost Priory

Warkworth Castle

The Old Manse

★ ★ ★ ★ ★ 🛏 GUEST ACCOMMODATION

Address: New Road, Chatton, WOOLER NE66 5PU
Tel: 01668 215343
Email: chattonbb@aol.com
Website: www.oldmansechatton.co.uk
Map ref: 10 NT92
Directions: 4m E of Wooler. On B6348 in Chatton
Rooms: 3 en suite (1GF) S £50-£90 D £80-£100
Notes: ⊗ on premises 🖐 under 14yrs **Parking:** 4
Closed: Nov-Feb

Built in 1875 and commanding excellent views over the open countryside, this imposing former manse stands on the edge of the pretty village of Chatton between the Cheviot Hills and the scenic North Northumberland Heritage Coast. Approached by a sweeping gravel drive, you can explore the extensive gardens, which include a wildlife pond. The Rosedale Suite is an elegant four-poster room with a Victorian-style bathroom en suite; Buccleuch has a sitting room and private patio. All rooms are well appointed, spacious and luxurious. Enjoy hearty breakfasts in the elegant conservatory dining room.

Recommended in the area

Alnwick Garden; Chillingham Castle and wild cattle; Bamburgh Castle

Statues at Blenheim Palace

The Angel at Burford

★★★★ ◉◉ RESTAURANT WITH ROOMS

Address: 14 Witney Street, BURFORD, OX18 4SN
Tel: 01993 822714
Fax: 01993 822069
Email: paul@theangelatburford.co.uk
Website: www.theangelatburford.co.uk
Map ref: 3 SP21
Directions: Off A40 at Burford rdbt, down hill, 1st right onto Swan Ln, 1st left to Pytts Ln, left at end onto Witney St
Rooms: 3 en suite D £85-£110
Notes: Wi-fi

Just 100 yards from Burford's bustling high street, The Angel is a haven of tranquillity and comfort. Built in 1652, this cosy restaurant with rooms is packed with original features. Old oak beams adorn the ceilings, and in the winter months flickering log fires reflect on the gleaming copper and brass, while in the summer you can relax in the peaceful courtyard or in the walled garden. The bedrooms are en suite, individually decorated for comfort and style, and have everything that you need to make you feel comfortable and at home. In the residents' lounge you will find information on local attractions, and literature to help you plan long or short walks. In the candlelit restaurant the menus reflect all that is good about the local Cotswold produce, with an imaginative range of seasonal dishes, incorporating game from local estates, great fish dishes, and stunning desserts, all created using the freshest and best ingredients available. In the bar you'll find well-kept Hook Norton Ales, and arguably the finest bar counter in Burford, made from the increasingly rare Burr Elm. You may also find some locals, enjoying a pint or two of Cotswold hospitality!

Recommended in the area

Blenheim Palace; Sudeley Castle; The Cotswolds

Burford House

★ ★ ★ ★ ★ 🏛 GUEST ACCOMMODATION

Address: 99 High Street, BURFORD, OX18 4QA
Tel: 01993 823151
Fax: 01993 823240
Email: stay@burfordhouse.co.uk
Website: www.burfordhouse.co.uk
Map ref: 3 SP21
Directions: Off A40 onto A361, on right half way down hill
Rooms: 8 en suite (1GF) **S** £115-£185
D £145-£185 **Notes:** Wi-fi ⊗ on premises

Set in picturesque Burford, a famous Cotswolds market town with many specialist shops, this charming 17th-century house is a landmark on the High Street. Marked by its half-timbered and stone exterior, it is a beautiful building in a great location, offering guests quality, space and comfort. The en suite bedrooms, including one family suite and some rooms with four-posters, are individually decorated and furnished to a very high standard. The host of thoughtful extras include Witney pure wool blankets, fine cotton bed linen, flat-screen TV/DVDs, bathrobes, Penhaligon's toiletries and complimentary mineral water. Wi-fi is available in all rooms. Guests are invited to make use of the two comfortable lounges, one furnished in contemporary style with a wood-burning stove and the other bright and airy with traditional furnishings and doors leading out to the wisteria-clad courtyard garden. Using fine-quality local produce, wonderful lunches and afternoon teas are available daily in the Centre Stage restaurant, with its theatre posters and pictures, while dinner is also available on Thursday, Friday and Saturday evenings. Morning coffee and afternoon tea may also be enjoyed in the lounges. A full bar service is available, and the house has a fine array of malt whiskies, cognacs and wines.

Recommended in the area

Ashmolean Museum; Batsford Arboretum; Blenheim Palace

St Mark's church, Thame

Chowle Farmhouse Bed & Breakfast

★ ★ ★ ★ FARMHOUSE
Address: FARINGDON, SN7 7SR
Tel: 01367 241688
Email: info@chowlefarmhouse.co.uk
Website: www.chowlefarmhouse.co.uk
Map ref: 3 SU29
Directions: From Faringdon rdbt on A420, 2m W on
right. From Watchfield rdbt 1.5m E on left
Rooms: 4 en suite (1GF) S fr £65 D fr £80
Notes: Wi-fi ☻ Parking: 10

This friendly establishment makes an ideal base for visiting the Thames Valley and surrounding area. All four bedrooms are very well equipped with tea- and coffee-making facilities, flat-screen TV, hairdryer, a spacious en suite bathroom (with either a bath or power shower) and complimentary toiletries. Breakfast is prepared to order using fresh, locally sourced ingredients – home-made preserves, the farm's own eggs and family reared bacon – and is served at private tables. Guest facilities include a heated pool, hot tub, sauna, a large garden, a patio area and secure parking.

Recommended in the area

Blenheim Palace; Kelmscott Manor; Buscot Park

The Miller of Mansfield

★ ★ ★ ★ ★ ◉ RESTAURANT WITH ROOMS

Address: High St, GORING, RG8 9AW
Tel: 01491 872829
Fax: 01491 873100
Email: reservations@millerofmansfield.com
Website: www.millerofmansfield.com
Map ref: 3 SU68
Rooms: 13 en suite S £100-£125 D £125-£225
Notes: Wi-fi **Parking:** 2

The newly renovated Miller of Mansfield occupies a quiet Thames-side village setting, overlooking the Chiltern Hills. Inside, this former coaching inn offers sumptuous en suite rooms and suites, all distinctively and individually styled and with all the home comforts guests could want and more. There are flatscreen digital TVs, marble bathrooms, free-standing stone resin baths and/or high-pressure showers, fluffy robes, Egyptian cotton linen, organic latex mattresses and REN's luxurious toiletries. Residents in some rooms can enjoy a good night's sleep in stunning antique French beds. The award-winning restaurant, which enjoys views over the terrace gardens, aims to provide an informal and enjoyable eating experience. Diners can expect impressive modern British cuisine featuring local, free-range and organic produce, home-cured and smoked fish and meats, hand-rolled pasta, home-made breads, ice creams and sorbets, coupled with an exciting wine list – with many wines available by the glass – and a selection of local real ales in the bar. From breakfast, light meals and afternoon tea through to three-course dinners, the menus at the Miller change regularly to reflect the best of seasonal produce. Free high-speed internet access is available at the Wi-fi Hotspot and there are also fully equipped meeting facilities for business travellers.

Recommended in the area

Basildon Park (NT); Beale Wildlife Park and Gardens; Henley-on-Thames

The Cherry Tree Inn

★★★★ ❀ INN

Address: Stoke Row, HENLEY-ON-THAMES, RG9 5QA
Tel: 01491 680430
Email: info@thecherrytreeinn.com
Website: www.thecherrytreeinn.com
Map ref: 3 SU78
Directions: W of Henley. Off B841 into Stoke Row
Rooms: 4 annexe en suite (4GF) D £95
Notes: Wi-fi **Parking:** 30 **Closed:** 25-26 Dec

This stylish inn, in a rural setting high up in The Chilterns, was originally three flint cottages; today the 400-year-old listed building successfully combines classic and contemporary features. The modern bedrooms, in a converted barn, have spacious en suites with power showers and luxury toiletries, plus king-sized beds, flat-screen TVs and beverage-making facilities; two can be converted into family rooms. The contemporary dining room is the setting for imaginative and hearty dishes from a 'classic European with a twist' menu. Food is prepared using fresh local ingredients and seasonal produce.

Recommended in the area

The Maharajah's Well; Windsor Castle; Basildon Park

The Tollgate Inn & Restaurant

★★★★ ⬤ INN

Address: Church Street, KINGHAM, OX7 6YA
Tel: 01608 658389
Email: info@thetollgate.com
Website: www.thetollgate.com
Map ref: 3 SP22
Rooms: 9 en suite (4GF)
Notes: Wi-fi **Parking:** 12

Situated in an idyllic Cotswold village, this Grade II listed Georgian farmhouse has been lovingly restored to provide a complete home-from-home. Inside, there is an informal yet stylish atmosphere, with flagstone floors, beamed ceilings and huge inglenook fireplaces. The Tollgate provides a range of comfortable, well-equipped en suite bedrooms; those on the ground floor have adjacent parking. Each room has its own identity – one features a four-poster, while the spacious Hayloft is designed as a family suite. The inn serves some of the best food in the area – including a hearty breakfast – from a constantly changing menu based on fresh local produce.

Recommended in the area

Blenheim Palace; Batsford Park Arboretum; Oxford

Byways

★ ★ ★ ★ 🛏 BED & BREAKFAST

Address: Old London Road, MILTON COMMON,
Thame, OX9 2JR
Tel/Fax: 01844 279386
Email: byways.molt@tiscali.co.uk
Website: www.bywaysbedandbreakfast.co.uk
Map ref: 3 SP60
Directions: Between M40 juncts 7 & 8A Rooms: 3
(2 en suite) (1 pri facs) (3GF) S £35-£40 D £60-£65
Notes: ⊗ on premises 📶 under 7yrs ⊛ Parking: 3

Situated in three acres with an interesting garden, yet just a few minutes from the M40, Byways is a TV-free establishment with the emphasis on providing a peaceful and relaxing stay away from it all. The bedrooms are comfortable and tastefully decorated, with extras such as robes and radios. Excellent breakfasts make use of organic and local produce where possible, and include home-made bread, home-grown fruit preserves and eggs from Byway's own free roaming chickens. Special diets can be catered for.

Recommended in the area

Waterperry Gardens; Le Manoir aux Quat'Saisons; The Swan Antique Centre

Duke of Marlborough Country Inn

★ ★ ★ ★ INN

Address: A44, Woodleys, WOODSTOCK, OX20 1HT
Tel: 01993 811460
Fax: 01993 810165
Email: sales@dukeofmarlborough.co.uk
Website: www.dukeofmarlborough.co.uk
Map ref: 3 SP41
Directions: 1m N of Woodstock on A44 x-rds
Rooms: 13 en suite (7GF) S £65-£95 D £80-£120
Notes: Wi-fi ⊗ on premises Parking: 42

This inn is located in a stunning rural location, just outside the popular town of Woodstock. It features a large garden area, making it popular with families, but it is also fully equipped to cater for business travellers. The bedrooms and en suite bathrooms are housed in an adjacent lodge-style building and offer high standards of quality and comfort. Dinner is served in either the bar restaurant, with its log fires, or in the modern function-room restaurant, and includes many tempting home-cooked dishes featuring seasonal ingredients and complemented by a good selection of ales and wines.

Recommended in the area

Blenheim Palace; Broughton Castle; Ashmolean Museum

SHROPSHIRE

Carding Mill valley

Broseley House

★★★★ GUEST HOUSE

Address: 1 The Square, Broseley,
IRONBRIDGE, TF12 5EW
Tel/Fax: 01952 882043
Email: info@broseleyhouse.co.uk
Website: www.broseleyhouse.co.uk
Map ref: 2 SJ60
Directions: 1m S of Ironbridge in Broseley town
centre **Rooms:** 6 en suite (1GF) **S** £40-£45
D £70-£80 **Notes:** Wi-fi 🐾 under 5yrs

This impressive and lovingly restored Georgian house prides itself on being 'the friendly place to stay'. It offers high-quality decor and soft furnishings throughout, and the thoughtfully and individually furnished en suite bedrooms, one of which is a family room, all come with homely extras such as TV with DVD/CD/video (with a free borrowing library) hairdryer, radio alarm, bathrobes and beverage tray. Self-catering accommodation is also available. Comprehensive breakfasts, ranging from full English to lighter alternatives, are freshly cooked from local produce and served in the elegant dining room.

Recommended in the area
Benthall Hall; Blists Hill Victorian Town; Buildwas Abbey

The Library House

★★★★★ 🏠 GUEST ACCOMMODATION

Address: 11 Severn Bank, IRONBRIDGE,
Telford, TF8 7AN
Tel: 01952 432299
Email: info@libraryhouse.com
Website: www.libraryhouse.com
Map ref: 2 SJ60
Directions: 50yds from Iron Bridge
Rooms: 4 en suite **S** £65-£75 **D** £75-£95
Notes: Wi-fi ⊗ on premises 🐾

Located just 60 yards from the famous Iron Bridge, this Grade II listed Georgian building is tucked away in a peaceful thoroughfare yet is close to good pubs and restaurants. Hanging baskets and window boxes enhance the creeper-covered walls of the former library, and in the spring and summer the gardens are immaculate. All of the bedrooms have a television with DVD, a small DVD library, and a hospitality tray. Excellent breakfasts are served in the pine-furnished dining room.

Recommended in the area
Ironbridge World Heritage Site; Telford International Exhibition Centre; Blists Hill Victorian Town

Woodlands Farm Guest House

★ ★ ★ ★ BED & BREAKFAST

Address: Beech Road, IRONBRIDGE, TF8 7PA
Tel: 01952 432741
Email: allen.woodlandsfarm@btinternet.com
Website: www.woodlandsfarmironbridge.co.uk
Map ref: 2 SJ60
Directions: Off B4373 rdbt in Ironbridge onto Church
Hill & Beech Rd, house on private lane 0.5m on right
Rooms: 5 en suite (3GF) S £30-£60 D £55-£85
(family room price on application)
Notes: Wi-fi ✸ under 5yrs Parking: 8 Closed: 24 Dec-2 Jan

This green oasis, set in 2 acres of garden, features a host of comforts and well-equipped suites. The three ground floor rooms have garden-facing lounges and upstairs studio bedrooms also provide comfortable seating arrangements. All suites have fridges and a generous selection of toiletries and refreshments are supplied. The grounds are open to guests and include pleasant seating areas and a car park. A comprehensive breakfast is served in the cheerful, welcoming dining room.

Recommended in the area

Ironbridge Gorge Museums; Telford International Exhibition Centre; Blists Hill Victorian Town

Top Farm House

★ ★ ★ ★ GUEST HOUSE

Address: KNOCKIN, SY10 8HN
Tel: 01691 682582
Fax: 01691 682070
Email: p.a.m@knockin.freeserve.co.uk
Website: www.topfarmknockin.co.uk
Map ref: 5 SJ32
Directions: Off B4396 in village centre
Rooms: 3 en suite S £35-£45 D £65-£75
Parking: 6

Set in pretty gardens and retaining many original features, including exposed beams and open log fires, Top Farm House combines traditional hospitality with elegant surroundings. The bedrooms are equipped with many thoughtful extras. There is a relaxing beamed drawing room with a grand piano, and imaginative and comprehensive breakfasts are served in the spacious period dining room which overlooks the garden. The village of Knockin is one of the prettiest in this part of Shropshire.

Recommended in the area

Shrewsbury; Powis Castle (NT); Llanthaedr Waterfall

Stokesay Castle

The Clive Bar & Restaurant with Rooms

★★★★★ ◉◉ RESTAURANT WITH ROOMS

Address: Bromfield, LUDLOW, SY8 2JR
Tel: 01584 856565 & 856665
Fax: 01584 856661
Email: info@theclive.co.uk
Website: www.theclive.co.uk
Map ref: 2 SO57
Directions: 2m N of Ludlow on A49 in village of Bromfield **Rooms:** 15 en suite (11GF) **S** £60-£85
D £85-£110 **Notes:** Wi-fi ⊗ on premises **Parking:** 100 **Closed:** 25-26 Dec

A stylish makeover of a former farmhouse has given The Clive a smart contemporary look. The well known restaurant has an emphasis on fresh produce ranging from local meats to Cornish fish. The spacious en suite bedrooms, situated in period outbuildings, have been tastefully refurbished to provide well-equipped, modern accommodation. Family suite and room with disability facilities are available.

Recommended in the area

Stokesay Castle, Craven Arms; Ludlow Food Hall; Ludlow Race Course and Golf Club; Offa's Dyke

De Greys of Ludlow

★★★★★ GUEST HOUSE
Address: 5-6 Broad Street, LUDLOW, SY8 1NG
Tel: 01584 872764
Fax: 01584 879764
Email: degreys@btopenworld.com
Website: www.degreys.co.uk
Map ref: 2 SO57
Directions: Off A49, in town centre, 50yds beyond clock tower
Rooms: 9 en suite (1GF) **S** £60-£120 **D** £80-£180
Notes: ⊗ on premises **Closed:** 26 Dec & 1 Jan

This 16th-century timber-framed property houses De Grey's Tea Rooms, a well-known establishment in Ludlow town centre. It now also provides high-quality accommodation with luxurious modern facilities. All of the individually decorated and spacious bedrooms – including two suites and one room on the ground floor – have been carefully renovated, the design of each governed by the labyrinth of historic timbers that comprise this Tudor building. Sporting evocative names such as The Buttercross, Valentines View, Castle View and Market View, all the rooms have en suite facilities, and some feature stunning bathrooms with roll-top baths and large, powerful showers; one even has 'his and hers' bathrooms separated by a 4-foot beam. Furnishings are tasteful, with lots of lush fabrics used throughout and four-poster beds in some rooms. Combined with the latest in entertainment technology, this creates a successful fusion of past and present, and guests are encouraged to return to their rooms, unwind and relax with a bottle of wine. Breakfast, taken in the adjacent tearoom/restaurant and bakery shop, includes award-winning breads and pastries freshly made on the premises, and is served by smartly dressed waitresses, helping make a stay at De Grey's even more memorable.

Recommended in the area
Ludlow Castle; Long Mynd; Cardin Mill Valley

Number Twenty Eight

 BED & BREAKFAST

Address: 28 Lower Broad Street, LUDLOW, SY8 1PQ
Tel: 01584 875466
Email: enquiries@no28ludlow.co.uk
Website: www.no28ludlow.co.uk
Map ref: 2 SO57
Directions: In town centre. Over Ludford Bridge onto Lower Broad St, 3rd house on right
Rooms: 2 en suite D £80-£90
Notes: ⊗ on premises ✻ under 16yrs **Closed:** Nov-May

A property with a wealth of period character, this half-timbered, 16th-century town house is just a stroll from the centre of historic Ludlow with its attractions. Guests have the use of a cosy sitting room and in fine weather you can relax in the pretty courtyard or on the roof terrace. The en suite bedrooms are well equipped and offer many thoughtful extras, such as welcoming home-made biscuits. Breakfast options include fresh orange juice, fruit salad, local bacon, sausages, eggs and breads, plus a fish and vegetarian option.

Recommended in the area

Berrington Hall; Stokesay Castle; Ironbridge World Heritage Site

Riseholme

★★★★ BED & BREAKFAST

Address: 4 Hampton Road, OSWESTRY, SY11 1SJ
Tel: 01691 656508
Email: ssparnell1234@googlemail.com
Map ref: 5 SJ22
Rooms: 3 en suite
Notes: Wi-fi ✻ under 12yrs ⊛

Riseholme is located in a residential area of Oswestry, a pretty market town that sits close to the Welsh border. The house is within easy walking distance of the town centre, taking in the attractive memorial gardens en route. Inside this attractive home, the comfortable bedrooms, which all provide tea- and coffee-making facilities, are complemented by smart, modern en suite bathrooms; one room is suitable for families. Comprehensive breakfasts are taken in a cosy dining room and a spacious guest lounge is also available.

Recommended in the area

Whittington Castle; Park Hall Farm; Erddig Hall (NT)

The River Severn, Shrewsbury

Fieldside Guest House

★ ★ ★ ★ GUEST HOUSE

Address: 38 London Road, SHREWSBURY, SY2 6NX
Tel: 01743 353143
Fax: 01743 354687
Email: robrookes@btinternet.com
Website: www.fieldsideguesthouse.co.uk
Map ref: 2 SJ41
Directions: A5 onto A5064, premises 1m on left
Rooms: 8 (5 en suite) (3 pri facs)
S £25-£45 D £50-£65
Notes: Wi-fi 😾 under 10yrs 🐾 **Parking:** 8

Fieldside, which dates back to 1835, is just one mile from the centre of Shrewsbury and a 5-minute walk from Shrewsbury Abbey. This delightful house is attractively furnished and decorated and offers both single and double/twin rooms. The bedrooms feature period-style furniture and are equipped with tea and coffee facilities. Breakfast is served at individual tables in the spacious dining room. Traditional English or vegetarian or lighter options are available. There is ample private parking.

Recommended in the area

Shrewsbury Castle and Abbey; Attingham Park (NT); Ironbridge Gorge and museums

Soulton Hall

★★★★ 🍽 GUEST ACCOMMODATION

Address: Soulton, Wem, SHREWSBURY, SY4 5RS
Tel: 01939 232786
Fax: 01939 234097
Email: enquiries@soultonhall.co.uk
Website: www.soultonhall.co.uk
Map ref: 6 SJ52
Directions: A49 between Shrewsbury & Whitchurch turn onto B5065 towards Wem. Soulton Hall 2m E of Wem on B5065

Rooms: 7 en suite (3GF) **S** £60.50-£80.50 **D** £90-£129 **Notes:** Wi-fi **Parking:** 50

The Ashton family can trace their tenure of this impressive manor house back to the 1400 and 1500s, and much evidence of the building's age remains. The family and their staff offer excellent levels of personal service where the care of guests is of the utmost importance. The welcoming entrance lounge leads into the well-stocked bar on one side and an elegant dining room on the other. Here a good range of freshly prepared dishes, using fresh local produce wherever possible, are served in a friendly and relaxed formal setting. After the meal, coffee and liqueurs are served in the lounge hall in front of a blazing log fire in season. The house has central heating as well as log fires. The bedrooms in the hall reflect the character of the house with mullioned windows and exposed timbers; one room also has wood panelling. The converted carriage house across the garden offers ground-floor accommodation in two spacious double rooms each with spa baths. Standing in its own grounds beyond the walled garden, Cedar Lodge provides a choice of a peaceful four-poster suite or more modest family accommodation. Soulton Hall stands in 500 acres of open farmland, parkland and ancient oak woodland and you are welcome to explore the grounds.

Recommended in the area

Chester; Ironbridge; Shrewsbury

SOMERSET

Roman baths and 16th-century Bath Abbey

Apsley House

★★★★★ 🛏 BED & BREAKFAST

Address: Newbridge Hill, BATH, BA1 3PT
Tel: 01225 336966
Fax: 01225 425462
Email: info@apsley-house.co.uk
Website: www.apsley-house.co.uk
Map ref: 2 ST76
Directions: 1.3m W of city centre on A431
Rooms: 11 en suite (2GF) **S** £55-£130 **D** £69-£175
Notes: Wi-fi ⊗ on premises **Parking:** 12
Closed: 3 days Xmas

Built by the Duke of Wellington in 1830, this country house in the city, owned by Nick and Claire Potts, offers a gracious taste of Georgian Bath at its finest. Here guests can really soak up the atmosphere of Britain's only World Heritage City. The location of Apsley House, in a peaceful residential area about a mile from the city centre, ensures a truly relaxing stay, and this is enhanced by the presence of a charming and secluded rear garden, to which two of the bedrooms have direct access. The on-site parking and walking distance into the heart of the Bath are also great benefits in a city that can at times seem besieged by traffic. Public rooms include a large drawing room with bar and a light and elegant dining room, where the outstanding, freshly cooked breakfasts are served. All of the bedrooms have en suite bathrooms, complete with Molton Brown toiletries, and each is individually decorated and furnished. The beds are either super king-size or four-posters, and other in-room facilities include flat-screen TVs, Freeview, hospitality trays, direct-dial telephones and Wi-fi internet access. Apsley House is an aristocrat among bed and breakfast establishments and, maintained to the highest standards, is, in fact, fit for a duke.

Recommended in the area

Roman Baths and Pump Room and the many museums in Bath; Longleat; Cheddar Gorge

The Bailbrook Lodge

★ ★ ★ ★ GUEST HOUSE
Address: 35/37 London Road West,
BATH, BA1 7HZ
Tel: 01225 859090
Fax: 01225 852299
Email: hotel@bailbrooklodge.co.uk
Website: www.bailbrooklodge.co.uk
Map ref: 2 ST76
Directions: M4 junct 18, A46 S to A4 junct, left
signed Batheaston. Lodge on left **Rooms:** 15 (14 en

suite) (1 pri facs) (1GF) **S** £60-£79 **D** £88-£180 **Notes:** Wi-fi ⊗ on premises **Parking:** 15

Bailbrook Lodge is a Grade II listed country house in a delightful location just one and a half miles from the city centre and only 10 minutes' drive from the M4, with free parking provided. The setting is peaceful and relaxed amid lovely lawns and gardens. The house, built in 1850, has been totally redecorated and refurbished. It offers five bedrooms with four-poster beds and eight rooms with views of the gardens, lawns and the Avon Valley. The remaining rooms overlook the grounds of Bailbrook House, a splendid Georgian mansion designed by the famous architect John Everleigh. All rooms are equipped with Freeview television, clock radios, hairdryers, trouser presses and complimentary tea and coffee, biscuits, mineral water and cotton slippers. The four-poster rooms have additional facilities, such as dressing gowns, DVD players and a private safe. Children are welcome, and cots, highchairs and children's portions are available on request. Bedroom rates include a full English breakfast together with a glass of champagne. Breakfast is served in the elegant dining room, and there is an inviting lounge with a small bar overlooking the patio. The proprietors are happy to recommend nearby restaurants for dinner.

Recommended in the area

Roman Baths; Bath Abbey; Thermal Spa

Brooks Guesthouse

★ ★ ★ ★ 🏠 GUEST ACCOMMODATION

Address: 1 & 1A Crescent Gardens, Upper Bristol Road,
BATH, BA1 2NA
Tel: 01225 425543
Fax: 01225 318147
Email: info@brooksguesthouse.com
Website: www.brooksguesthouse.com
Map ref: 2 ST76
Directions: On A4, 350yds W of Queens Square, before Royal
Victoria Park **Rooms:** 21 en suite (7GF) **S** £65-£90 **D** £75-£110
Notes: Wi-fi ⊗ on premises **Closed:** 25 Dec

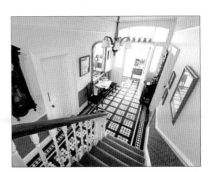

Conveniently located just a few minutes' stroll from the centre of
Bath, Brooks Guesthouse offers guests a relaxed atmosphere and upgraded en suite accommodation.
The bedrooms and bathrooms are well decorated, with pocket-sprung mattresses, goose-down duvets,
and flat-screen TVs. An open fire features in the guest living room and there's an honesty bar, while the
delicious breakfasts – which emphasise local British suppliers – are served in the breakfast room.

Recommended in the area

Jane Austen Centre; Stonehenge; The Grand Pump Room

Cheriton House

★ ★ ★ ★ ★ GUEST ACCOMMODATION

Address: 9 Upper Oldfield Park, BATH, BA2 3JX
Tel: 01225 429862
Fax: 01225 428403
Email: info@cheritonhouse.co.uk
Website: www.cheritonhouse.co.uk
Map ref: 2 ST76
Directions: A36 onto A367 Wells Rd, 1st right
Rooms: 11 en suite (2GF) **S** £60-£90 **D** £85-£130
Notes: Wi-fi ⊗ 👶 under 12yrs **Parking:** 11

This grand Victorian house has panoramic views over Bath and is only a short walk from the city centre.
Expect a friendly welcome from the proprietors who work hard to achieve a relaxed atmosphere. The
carefully restored en suite bedrooms are charmingly individual, and include a two-bedroom suite in a
converted coach house. All rooms have a TV and a well-stocked hospitality tray. A substantial breakfast
is served in the large conservatory overlooking beautifully manicured gardens. Plan your day in the
comfortable lounge, where you can browse the brochures and guide books.

Recommended in the area

The Abbey & many museums in Bath; Cheddar Gorge; Wells; Longleat

Chestnuts House

★★★★★ ≜ GUEST ACCOMMODATION

Address: 16 Henrietta Road, BATH, BA2 6LY
Tel: 01225 334279
Fax: 01225 312236
Email: reservations@chestnutshouse.co.uk
Website: www.chestnutshouse.co.uk
Map ref: 2 ST76
Rooms: 5 en suite (2GF)
Notes: Wi-fi ⊗ on premises Parking: 5

Chestnuts House, a fine Edwardian house with an enclosed garden, is ideally situated off the main road and adjacent to Henrietta Park, but is within a few minutes' level stroll of the city centre with its many attractions. Built from natural Bath stone, it offers fresh, airy accommodation. The bedrooms feature stylish contemporary furnishings and decor, and some have king-size and wrought-iron beds. All offer colour TV, broadband wireless internet connection, hairdryer and refreshment tray; one has its own private patio area. Breakfast features an extensive buffet and daily specials, and there is a cosy lounge.

Recommended in the area

Bath's Roman Baths; Royal Crescent; Thermae Bath Spa

Devonshire House

★★★ GUEST ACCOMMODATION

Address: 143 Wellsway, BATH, BA2 4RZ
Tel: 01225 312495
Email: enquiries@devonshire-house.uk.com
Website: www.devonshire-house.uk.com
Map ref: 2 ST76
Directions: 1m S of city centre. A36 onto A367 Wells Rd
& Wellsway Rooms: 4 en suite (1GF) S £50-£70 D £70-£90
Notes: Wi-fi ⊗ on premises Parking: 6

Located within walking distance of the city centre, this charming house, built in 1880, maintains its Victorian style. The attractive en suite bedrooms, some appointed to a high standard, have TVs and tea- and coffee-making facilities. There is a small lounge area. Continental breakfast choices are abundant and English breakfast is available at a supplement; all are served in the pleasant dining room, which was originally a Victorian grocer's shop. Secure parking is in the walled courtyard, and the proprietors make every effort to ensure your stay is pleasant and memorable.

Recommended in the area

Roman Baths; Longleat House and Safari Park; Wells Cathedral

Dorian House

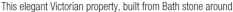

★★★★★ GUEST ACCOMMODATION

Address: 1 Upper Oldfield Park, BATH, BA2 3JX
Tel: 01225 426336
Fax: 01225 444699
Email: info@dorianhouse.co.uk
Website: www.dorianhouse.co.uk
Map ref: 2 ST76
Directions: A36 onto A367 Wells Rd, right onto Upper Oldfield Park, 3rd building on left
Rooms: 13 en suite (2GF) **S** £55-£165 **D** £65-£165
Notes: Wi-fi ⊗ on premises **Parking:** 9

This elegant Victorian property, built from Bath stone around 1880, has stunning views over the city. The house is just 10 minutes' walk from the city centre and is also close to many fine gardens and pretty villages, making it a good base. Dorian House is owned by Tim Hugh, Principal Cellist with the London Symphony Orchestra, and music influences the overall character and ambience of the property, with bedrooms bearing names such as Vivaldi, Gershwin and Rossini. The house was extensively refurbished in 2009 and one new room, which contains a beautiful four-poster, has been named Slava in honour of the Russian cellist Rostropovich. All of the en suite bedrooms, which feature opulent fabrics and stunning decor and have good views over Bath's famous Georgian Royal Crescent or the well-tended gardens, provide a range of extras such as marble bathrooms with high-pressure showers, crisp cotton sheets, fluffy towels and hairdryers. The attractive lounge has an open fireplace, large comfortable sofas, a bar and views of the terraced gardens. Delicious breakfasts offer treats such as freshly baked croissants and fresh fruit juices, as well as the traditional full English. Parking is very steep but free.

Recommended in the area

Thermae Bath Spa; Bath Abbey; Westonbirt Arboretum

The Kennard

★★★★ 🏨 GUEST ACCOMMODATION

Address: 11 Henrietta Street, BATH, BA2 6LL
Tel: 01225 310472
Fax: 01225 460054
Email: reception@kennard.co.uk
Website: www.kennard.co.uk
Map ref: 2 ST76
Directions: A4 onto A36 Bathwick St, 2nd right onto Henrietta Rd & Henrietta St
Rooms: 12 (10 en suite) (2GF) S £58-£89
D £98-£140 Notes: Wi-fi ⊗ on premises 👶 under 8yrs Closed: 2 wks Xmas

This Georgian town house, now charmingly restored and with its own special character, was built as a lodging house in 1794. Situated just off the famous Great Pulteney Street, it is only five minutes from the Abbey, the Roman Baths, the new spa complex and the railway station. All of the bedrooms are thoughtfully and individually furnished, most are en suite, and some are located at ground-floor level. Breakfast includes a cold buffet as well as a selection of hot items.

Recommended in the area

Stonehenge; Castle Combe; Wells

Marlborough House

★★★★ GUEST ACCOMMODATION

Address: 1 Marlborough Lane, BATH, BA1 2NQ
Tel: 01225 318175
Fax: 01225 466127
Email: mars@manque.dircon.co.uk
Website: www.marlborough-house.net
Map ref: 2 ST76
Directions: 450yds W of city centre, at A4 junct
Rooms: 6 en suite (1GF) S £75-£95 D £85-£135
Notes: Wi-fi Parking: 3 Closed: 24-26 Dec

This enchanting Victorian town house is owned and run in a friendly and informal style by Peter Moore. The location is walking distance from Bath's major attractions. This large and impressive house has spacious, well proportioned bedrooms, all fully en suite and presented with complimentary organic shampoo, conditioners and soap. The rooms are elegantly furnished with antiques, including some antique four-poster or king-size beds, and feature free Wi-fi and flat-screen TVs with Freeview. A hospitality tray is provided including organic teas and coffees and a decanter of sherry.

Recommended in the area

Roman Baths; Abbey Tower Tour; Thermae Bath Spa

Priddy

Whittles Farm

★ ★ ★ ★ FARMHOUSE
Address: BEERCROCOMBE, TA3 6AH
Tel/Fax: 01823 480301
Email: djcm.mitchem@btinternet.com
Website: www.whittlesfarm.co.uk
Map ref: 2 ST32
Directions: Off A358 through Hatch Beauchamp to
Beercrocombe, keep left through village, Whittles
Farm 1st lane on right, no through road
Rooms: 2 en suite **S** £40-48 **D** £60-68
Notes: ⊗ on premises ⚄ under 12yrs ⊛ **Parking:** 4 **Closed:** Dec & Jan

This 200-year-old farmhouse, with lots of character and luxurious furnishings, is ideally set on a
no-through road, with lovely walks nearby. The en suite bedrooms, with zip-link beds, are light and
spacious, and guests have their own cosy lounge with an inglenook fireplace, and a dining room with
a large dining table where excellent breakfast are served. Owners John and Claire Mitchem have been
receiving guests here for more than 25 years, and their friendly hospitality is the highlight of any stay.
Recommended in the area
Montacute House; Forde Abbey; Barrington Court (NT)

Clanville Manor

★ ★ ★ ★ 🚇 FARMHOUSE

Address: CASTLE CARY, BA7 7PJ
Tel: 01963 350124 & 07966 512732
Fax: 01963 350719
Email: info@clanvillemanor.co.uk
Website: www.clanvillemanor.co.uk
Map ref: 2 ST63
Directions: A371 onto B3153, 0.75m entrance to Clanville Manor via white gate & cattle grid under bridge
Rooms: 4 en suite S £35-£45 D £70-£90
Notes: Wi-fi ⊗ on premises 🚼 under 12yrs **Parking:** 6
Closed: 21 Dec-2 Jan

Clanville Manor, with its wisteria-clad Carystone walls, polished English oak stairs and flagstone hall, has been the home to the Snook family for 110 years. Guests can enjoy a cup of tea and home-made cakes by the log fire in the elegant drawing room, or under the walnut tree in summer, walk beside the River Brue, relax in the walled garden, or swim in the heated outdoor pool in June, July and August. Perhaps just sit on the swing seat and watch the suckler beef herd grazing. There are four bedrooms including one with a luxurious four-poster with 'candlelight', and a pretty single room; each room has a flat-screen TV, radio, hairdryer, complimentary biscuits, teas and real coffee. In the morning there is a choice of traditional, locally sourced English breakfast cooked on the Aga, local smoked salmon and fresh creamy eggs from the manor's own hens, or one of the lighter options, all served in the Georgian dining room overlooking the farm pond. Wi-fi access is available. Clanville Manor is within easy reach of Wells, Glastonbury, Longleat, Cheddar and many National Trust properties.

Recommended in the area

Glastonbury; Stourhead (NT); Wells Cathedral; Cheddar Gorge and Wookey Hole Caves; Glastonbury Tor

Bellplot House

★★★★★ GUEST ACCOMMODATION

Address: High Street, CHARD, TA20 1QB
Tel/Fax: 01460 62600
Email: info@bellplothouse.co.uk
Website: www.bellplothouse.co.uk
Map ref: 2 ST30
Directions: In town centre, 500yds from Guildhall
Rooms: 7 en suite (2GF) **S** £79.50 **D** £89.50
Notes: Wi-fi ⊗ on premises **Parking:** 12

This Grade II listed town house is a delightful Georgian bolthole, with its own private car park, Chard is surrounded by beautiful countryside in an area with many historical houses and gardens to explore. You arrive to a warm welcome from Betty and Dennis, who ensure that their guests have all they need. The bedrooms are named after the women who once owned Bellplot, and offer en suite facilities, free Wi-Fi and complimentary tea and coffee. Breakfast is a feast of excellent local ingredients.

Recommended in the area

Forde Abbey and Gardens; Barrington Court; East Lambrook Manor Gardens; River Cottage

Tarr Farm Inn

★★★★★ ⊛ 🏚 INN

Address: Tarr Steps, Exmoor National Park, DULVERTON, TA22 9PY
Tel: 01643 851507
Fax: 01643 851111
Email: enquiries@tarrfarm.co.uk
Website: www.tarrfarm.co.uk
Map ref: 2 SS92
Directions: 4m NW of Dulverton. Off B3223 signed Tarr Steps, signs to Tarr Farm Inn
Rooms: 9 en suite (4GF) **S** £75-£90 **D** £150 **Notes:** Wi-fi 🐾 under 14yrs **Parking:** 10

Tarr Farm dates from the 16th century and nestles just above Tarr Steps and the River Barle. The new bedrooms with en suite bathrooms display careful attention to detail with thick fluffy bathrobes, fridges, organic toiletries and much more. When it comes to food you will not be disappointed with wonderful cream teas, scrumptious breakfasts and excellent dinners with ingredients sourced from Devon and Somerset farms and suppliers. The farm is set in beautiful countryside ideal for walkers.

Recommended in the area

Exmoor National Park; South West Coast Path; Dunster Castle (NT)

Cannards Grave Farmhouse

★★★★ GUEST ACCOMMODATION

Address: Cannards Grave, SHEPTON MALLET,
BA4 4LY
Tel/Fax: 01749 347091
Email: sue@cannardsgravefarmhouse.co.uk
Website: www.cannardsgravefarmhouse.co.uk
Map ref: 2 ST64
Directions: On A37 between Shepton Mallet & The
Bath & West Showground, 100yds from Highwayman
pub towards showground on left
Rooms: 5 en suite (1GF) **S** £40-£60 **D** £60-£80
Notes: Wi-fi ⊗ on premises Parking: 6

Charming host Sue Crockett offers quality accommodation at this welcoming 17th-century farmhouse.
The bedrooms are delightful and have thoughtful touches such as hospitality trays, mineral water,
biscuits and mints. One room has a four-poster bed and a fridge with fresh milk. Delicious breakfasts
are served in the garden conservatory and there is a comfortable lounge to relax in.

Recommended in the area

Bath and West Showground; Historic Wells; Glastonbury Tor; City of Bath

Lower Farm

★★★★ FARMHOUSE

Address: Thornfalcon, TAUNTON, TA3 5NR
Tel: 01823 443549
Email: doreen@titman.eclipse.co.uk
Website: www.thornfalcon.co.uk
Map ref: 2 ST22
Directions: M5 junct 25, 2m SE on A358, left opp
Nags Head pub, farm signed 1m on left
Rooms: 11 (8 en suite) (3 pri facs) (7GF)
S £45-£50 **D** £70-£75
Notes: Wi-fi ⊗ on premises 🐾 under 5yrs Parking: 10

This charming thatched 15th-century longhouse is full of character. Lovely gardens and open farmland
surround this pretty property, where beamed ceilings and inglenook fireplaces testify to its age. The
bedrooms include some in a converted granary and byre, and all are en suite or have private facilities.
All rooms have high standards of furnishings. A hearty breakfast is cooked on the Aga and served in the
farmhouse kitchen, using local bacon and sausages, and eggs from the proprietor's own hens.

Recommended in the area

Hestercombe Gardens; Willow and Wetlands Visitors Centre; Quantock Hills

The Old Court

★★★★ GUEST ACCOMMODATION

Address: Main Road, TEMPLE CLOUD, BS39 5DA
Tel: 01761 451101
Fax: 01761 451223
Email: oldcourt@gifford.co.uk
Website: www.theoldcourt.com
Map ref: 2 ST65
Rooms: 5 (4 en suite) (1 pri facs)
S £60-£125 **D** £70-£150

This truly unique Grade II-listed property, constructed in 1857, was a courthouse in a previous life and is well located for many attractions. Now tastefully converted into plush family-run accommodation, it skilfully combines modern amenities with original features, such as flagstone floors and a grand sweeping staircase. The plentiful and spacious public areas include the large courtroom with its high-vaulted ceiling, now converted into a comfortable lounge with an adjoining games room. There's also a Roman-style jacuzzi and sauna room, with views of the surrounding countryside, including Old Court's own outdoor pond and waterfall. The bedrooms, with evocative names such as The Judge's Master Suite and The Barrister's Room, vary in size, but all are comfortably furnished with power showers, satellite TV and free Wi-fi and are based in the main building. Should guests wish, there is the option to stay in one of the three smaller converted cells, which feature hatches to feed the prisoners, and can also be rented together as a self-contained apartment, with a separate kitchen and patio area. Freshly prepared breakfast, ranging from full English to American pancakes, is a highlight. Dinners are available by prior arrangement, and very welcoming hospitality is assured from the resident American owner.

Recommended in the area

Longleat Safari Park; Wookey Hole Caves; Wells Cathedral

Crown & Victoria

★★★★ ◉ INN

Address: Farm Street, TINTINHULL,
Yeovil, BA22 8PZ
Tel: 01935 823341
Fax: 01935 825786
Email: info@thecrownandvictoria.co.uk
Website: www.thecrownandvictoria.co.uk
Map ref: 2 ST41
Directions: Off A303, signs for Tintinhull Gardens
Rooms: 5 en suite S £65 D £85
Notes: Wi-fi Parking: 60

The Crown and Victoria country inn stands in the heart of the pretty village of Tintinhull. In days gone by, as well as being the village pub, the inn was also a private school – lessons took place where the existing bar is situated. Today, above the new restaurant, the unfussy bedrooms are light and airy and very well equipped with hairdryers, TVs with DVD players, tea and coffee facilities, and wireless broadband internet access. The staff ensure you are well cared for. The contemporary bar and restaurant offers a successful combination of traditional pub atmosphere and quality dining. Carefully presented dishes are available for lunch and dinner under the direction of head chef, London-trained Stephen Yates. The menu ranges from traditional English dishes such as steak and ale pie to the more elaborate pan-roasted breast of duck on a bed of spinach with a potato rösti, plum and port jus. The extensive wine list includes ten fine house wines and there is a choice of local real ales. When the weather is kind, guests can relax in the garden with a drink or a light meal or enjoy a candlelit dinner in the conservatory with lovely garden views.

Recommended in the area

Tintinhull House Garden (NT); Montacute House (NT); Barrington Court (NT); Yeovil; Fleet Air Arm Museum, Yeovilton

Glastonbury Tor

Double-Gate Farm

★ ★ ★ ★ FARMHOUSE
Address: Godney, WELLS, BA5 1RX
Tel: 01458 832217
Fax: 01458 835612
Email: doublegatefarm@aol.com
Website: www.doublegatefarm.com
Map ref: 2 ST54
Directions: A39 from Wells towards Glastonbury, at Polsham right signed Godney/Polsham. 2m to x-rds, continue to farmhouse on left after inn

Rooms: 10 en suite (5GF) Notes: ⊗ on premises Parking: 10 Closed: 22 Dec-5 Jan

A special welcome awaits you, not just from the owners but from Jasper and Paddy, the friendly retrievers, at this lovely old farmhouse situated on the banks of the River Sheppey on the Somerset Levels, which has good views of Glastonbury Tor and the Mendip Hills. There's fishing at the bottom of the garden and cycle rides from the farm on the quiet roads which abound with birds and wildlife. There's even a resident barn owl in the chimney! Guests can play table tennis or snooker in the games room, or watch their own DVDs in the well equipped, en suite bedrooms. There is free internet access in the guest lounge. There are now luxury Riverside Suites (£45-50pppn) suitable for two to four guests that have spacious bedrooms with fridges, ceiling fans, mood lighting and access onto an extensive patio. Each of these large en suites can be adapted for disabled use (NAS 3). Double-Gate Farm is well known for its beautiful summer flower garden and home-grown tomatoes and fruit. Delicious breakfasts are served in the garden dining room that has panoramic views of the garden and meadow, and the options are extensive – cereals, juice, yoghurt, compote, local cheeses, home-made bread, full farmhouse breakfast, kippers and mouth-watering pancakes.

Recommended in the area

Wells Cathedral and Bishop's Palace; Cheddar Gorge; Bath & Glastonbury

Cheddar Gorge

Camellia Lodge

★★★★ BED & BREAKFAST

Address: 76 Walliscote Road,
WESTON-SUPER-MARE, BS23 1ED
Tel/Fax: 01934 613534
Email: dachefscamellia@aol.com
Website: www.camellialodge.net
Map ref: 2 ST36
Directions: 200yds from seafront
Rooms: 5 en suite S £27.50-£30 D £60-£65
Notes: Wi-fi

With the mile-long promenade and pier right on the doorstep, Camellia Lodge is a great choice for a seaside break. The proprietors create a warm atmosphere – they will even collect you from the train or bus stations. Inside their three-storey Victorian home you will find immaculate, mainly good size, well equipped bedrooms. Breakfast is a wide choice using local produce and excellent home-cooked evening meals are available by prior arrangement. Both are served the dining room.

Recommended in the area

Weston Golf Club; Sea Life Centre; Cheddar Gorge

STAFFORDSHIRE

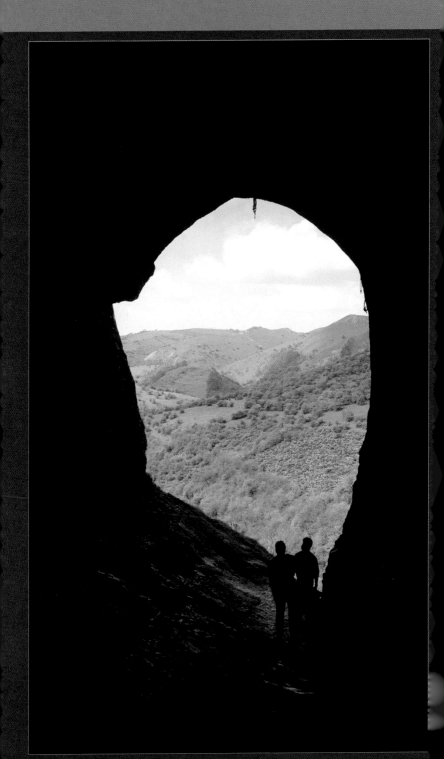

Thor's Cave, Peak District National Park

The Church Farm

★★★★ FARMHOUSE

Address: Holt Lane, KINGSLEY,
Stoke-on-Trent, ST10 2BA
Tel: 01538 754759
Email: thechurchfarm@yahoo.co.uk
Website: www.bandbatthechurchfarm.co.uk
Map ref: 7 SK04
Directions: Off A52 in Kingsley onto Holt Ln,
150mtrs on right opposite school drive
Rooms: 3 en suite S £28-£30 D £50-£55
Notes: ⊗ on premises ⊛ Parking: 6

The Church Farm, a listed 18th-century farmhouse situated in the quaint village of Kingsley, is still a working dairy farm and family home. It sits amid 100 acres of farmland and makes a good base for exploring the Potteries and the Peak District; it is also ideal for those who simply fancy a well-earned break. Inside, it provides friendly, relaxed accommodation in a number of beautiful, individually decorated rooms, complete with original antique furniture. There's also a log fire where guests can put their feet up during the winter season and relax. The thoughtfully equipped en suite bedrooms within the main house also contain stylish furnishings, and guests are provided with a range of little extras. Breakfast here is not to be missed, as you will be offered a hearty Staffordshire farmhouse plate, containing locally sourced ingredients and home-produced free-range eggs, all served on individual tables overlooking the cottage gardens. One charming feature is Church Farm's scented garden, which is a haven for birds and butterflies during the summer, or you can wander down the walkable paths that lead from the house to the beautiful Churnet Valley.

Recommended in the area

Bakewell; Chatsworth House; Churnet Valley Steam Railway

The Beehive Guest House

★★★★ GUEST HOUSE

Address: Churnet View Road,
OAKAMOOR, ST10 3AE
Tel: 01538 702420
Fax: 01538 703735
Email: thebeehiveoakamoor@btinternet.com
Website: www.thebeehiveguesthouse.co.uk
Map ref: 7 SK04
Directions: Off B5417 in village N onto Eaves Ln,
sharp left onto Churnet View Rd
Rooms: 5 en suite (1GF) S £35-£54 D £54-£60 Notes: ⊗ on premises ✿ under 5yrs Parking: 6

This spacious detached house offers a choice of thoughtfully equipped and comfortable bedrooms, one of which is a triple. All of the rooms, which benefit from central heating, TV, hairdryer and tea- and coffee-making facilities, are en suite and come with four-poster beds, making this an ideal place for a romantic break or just a stress-free trip away from it all. The family-run Beehive has a comfortable lounge/dining room, where individually prepared breakfasts are served.

Recommended in the area

Peak District National Park; Stoke-on-Trent potteries; Chatsworth House

Haywood Park Farm

★★★★ FARMHOUSE

Address: Shugborough, STAFFORD, ST17 0XA
Tel/Fax: 01889 882736
Email: haywood.parkfarm@btopenworld.com
Website: www.haywoodparkfarm.co.uk
Map ref: 7 SJ92
Directions: 4m SE of Stafford off A513. Brown signs
to Shugborough, on right 400yds past estate exit
Rooms: 2 en suite S £60-£75 D £80-£85 Notes: ⊗
on premises ✿ under 14 yrs ⊛ Parking: 4

The attractive farmhouse stands on a 120-acre arable and sheep farm on Cannock Chase, part of the Shugborough Estate. The large, attractively furnished bedrooms have a host of extras such as fresh flowers, fruit, tea facilities and shortbread. Large fluffy towels are provided in the luxury bathrooms. Breakfast, using local produce, is served in the lounge-dining room. The area is a paradise for walkers and cyclists. Fishing is offered in the lake, which is well stocked with carp and other coarse fish.

Recommended in the area

Shugborough Estate (NT); Wedgwood Museum; Alton Towers; Trentham Gardens

SUFFOLK

River Blyth, Blythburgh

The Chantry

★★★★ GUEST ACCOMMODATION

Address: 8 Sparhawk Street, BURY ST EDMUNDS, IP33 1RY
Tel: 01284 767427
Fax: 01284 760946
Email: chantryhotel1@aol.com
Website: www.chantryhotel.com
Map ref: 4 TL86
Directions: From cathedral S onto Crown St, left onto
Sparhawk St
Rooms: 15 en suite (1GF) S £69-£89 D £89-£99
Notes: Wi-fi Parking: 16

A delightful Grade II listed building where parking for each
room is provided via a 19th-century carriage access. Bedrooms are decorated in period style, and
the spacious superior double rooms have antique beds. There is a cosy lounge bar, and breakfast
and dinner are served in the restaurant. Dishes are home cooked and prepared from the freshest
of ingredients.

Recommended in the area
Abbey Gardens and ruins; Theatre Royal (NT); Ickworth House, Park & Gardens (NT)

Clarice House

★★★★★ ⊛ GUEST ACCOMMODATION

Address: Horringer Court, Horringer Road,
           BURY ST EDMUNDS, IP29 5PH
Tel: 01284 705550
Fax: 01284 716120
Email: bury@claricehouse.co.uk
Website: www.claricehouse.co.uk
Map ref: 4 TL86
Directions: 1m SW from town centre on A143 towards Horringer
Rooms: 13 en suite S £65-£105 D £100-£125
Notes: ⊗ on premises ⭍ under 5yrs Parking: 85
Closed: 24-26 Dec & 31 Dec-1 Jan

This large mansion is set in 20 acres of landscaped grounds just a short drive from Bury St Edmunds.
The family-run residential spa, with superb leisure facilities, has spacious, well-equipped bedrooms.
Public rooms include a smart lounge bar, an intimate restaurant offering quality food and a changing
menu, a further lounge and a conservatory.

Recommended in the area
Bury St Edmunds; Abbey Gardens; Ickworth House, Park and Gardens (NT)

Valley Farm

★★★★★ BED & BREAKFAST

Address: Bungay Road, HOLTON, IP19 8LY
Tel: 01986 874521
Email: mail@valleyfarmholton.co.uk
Website: www.valleyfarmholton.co.uk
Map ref: 4 TM47
Directions: A144 onto B1123 to Holton, left at fork in village, left at school, 500yds on left
Rooms: 2 en suite **S** £65-£75 **D** £65-£85
Notes: Wi-fi ⊗ on premises ⊛ **Parking:** 15

The owners of Valley Farm are keen advocates of green tourism, and this is reflected in many aspects of the charming red brick farmhouse situated in a peaceful rural location, a short drive or walk from the small market town of Halesworth. The individually decorated en suite bedrooms are tastefully appointed with many thoughtful touches. Breakfast, featuring locally sourced and home-grown produce, is served at a large communal table in the smartly appointed dining room. The property also boasts two and a half acres of lovely landscaped grounds and an indoor heated swimming pool.

Recommended in the area

Southwold; Minsmere RSPB sanctuary; The Cut arts centre

Lavenham Old Rectory

★★★★★ BED & BREAKFAST

Address: Church Street, LAVENHAM, CO10 9SA
Tel: 01787 247572
Email: susie_dwright@hotmail.co.uk
Website: www.lavenhamoldrectory.co.uk
Map ref: 4 TL94
Rooms: 3 en suite **S** £130-£150 **D** £155-£190
Notes: Wi-fi ⊗ on premises ⓧ **Parking:** 10
Closed: 24-26 Dec

The Lavenham Old Rectory is a stunning boutique-style residence situated in three acres of landscaped grounds. Ranked as one of the top places to stay, the three large and individually designed en suite rooms offer traditional decor with a host of interesting features. Two new suites are due for completion by summer 2010. An extensive breakfast menu is offered and there is private dining for parties of up to ten. Prepared by a professional chef, food is always fresh and locally sourced, with vegetables from the kitchen garden and eggs from the rectory's own hens, accompanied by wine from an interesting cellar.

Recommended in the area

Lavenham Guildhall (NT); Lavenham Airfield; Church of St Peter & St Paul

Sandpit Farm

★★★★ BED & BREAKFAST
Address: Bruisyard, SAXMUNDHAM, IP17 2EB
Tel: 01728 663445
Email: smarshall@aldevalleybreaks.co.uk
Website: www.aldevalleybreaks.co.uk
Map ref: 4 TM36
Directions: 4m W of Saxmundham. A1120 onto
B1120, 1st left for Bruisyard, house 1.5m on left
Rooms: 2 en suite S £50-£60 D £65-£80
Notes: Wi-fi ☺ Parking: 4 Closed: 24-26 Dec

This delightful Grade II listed farmhouse set in 20 acres of grounds, with the River Alde meandering along the boundary of the gardens, is well located for visiting the many places of interest in Suffolk. The en suite bedrooms have lots of thoughtful touches and enjoy lovely country views; one is located in its own wing of the house. There is also a cosy sitting room for relaxing, as well as a secret garden, a wild-flower orchard and a hard tennis court. Breakfast features quality local and home-made produce as well as freshly laid free-range eggs.

Recommended in the area

Framlingham; Minsmere RSPB reserve; Sutton Hoo (NT)

Sutherland House

★★★★★ ❀❀ RESTAURANT WITH ROOMS
Address: 56 High Street, SOUTHWOLD, IP18 6DN
Tel: 01502 724544
Email: enquiries@sutherlandhouse.co.uk
Website: www.sutherlandhouse.co.uk
Map ref: 4 TM57
Directions: A1095 into Southwold, on High St on left after
Victoria St Rooms: 4 en suite S £120-£220 D £120-£250
Notes: Wi-fi ⊗ on premises Parking: 1

This delightful 15th-century house is at the heart of the bustling town centre. It displays real attention to detail – alongside its wealth of period character, such as oak beams, exposed brickwork and open fireplaces, guests will find rich contemporary furnishings and sumptuous fabrics. The stylish en suite bedrooms, all with king-sized beds, have many thoughtful touches such as flat-screen TVs and DVD players with a choice of films. Public rooms feature a large restaurant with a regularly changing menu based on locally sourced ingredients.

Recommended in the area

Southwold Railway; Walberswick; Electric Picture Palace

Dunwich Heath

Bays Farm

★ ★ ★ ★ ★ GUEST ACCOMMODATION
Address: Forward Green, STOWMARKET, IP14 5HU
Tel: 01449 711286
Email: information@baysfarmsuffolk.co.uk
Website: www.baysfarmsuffolk.co.uk
Map ref: 4 TM05
Directions: A14 junct 50, onto A1120. 1m after
Stowupland, turn right at sharp left bend signed
Broad Green. Bays Farm 1st house on right
Rooms: 3 en suite S £60-£100 D £70-£110
Notes: ⚑ under 12yrs **Parking:** 3

Lavish restoration has turned this charming 17th-century farmhouse into a quality destination. A moat and 4 acres of mature gardens surround the property, while the interior has a wealth of oak beams and a roaring open fire. The individually designed bedrooms are luxuriously furnished with antiques, colour co-ordinated fabrics and en suite facilities. Extras include goose-down duvets, Egyptian cotton bed linen, bathrobes and hand-made toiletries. Breakfasts are served in the oak-beamed dining room.
Recommended in the area
Museum of East Anglian Life; Mechanical Music Museum and Bygones; Otley Hall

West Warren woods, North Downs Way

Pembroke House

★★★★ GUEST ACCOMMODATION
Address: Valley End Road, CHOBHAM, GU24 8TB
Tel: 01276 857654
Fax: 01276 858445
Email: pembroke_house@btinternet.com
Map ref: 3 SU96
Directions: A30 onto B383 signed Chobham, 3m right onto Valley End Rd, 1m on left
Rooms: 4 (2 en suite) (2 pri facs)
S £40-£50 D £90-£110
Notes: Wi-fi 🌐 **Parking:** 10

Julia Holland takes great pleasure in treating guests as friends at this spacious neo-Georgian home set amid rolling fields. The elegant public areas include an imposing entrance hall and a dining room with views over the surrounding countryside. The bedrooms are filled with thoughtful extras. Two single rooms share a bathroom, while the other rooms are en suite. There are many top-class golf clubs in the vicinity, as well as polo, horseracing and shooting. There is a tennis court in the attractive grounds.
Recommended in the area
Windsor Castle; Wisley RHS Gardens; shooting at Bisley

Bentley Mill

★★★★★ BED & BREAKFAST
Address: Gravel Hill Road, Bentley, FARNHAM, GU10 5JD
Tel: 01420 23301 & 07768 842729
Fax: 01420 22538
Email: ann.bentleymill@supanet.com
Website: www.bentleymill.com
Map ref: 3 SU84
Directions: Off A31 (Farnham-Alton road), opposite Bull Inn, turn left onto Gravel Hill Rd
Rooms: 2 en suite (1GF) S £85-£100 D £105-£140
Notes: Wi-fi ⊗ on premises 🧒 under 8yrs **Parking:** 6

David and Ann welcome you to their lovely home, a former corn mill beside the River Wey and set in five acres of beautiful grounds. The two spacious suites are former mill rooms with original beams; each has its own private entrance that is separate from the main house. They have countryside and river views and feature antiques, luxurious beds and deep sofas. A full breakfast is cooked on the Aga.
Recommended in the area
Jane Austen's House, Chawton; The Watercress Line, Alresford; Portsmouth Historic Dockyard

Pathway leading to North Downs Way

Asperion Hillside

★ ★ ★ ★ ⬡ GUEST ACCOMMODATION

Address: Perry Hill, Worplesdon,
         GUILDFORD, GU3 3RF
Tel: 01483 232051
Fax: 01483 237015
Email: info@thehillsidehotel.com
Website: www.asperionhillside.com
Map ref: 3 SU94 Rooms: 15 en suite (6GF)
S £65 D £80-£120 Notes: Wi-fi ⊗ on premises
Parking: 15 Closed: 21 Dec-7 Jan

Located just a short drive from central Guildford, this high-quality accommodation, which uses organic and Fairtrade produce, is popular with both business and leisure travellers. The en suite bedrooms are comfortable and well equipped with good facilities, including free Wi-fi; one suite features a king-size four-poster bed. There is a lounge bar and a bistro-style restaurant. The gardens, including a Koi carp pond, include a guest terrace. Asperion Hillside specialises in intimate high quality weddings, parties and small conferences.

Recommended in the area

St Mary's Church, Worplesdon; RHS Garden, Wisley; Clandon Park (NT)

EAST SUSSEX

Sandy beach and rock pools near Fairlight

Brighton House

★★★★ 🛎 GUEST ACCOMMODATION
Address: 52 Regency Square, BRIGHTON, BN1 2FF
Tel: 01273 323282
Email: info@brighton-house.co.uk
Website: www.brighton-house.co.uk
Map ref: 3 TQ30
Directions: Opposite West Pier
Rooms: 16 en suite Notes: ⊗ on premises 👣 under 12yrs

This charming Regency town house is perfectly placed for all Brighton's attractions. The owners try to minimise the impact that the house has on the environment without compromising guests' comfort. Their electricity supplies are from renewable sources, such as wind, and the kitchen extension has a sedum roof. Recycling is taken seriously, with packaging kept to a minimum. The smartly furnished bedrooms have high quality beds and linens, TVs, Wi-fi, hairdryers, beverage-making facilities and fans for summer use. The continental-style buffet breakfast provides a broad choice of primarily organic and locally sourced produce. No children under 12.

Recommended in the area

Brighton Pavilion; Brighton seafront; South Downs

Five

★★★★ GUEST ACCOMMODATION
Address: 5 New Steine, BRIGHTON, BN2 1PB
Tel: 01273 686547
Fax: 01273 625613
Email: info@fivehotel.com
Website: www.fivehotel.com
Map ref: 3 TQ30
Directions: On A259 towards E, 8th turn on left into square
Rooms: 10 en suite S £45-£75 D £70-£140
Notes: Wi-fi ⊗ on premises

Five, a period town house overlooking a classic Regency square, has far-reaching views and is only a few steps to the beach, bars and restaurants of the famous Lanes. The contemporary rooms are comfortable and well equipped, and benefit from crisp white linen, luxurious duvet, TV (some have DVD), Wi-fi and tea and coffee facilities. Some triple and family rooms are available. Breakfast, which includes organic bacon, eggs, mushrooms and fresh berries, is served in the bay-fronted dining room.

Recommended in the area

Brighton Pier; Brighton Pavilion; shopping in The Lanes

Lansdowne Guest House

★★★★ 🛏 GUEST ACCOMMODATION

Address: 3 The Red House, 21 Lansdowne Road,
HOVE, BN3 1FE
Tel: 07803 484775
Fax: 01273 773718
Email: lansdowneguesthouse@hotmail.co.uk
Map ref: 3 TQ30
Rooms: 2 (1 en suite) (1 pri facs)
S £65-£75 **D** £75-£85
Notes: ⊗ on premises **Closed:** 24-27 Dec

Lansdowne Guest House is set in the middle of 'Pimlico-by-the-Sea', with its grand white Regency terraces close to the beach and promenade. The building is a 1920s mansion, built for a lord's mistress, with its own grounds just a few minutes' walk from the main shopping centre and the cobbled Lanes. Attentive, interesting, well-travelled hosts welcome guests into a big, friendly sitting room with a fire and candles for winter nights. The under-the-eaves bedrooms are stylish and modern with sitting areas, TVs, internet, fridges and kettles, and the compact bathrooms are stocked with toiletries.

Recommended in the area

Brighton Pavilion; The Lanes, Brighton Beach & Pier

New Steine

★★★★ 🛏 ☕ GUEST ACCOMMODATION

Address: 10-11 New Steine, BRIGHTON, BN2 1PB
Tel: 01273 695415 & 681546
Fax: 01273 622663
Email: reservation@newsteinehotel.com
Website: www.newsteinehotel.com
Map ref: 3 TQ30
Directions: A23 to Brighton Pier, left onto Marine Parade, New Steine on left after Wentworth St
Rooms: 20 (16 en suite) (2GF) **S** £39-£55
D £65-£105 **Notes:** Wi-fi ✖ under 4yrs

Elegant and fashionable, this five-storey Georgian town house is located in central Brighton and is favoured by both business travellers and leisure guests. Decorated in chocolate and cream contemporary design, chic bedrooms are equipped with free Wi-fi, desk space, hairdryers, flat-screen LCD TVs, tea and coffee facilities and luxury toiletries. French food is served in the New Steine Bistro, prepared from local produce. A concierge service is 24 hours, and conference rooms are available.

Recommended in the area

The Royal Pavilion; Devil's Dyke; Brighton Museum & Art Gallery

The Twenty One Guest House

★ ★ ★ ★ GUEST ACCOMMODATION

Address: 21 Charlotte Street, Marine Parade,
BRIGHTON, BN2 1AG
Tel: 01273 686450
Email: enquiries@thetwentyone.co.uk
Website: www.thetwentyone.co.uk
Map ref: 3 TQ30
Directions: From Brighton Pier turn left onto Marine Parade,
16th turning on left **Rooms:** 8 en suite **S** £50-£60 **D** £90-£149
Notes: Wi-fi ⊗ on premises

Located in a quiet residential side street in the lively and
cosmopolitan Kemp Town area of Brighton, this stylishly
refurbished Regency townhouse is nevertheless within easy reach of the town's major attractions,
clubs, bars and restaurants and is just a few steps from the famous seafront. Within the house, guests
can relax in the refurbished, elegantly furnished and comfortable bedrooms, which have either smart
and modern en suite shower rooms or bathrooms. Each room has an abundance of thoughtful extras,
such as flatscreen TVs with Freeview, DVD players, digital radio alarms, use of towelling bathrobes and
slippers, well-stocked hospitality trays, mini-bars with complimentary mineral water, and iPod docking
stations. Some of the rooms have oblique sea views, and one of these, a large high-ceilinged double
with a brass bed and the original cornicing intact, has bay windows and its own private balcony. A
family room is also available. The smart dining room is the setting for an extensive buffet breakfast
comprising a choice of cereals, fresh fruit, yoghurt, croissants, fruit smoothies and freshly brewed
coffee, in addition to a freshly cooked hot breakfast, with a vegetarian alternative available. Locally
sourced ingredients are used as far as possible.

Recommended in the area

Brighton Pier; The Lanes; Brighton Marina

Eastbourne

Cuckmere river

Tovey Lodge

★★★★★ GUEST ACCOMMODATION
Address: Underhill Lane, DITCHLING, BN6 8XE
Tel: 08456 120544
Email: info@sussexcountryholidays.co.uk
Website: www.sussexcountryholidays.co.uk
Map ref: 3 TQ31
Directions: From Ditchling village, N on Beacon Rd.
After 0.5m left onto Underhill Ln, 100yds 1st drive on
left Rooms: 5 en suite (2GF) S £55-£80 D £80-£140
Notes: Wi-fi ❷ Parking: 28

Set within three acres of garden and enjoying great views of the South Downs, Tovey Lodge provides guests with an indoor swimming pool, sauna and jacuzzi. The bedrooms and en suite bathrooms are spacious and stylishly decorated and come with extras such as Wi-fi and plasma-screen TVs with DVD players. Three rooms are suitable for families, and two rooms are on the ground floor. There is also a spacious guest lounge, which backs onto a patio offering additional space to relax and features a 50-inch plasma-screen TV. A cooked or continental breakfast can be enjoyed in the dining room.

Recommended in the area

South Downs National Park; Wings Place; St Margaret's Church

The Manse B & B

★ ★ ★ ★ ★ BED & BREAKFAST
Address: 7 Dittons Road, EASTBOURNE, BN21 1DW
Tel: 01323 737851
Email: anne@themansebb.com
Website: www.themansebb.com
Map ref: 4 TV69
Directions: A22 to town centre railway station, onto Old Orchard Rd, right onto Arlington Rd
Rooms: 3 en suite S £50-£55 D £76-£90
Notes: Wi-fi Parking: 2

Originally built in 1906 as a Presbyterian manse, this characterful property, designed in the Arts and Crafts style, retains many of its original features, such as stained-glass windows, oak panelling and oak floors. The property benefits from a quiet location, yet is just a five-minute stroll from Eastbourne's lively town centre, with its many shops, theatres, pubs and restaurants. The start of the South Downs is within a ten-minute walk and there are many lovely walks and places to visit in the nearby area. Inside, the spacious, beautifully decorated en suite bedrooms provide armchairs, digital TVs, DVD/CD players, Wi-fi access, hospitality trays and fridges. Guests can enjoy a good night's sleep in king size beds with deep pocket-sprung mattresses. The wide selection of breakfast options, many of them locally sourced and free-range and/or organic, is served in the south-facing dining room, which has French doors leading to the rear garden. Here, guests are welcome to relax with tea or coffee after breakfast, weather permitting, or they are free to make use of the sitting room, which has large comfortable chairs and a sofa from which to pore over local information, read or listen to music. Off-street and unrestricted street parking is available.

Recommended in the area
South Downs and Beachy Head; Charleston Farmhouse (Bloomsbury Group); Michelham Priory

Ocklynge Manor

★ ★ ★ ★ ★ BED & BREAKFAST

Address: Mill Road, EASTBOURNE, BN21 2PG
Tel: 01323 734121 & 07979 627172
Email: ocklyngemanor@hotmail.com
Website: www.ocklyngemanor.co.uk
Map ref: 4 TV69
Directions: From Eastbourne Hospital follow town
centre/seafront sign, 1st right onto Kings Av,
Ocklynge Manor at top of road
Rooms: 3 (2 en suite) (1 pri facs)
S £50-£80 **D** £80-£90 **Notes:** Wi-fi ⊗ on premises 🐾 under 16yrs ⊚ **Parking:** 3

Instantly inviting, this 300-year-old house is set in extensive grounds and it's hard to imagine that you are just 10 minutes' walk from the centre of Eastbourne. The manor is on land that was previously occupied by a monastery, and this was also the site of a 12th-century Commandery of the Knights of St John of Jerusalem. More recently, according to a blue plaque, the house was once the home of the renowned children's book illustrator Mabel Lucie Atwell. Today, David and Wendy Dugdill welcome guests to the manor, providing a charming personal touch to every aspect of the place. The bedrooms, all accessed via the main staircase, are spacious and sunny, with views across the garden from the large windows. The decor and furnishings are comfortable and elegant, and top quality Egyptian cotton bed linen and towels are provided. Fresh flowers, a TV, DVD, radio, hairdryer and plenty of lamps are among the extra touches that so enhance a stay here. The bathrooms are modern and luxurious, and two adjoining rooms can be used as a suite which sleeps three. The public rooms include a gracious drawing room with grand piano and the beautiful garden is a lovely place to stroll on a summer evening. A full English breakfast is served in the dining room.

Recommended in the area

South Downs Way; Beachy Head; Great Dixter; Bodiam Castle (NT); Bateman's

Parkside House

★★★★ GUEST ACCOMMODATION

Address: 59 Lower Park Road,
HASTINGS, TN34 2LD
Tel: 01424 433096
Fax: 01424 421431
Email: bkentparksidehse@aol.com
Map ref: 4 TQ80
Directions: A2101 to town centre, right at rdbt,
1st right
Rooms: 5 (4 en suite) S £30-£50 D £65-£75
Notes: Wi-fi ⊗ on premises

Parkside House is in a quiet conservation area opposite Alexandra Park, with its lakes, tennis courts and bowling green, yet is only a 15-minute walk from the seafront. The rooms are stylishly furnished, with many antique pieces, and generously equipped with video recorders, hairdryers, tongs, toiletries, bathrobes, and beverage trays. A good choice of breakfast – English or continental – is served at individual tables in the elegant dining room, and there is also an inviting lounge.

Recommended in the area

Battle Abbey; Bodiam Castle (NT); Michelham Priory

Holly Grove

★★★★ BED & BREAKFAST

Address: Little London, HEATHFIELD, TN21 0NU
Tel: 01435 863375
Email: joedance@btconnect.com
Website: www.hollygrovebedandbreakfast.co.uk
Map ref: 4 TQ52
Directions: A267 to Horam, turn right at Little
London garage, proceed to bottom of lane
Rooms: 3 (2 en suite) (1 pri facs) (2GF) S £50-£70
D £60-£85 **Notes:** Wi-fi ⋈ under 12yrs **Parking:** 5

Holly Grove is set in a quiet rural location in the heart of East Sussex, yet has easy access to many attractions. Set in over 2 acres of garden, it offers guests use of the heated outdoor swimming pool from May to October. Inside guests will enjoy the luxury, comfort and warm welcome offered by the Christie family. The bedrooms are appointed to a very high standard, with flatscreen TVs and many thoughtful extras. There is a separate guest lounge with open fire and a games room, for the sole use of guests. Breakfast is served in the dining room or on the terrace.

Recommended in the area

Bentley Wildfowl and Motor Museum; Glyndebourne; Bateman's

The Blacksmiths Arms

★★★★ 🛏 INN

Address: London Road, Offham, LEWES, BN7 3QD
Tel: 01273 472971
Email: blacksmithsarms@tiscali.co.uk
Website: www.theblacksmithsarms-offham.co.uk
Map ref: 3 TQ41
Directions: 2m N of Lewes. On A275 in Offham
Rooms: 4 en suite
Notes: Wi-fi ⊗ on premises 👶 under 5yrs
Parking: 22

Situated just outside Lewes, this charming 18th-century inn is set amid beautiful surroundings in an Area of Outstanding Natural Beauty. Nestled beneath the Sussex Downs, this is a great location for touring the south coast. Each of the high-quality, comfortable double bedrooms at the Blacksmiths Arms features en suite bathroom, flat-screen TV and tea- and coffee-making facilities. All have been refurbished and are delightfully decorated. Downstairs, open log fires and a warm, relaxed atmosphere welcome you to the cosy bar, where excellent dinners and hearty breakfasts are freshly cooked to order. Evening diners can choose from the inventive brasserie-style menu, which draws from only the best local produce wherever possible, including fresh fish and seafood landed at local ports. Dishes here are much more than pub food, and might include roast local estate free-range venison, wild sea bass fillets on a seafood risotto with a lobster velouté drizzle, or Auntie Kate's fresh crispy roast duckling. Bernard Booker, the owner and chef of the Blacksmiths, has won awards for his seafood dishes, and award-winning, locally brewed Harveys Sussex Bitter is properly served in superb condition; another indication that the owners here like to do things properly.

Recommended in the area

Brighton; South Downs Way; Sheffield Park Gardens; Bluebell Railway; Glyndebourne Opera House

Nightingales

★ ★ ★ ★ GUEST ACCOMMODATION
Address: The Avenue, Kingston, LEWES, BN7 3LL
Tel/Fax: 01273 475673
Email: nightingalesbandb@googlemail.com
Website: www.nightingalesbandb.co.uk
Map ref: 3 TQ41
Directions: Please telephone for directions
Rooms: 2 en suite (2GF)
S (occupancy) £45-£65 D £70-£85
Notes: ⊗ on premises ⅋
Parking: 2

A spacious bungalow with a light and airy feel, Nightingales is set in a tree-lined avenue in the village of Kingston, with off-street parking provided. A footpath from the gardens leads directly to the South Downs Way, so it is a perfect base from which to explore this lovely area. Bedrooms are furnished with comfortable beds and equipped with flat-screen TVs and tea- and coffee-making facilities. Aga-cooked breakfasts are prepared from locally sourced produce, with eggs from the household hens.

Recommended in the area

Lewes Castle; Anne of Cleves House; Charleston; Glyndebourne Opera

Manor Farm Oast

★ ★ ★ ★ ★ ⅊ ⌣ GUEST ACCOMMODATION
Address: Windmill Lane, ICKLESHAM, TN36 4WL
Tel: 01424 813787
Email: manor.farm.oast@lineone.net
Website: www.manorfarmoast.co.uk
Map ref: 4 TQ92
Directions: 4m SW of Rye. A259 W past church, left onto Windmill Ln Rooms: 3 (2 en suite) (1 pri facs)
S £56 D £99 Notes: Wi-fi ⊗ on premises ⅋ under 11yrs Parking: 7 Closed: 23 Dec-15 Jan

Built in 1860 and surrounded by a working orchard on the edge of the Icklesham, Manor Farm Oast is ideal for a quiet break. The oast house has been converted to keep the unusual original features both inside and out – the double bedroom in one tower is completely round. Your host Kate Mylrea provides a very friendly welcome. Kate is passionate about food: as well as a traditional English breakfast or a healthier alternative, she can prepare a top quality five-course dinner by arrangement on Fridays and Saturdays.

Recommended in the area

Battle Abbey; historic Rye; Ellen Terry's House (NT)

The Seven Sisters

Strand House

★★★★ ♒ ⇔ GUEST ACCOMMODATION

Address: Tanyards Lane, Winchelsea, RYE, TN36 4JT
Tel: 01797 226276
Fax: 01797 224806
Email: info@thestrandhouse.co.uk
Website: www.thestrandhouse.co.uk
Map ref: 4 TQ92
Directions: M20 junct 10 onto A2070 to Lydd.
Follow A259 through Rye to Winchelsea, 2m past Rye
Rooms: 10 (9 en suite) (1 pri facs) (1GF)
S £55-£75 D £65-£125 Notes: Wi-fi ✈ under 12yrs Parking: 12

Strand House provides a calm retreat from the stresses of modern living, with elegant rooms set in a historic Tudor house full of period detail, such as low, oak-beamed ceilings, winding stairs and inglenook fireplaces in the large lounge. Bedrooms are full of quality furniture and include thoughtful extras such as hand-made biscuits. Sussex breakfasts are provided. Afternoon tea, packed lunches and evening meals are all available – using organic local meat, fish from the boats at Rye Bay, plus home-made cakes.

Recommended in the area

Great Dixter; Sissinghurst; Romney Hythe and Dymchurch Railway

Ab Fab Rooms

★ ★ ★ ★ BED & BREAKFAST

Address: 11 Station Road, Bishopstone,
SEAFORD, BN25 2RB
Tel: 01323 895001
Fax: 0870 127 1624
Email: stay@abfabrooms.co.uk
Website: www.abfabrooms.co.uk
Map ref: 3 TV49
Directions: Close to train station
Rooms: 3 en suite S £45-£50 D £65-£75
Notes: Wi-fi ⊗ on premises 🐾
Parking: 2

Situated in Bishopstone, close to the train station and on the outskirts of the pretty Sussex town of
Seaford, Ab Fab Rooms is just a short walk from sandy beaches and the South Downs, making it an
ideal base for visiting local sights and attractions. The stylish, contemporary-styled en suite bedrooms
enjoy stunning views of the end of Seaford Bay and on to the ferry port of Newhaven and beyond.
Each room offers a superior level of comfort and amenities, such as fluffy towels, TV/DVDs and well-
stocked hospitality trays, which include such treats as home-baked biscuits and cakes. One room
has a chocolate brown leather bed and tub chairs in which to relax. Breakfast, served in the garden
conservatory, is a special feature and includes home-made jams and marmalade alongside local Sussex
produce. Sunsets in this part of the world are spectacular, and the friendly owners are happy to provide
sunset picnic baskets, packed with delicious home-made food, for guests to sit back and enjoy on the
beach. They'll even chill the wine beforehand. Guest parking is available.

Recommended in the area

Brighton & Hove; Glyndebourne; Charleston Farmhouse

The Avondale

★ ★ ★ GUEST ACCOMMODATION
Address: Avondale Road, SEAFORD, BN25 1RJ
Tel: 01323 890008
Fax: 01323 490598
Email: avondalehotel@btconnect.com
Website: www.theavondale.co.uk
Map ref: 3 TV49
Directions: In town centre, off A259 behind
war memorial
Rooms: 14 (8 en suite) S £30-£42 D £55-£75
Notes: Wi-fi ⊗ on premises

The Avondale is conveniently positioned for both the town centre and the seafront, with Seaford Leisure Centre close by and Brighton, Eastbourne, the South Downs and many other places of interest are within easy reach. Guests frequently comment on how well they sleep in the spotlessly clean bedrooms. The beds are certainly comfortable, but the friendly service, relaxed atmosphere and fresh flowers also play their part in the home-from-home experience. Jane and Martin Home and their experienced staff spare no effort in making your stay relaxing and enjoyable, offering a perfect blend of modern comforts and traditional courtesy and service. All bedrooms are accessible by stair lift and eight rooms have en suite facilities. Each room has free Wi-fi access, a hospitality tray, complimentary toiletries, radio and TV, with a DVD player on request. An inviting lounge is available during the day for guests' use, and breakfast is served at individual tables in the spacious dining room. Guests appreciate the quality and choice of the breakfasts, and dinners and hot/cold buffets featuring home-cooked local produce can be catered for by arrangement. There are also plenty of good pubs and restaurants serving food in the area.

Recommended in the area

Beachy Head Countryside Centre; Firle Place; Clergy House Alfriston (NT)

West Wittering

South Downs Way

The Townhouse

★ ★ ★ ★ ⑥ RESTAURANT WITH ROOMS
Address: 65 High Street, ARUNDEL, BN18 9AJ
Tel: 01903 883847
Email: enquiries@thetownhouse.co.uk
Website: www.thetownhouse.co.uk
Map ref: 4 TQ00
Directions: A27 to Arundel, onto High Street
Rooms: 4 en suite S £70-£85 D £85-£120 **Notes:**
Wi-fi ⊗ on premises **Closed:** 2wks Feb & 2wks Oct

The Townhouse, an elegant Grade II listed building dating from around the 1800s, occupies a prime position opposite Arundel Castle. The spectacular carved ceiling in its dining room, however, is much older than the rest of the house; it originated in Florence and is a beautiful example of late Renaissance architecture. All of the en suite bedrooms here are sympathetically and tastefully decorated, and all benefit from TV, hairdryer and tea- and coffee-making facilities. The restaurant, too, is stylish, though informal, with owner/chef Lee Williams offering a diverse menu based on local produce and featuring fresh bread made on the premises, earning The Townhouse an AA Rosette.

Recommended in the area

Glorious Goodwood; Arundel Castle; Chichester Theatre

The Boathouse Bosham

★ ★ ★ ★ GUEST ACCOMMODATION

Address: Main Road, BOSHAM, PO18 8EH
Tel/Fax: 01243 572572
Email: info@bosham-boathouse.com
Website: www.bosham-boathouse-bed-and-breakfast.co.uk
Map ref: 3 SU80
Directions: On A259, opp Chequers Ln
Rooms: 4 en suite (4GF) **S** £60-£85 **D** £65-£99
Notes: Wi-fi **Parking:** 6

Guests at this modern, family-run establishment in the historic sailing village of Bosham, two miles from Chichester, can enjoy boutique-style rooms, each with its own independent access. All of the rooms have been tastefully decorated and provide sumptuous – and very expensive – beds, luxury Egyptian cotton bed linen, Hungarian goose-down duvets and pillows, fluffy towels and Freeview TV, among other thoughtful touches. Some of the rooms have their own decked areas and one bedroom has been adapted for less mobile guests. A separate decked area is also available, and from here guests can enjoy views of Kingley Vale over the rolling South Downs or watch the sun go down and the stars come out, far away from any light pollution, snuggled under one of the sofa throws. A delicious home-cooked breakfast, featuring award-winning sausages and free-range eggs along with a selection of fruit and cereal and Fairtrade coffee, can be served outside in the attractive garden during warmer months and enjoyable evening meals are available by prior arrangement. Access to the dining room is via a deck with anti-slip walkways, overlooking a large, illuminated Koi carp pond with a fountain. Off-road car parking is provided.

Recommended in the area

West Wittering Beach; Amberley Museum; Arundel Castle

Rooks Hill

★ ★ ★ ★ ★ 🛎 GUEST HOUSE

Address: Lavant Road, Lavant, CHICHESTER,
          PO18 0BQ
Tel: 01243 528400
Email: enquiries@rookshill.co.uk
Website: www.rookshill.co.uk
Map ref: 3 SU80
Rooms: 6 en suite (2GF) S £65-£110 D £75-£165
Notes: Wi-fi ⊗ on premises 🐾 under 12yrs
Parking: 6

This charming Grade II-listed country house is situated on the edge of the Sussex Downs, and enjoys stunning views over Goodwood. Rooks Hill has been lovingly restored by Ron and Lin Allen, the friendly proprietors, and the tasteful result combines character and contemporary style. Accommodation is in the form of superbly finished, light and airy bedrooms, two of which are on the ground floor. All have pristine en suite bathrooms with power showers and White Company toiletries, as well as pocket-sprung mattresses and white cotton bed linen, LCD flatscreen televisions, hairdryers, hospitality trays and other thoughtful extras. Free Wi-fi is available. The delicious breakfast includes a choice of full English breakfast, fresh fruit, cereals, yoghurts, organic free-range eggs, freshly baked bread and preserves made using organic fruit from the garden. This feast is served in the stylish oak-beamed breakfast room, with its log burner in cooler months. In warmer weather the French doors are opened on to a beautiful wisteria-clad courtyard. Guests may also enjoy afternoon tea in the courtyard, or relax in the cosy guest lounge, which is well stocked with books, magazines and newspapers. There are good pubs and restaurants in the vicinity for evening meals.

Recommended in the area

Chichester Festival Theatre and Cathedral; Goodwood Racecourse; West Wittering Beach

West Stoke House

★★★★★ ⊛⊛⊛ RESTAURANT WITH ROOMS

Address: Downs Road, West Stoke,
CHICHESTER, PO18 9BN
Tel: 01243 575226
Fax: 01243 574655
Email: info@weststokehouse.co.uk
Website: www.weststokehouse.co.uk
Map ref: 3 SU80
Directions: 3m NW of Chichester. Off B286 to West
Stoke, next to St Andrew's Church
Rooms: 8 (7 en suite) (1 pri facs) S £95-£115 D £130-£215
Notes: Wi-fi **Parking:** 20 **Closed:** 24-28 Dec

This fine country house, part Georgian and part medieval, with over 5 acres of manicured lawns and gardens, lies on the edge of the South Downs. Guests can enjoy a game of croquet on the lawn, or view the artworks exhibited in the semi-permanent West Stoke House Art Space. The large, uncluttered bedrooms at this exclusive restaurant with rooms have smart modern bathrooms and great country views, and parts of the original timber beams can still be seen in the attic bedrooms. Thoughtful touches include white linen bedding and fresh flowers in every room, as well as flat-screen televisions and DVD players. For those looking for something different, one room has a round double bed, providing Hollywood glamour. The restaurant has a relaxed atmosphere and produces exceptional food from a modern British menu with French influences; wines can be chosen from an interesting and varied list. Hearty breakfasts are made from local produce where possible, with eggs coming from West Stoke free-range hens. Public rooms, including the spacious Grand Ballroom, have a light-filled elegance and are adorned with an eclectic mix of period furniture and contemporary art.

Recommended in the area

The Witterings; Chichester Cathedral; Goodwood

The Beacons

★★★★ GUEST ACCOMMODATION
Address: 18 Shelley Road, WORTHING, BN11 1TU
Tel: 01903 230948
Email: thebeacons@btconnect.com
Map ref: 3 TQ10
Directions: 0.5m W of town centre. Off A259
Richmond Rd onto Crescent Rd & 3rd left
Rooms: 8 en suite (3GF) **S** £40-£45 **D** £70-£80
Notes: Wi-fi **Parking:** 8

The Beacons is conveniently situated for all local amenities, including the shopping centre, marine garden, theatres, nightclubs, pier and promenade. The bowling greens at Beach House Park and Marine Gardens are only a short walk from the house. It is also well placed for touring the south coast and the towns of Brighton, Chichester and Arundel are within easy reach. The bedrooms all have TV, tea- and coffee-making facilities, hairdryer and clock. Breakfast, served at individual tables, is taken in the dining room and there is a comfortable lounge to relax in after a busy day sightseeing. There is ample parking on the premises. Dogs are allowed in rooms with prior arrangement.

Recommended in the area

Brighton Pavilion; The Lanes, Brighton; South Downs

The Conifers

★★★★ GUEST ACCOMMODATION
Address: 43 Parkfield Road, WORTHING, BN13 1EP
Tel: 01903 265066 & 07947 321096
Email: conifers@hews.org.uk
Website: www.theconifers.org.uk
Map ref: 3 TQ10
Directions: A24 or A27 onto A2031 at Offington
rdbt, over lights, Parkfield Rd 5th right
Rooms: 2 (1 pri facs) **S** £37.50-£40 **D** £70-£75
Notes: ⊗ on premises ⬩ under 12yrs ⊚
Parking: On-street (free) **Closed:** Xmas

The Conifers is an immaculately kept Art Deco house quietly located in West Worthing, that offers high standards in a home-from-home atmosphere. Complimentary tea and home-made cakes are served in the award-winning garden on arrival. South-facing bedrooms (a twin and a large double with a king-size bed) have TVs, courtesy trays, hairdryers, robes and chocolates. A varied menu is offered at breakfast, including the full English or buffet with rolls, croissants, cold meats, cheese, yoghurts and fresh fruit.

Recommended in the area

Tarring village; Highdown Gardens; Arundel

Moorings

★★★★ GUEST ACCOMMODATION

Address: 4 Selden Road, WORTHING, BN11 2LL
Tel: 01903 208882
Email: themooringsworthing@hotmail.co.uk
Website: www.mooringsworthing.co.uk
Map ref: 3 TQ10
Directions: 0.5m E of pier off A259 towards Brighton
Rooms: 6 en suite S £40-£45 D £50-£60
Notes: Wi-fi ⊗ on premises

Colourful container plants and window boxes greet guests to this fine Victorian house, in a quiet residential area yet handy for the seafront and town centre. Inside, the spacious rooms are beautifully decorated, in keeping with the age of the house, and the good-sized bedrooms have co-ordinated colour schemes, original fireplaces, teddy bears on the beds and light flooding in from the big windows. Each has a TV and tea- and coffee-making facilities, and two are large enough to accommodate a family. In addition to the stylish dining room, there's a cosy lounge, with books, magazines and games.

Recommended in the area

Pier and seafront; Aquarena; Bowling Greens

Olinda Guest House

★★★★ GUEST ACCOMMODATION

Address: 199 Brighton Road, WORTHING, BN11 2EX
Tel: 01903 206114
Email: info@olindaguesthouse.co.uk
Website: www.olindaguesthouse.co.uk
Map ref: 3 TQ10
Directions: 1m E of pier on Brighton Rd along Worthing seafront
Rooms: 6 (3 en suite)
Notes: Wi-fi ⊗ on premises 🐾 under 12yrs

Guests can enjoy a seafront location at this smart guest house, which is a 15-20 minute level stroll from the town centre. Named after the Olinda Lighthouse in Brazil, where a sea captain who once lived in the house met his wife, it makes a good base for exploring this stretch of the English coastline. The bedrooms, some en suite, are cosy and comfortable, with TVs and tea- and coffee-making facilities provided; some of the rooms have their own sea-facing balconies. Hearty breakfasts, which include a range of choices, are taken in the attractively appointed dining room overlooking the sea.

Recommended in the area

Field Place; Worthing Museum and Art Gallery; Highdown Gardens

TYNE & WEAR

The Angel of The North

The Stables Lodge

★★★★★ 🏠 GUEST HOUSE

Address: South Farm, Lamesley,
GATESHEAD, NE11 0ET
Tel: 0191 492 1756
Fax: 0191 410 6192
Email: janet@thestableslodge.co.uk
Website: www.thestableslodge.co.uk
Map ref: 7 NZ26
Directions: From A1, take Team Valley/Retail World
slip road and turn off towards Lamesley/Kibblesworth

Rooms: 3 en suite (1GF) **S** £49-£65 **D** £69-£89 **Notes:** ⊗ on premises **Parking:** 6

The Stables Lodge enjoys an easily accessible yet semi-rural setting not far from Newcastle, Gateshead and the A1, with the Metro Centre and the Angel of the North only minutes away. The establishment has been thoughtfully converted by experienced owners with a background in interior design, presenting a 'Hunting Lodge' theme throughout. Notable features include luxurious surroundings and excellent guest care – The Stables was the AA's Guest Accommodation of the Year for England in 2008–2009. Each of the en suite bedrooms has a unique character and provides a host of indulgent extras such as chocolates, satellite TV and DVD player, mini-fridge, towelling bathrobes, guest slippers and Molton Brown toiletries. The Red Room has its own spa bath, sauna and steam room, while the Garden Room has an outside seating area. Breakfast, taken in the main lounge, is an informal affair and majors on local, organic and Fairtrade ingredients. As well as lighter options, such as fresh fruit and freshly baked croissants, traditional full English breakfasts are prepared on the Aga, and a pre-ordered luxury option, featuring champagne and strawberries, scrambled eggs with smoked salmon, and creamed chestnut mushrooms with Wiltshire ham on toasted muffins, is also available.

Recommended in the area

Grey's Monument; The Angel of the North; Segedunum Roman Fort

The Millennium and Tyne Bridges, Newcastle upon Tyne

Park Lodge

★★★★ GUEST HOUSE

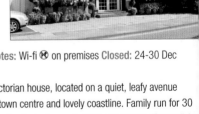

Address: 158/160 Park Avenue, WHITLEY BAY,
NE26 1AU
Tel: 0191 253 0288
Fax: 0191 252 6879
Email: parklodgehotel@hotmail.com
Website: www.parklodgewhitleybay.com
Map ref: 8 NZ37
Directions: A19 onto A1058 to seafront. Turn left,
after 2m left at lights onto A191
Rooms: 5 en suite (2GF) S £60-£75 D £90-£95 **Notes:** Wi-fi ⊗ on premises **Closed:** 24-30 Dec

A friendly atmosphere prevails at this refurbished Victorian house, located on a quiet, leafy avenue overlooking Whitley Park and just minutes from the town centre and lovely coastline. Family run for 30 years, it makes an ideal base for exploring the region thanks to its excellent transport links. The stylish en suite bedrooms, one a family room, are very comfortable. All have wet-room showers, Freeview TV, DVD players and hospitality trays. A hearty breakfast is served and free Wi-fi is available.
Recommended in the area
Alnwick Castle; Hadrian's Wall; The Sage, Gateshead

WARWICKSHIRE

Warwick Castle

Chapel House

★★★★★ ⊛ RESTAURANT WITH ROOMS
Address: Friar's Gate, ATHERSTONE, CV9 1EY
Tel: 01827 718949
Fax: 01827 717702
Email: info@chapelhouse.eu
Website: www.chapelhouse.eu
Map ref: 3 SP39
Directions: A5 to town centre, right onto Church St.
Right onto Sheepy Rd & left onto Friar's Gate
Rooms: 12 en suite Notes: Wi-fi ⊗ on premises
Closed: Etr wk, Aug BH wk & Xmas wk

Peacefully set in the heart of a charming market town, this fine Georgian town house glows with a mellow ambience that befits its age. Built in 1728, it retains many original features and is set in a pretty walled garden. Each of the spacious bedrooms has individual decor, luxurious linens and the en suite bathrooms have power showers. Wi-fi internet access is available. Dinner is a highlight, offering a menu of impressive dishes. Crisp white linen, fine silverware and candlelight add to the atmosphere.
Recommended in the area
Warwick Castle; National Exhibition Centre; National Memorial Arboretum

Bubbenhall House

★★★★ GUEST ACCOMMODATION
Address: Paget's Lane, BUBBENHALL, CV8 3BJ
Tel: 024 7630 2409 & 07746 282541
Fax: 024 7630 2409
Email: wharrison@bubbenhallhouse.freeserve.
co.uk
Website: www.bubbenhallhouse.com
Map ref: 3 SP36
Directions: 5m NE of Leamington. Off A445 at
Bubbenhall S onto Paget's Ln, 1m on single-track
lane (over 4 speed humps) Rooms: 5 en suite (1GF) S £50 D £70-£75 Notes: Wi-fi ⊛ Parking: 12

This impressive late Edwardian house was once the home of Alexander Issigonis, designer of the Mini. Set in five acres of ancient woodland, the house contains many interesting features including a Jacobean-style staircase. The large, individually styled, en suite bedrooms are well equipped and have flat-screen TVs and hospitality trays; a four-poster room is available. Guests have a wide choice at breakfast time: a full English plus vegetarian dishes, or a champagne or continental breakfast.
Recommended in the area
Warwick Castle; Stratford-upon-Avon; The Cotswolds

Holly End Bed & Breakfast

★ ★ ★ ★ 🏠 BED & BREAKFAST

Address: London Road, SHIPSTON ON STOUR, CV36 4EP

Tel: 01608 664064

Email: hollyend.hunt@btinternet.com

Website: www.holly-end.co.uk

Map ref: 3 SP24

Directions: 0.5m S of Shipston on Stour on A3400

Rooms: 3 (2 en suite) (1 pri facs) S £50-£65 D £75-£100

Notes: Wi-fi ⊗ on premises 👶 under 9yrs ⊗ **Parking:** 6

Holly End provides top-drawer accommodation on the edge of the Cotswolds, midway between Moreton-in-Marsh and Stratford-upon-Avon. Whether your preferences lie with long country hikes and exploring quaint Cotswold villages or discovering the history and culture of Shakespeare country, this bed and breakfast is suitably placed for both. The modern detached family house, immaculately maintained and spotlessly clean, is just a short walk from the centre of Shipston on Stour. Shipston, once an important sheep market town, was also an important stop for coaches, and many of the inns in the High Street date from that era. The spacious, comfortable bedrooms – king-size, twin and double – with subtle soft furnishings and decor have shower-baths, while dormer windows add to the character. You can pamper yourself with the Sanctuary spa products provided in each room. Colour televisions and tea- and coffee-making facilities are also provided. A comprehensive freshly cooked English breakfast uses the best of local produce (organic wherever possible). Afternoon tea or sherry and snacks are offered on arrival. There is a beautiful sunny garden with a lawn and patio dotted with many container plants.

Recommended in the area

Stratford-upon-Avon; Hidcote Manor (NT); Warwick Castle; Cotswold Falconry Centre; Cotswolds

HAMLET.

Shakespeare and Hamlet statues, Stratford Upon Avon

Ambleside Guest House

★ ★ ★ ★ GUEST HOUSE

Address: 41 Grove Road, STRATFORD-UPON-AVON, CV37 6PB
Tel: 01789 297239
Fax: 01789 295670
Email: ruth@amblesideguesthouse.com
Website: www.amblesideguesthouse.com
Map ref: 3 SP25
Directions: On A4390 opp Firs Park
Rooms: 7 (5 en suite) (2GF) **S** £28-£35 **D** £55-£75
Notes: Wi-fi ⊗ on premises 🚼 under 5yrs **Parking:** 7

Ambleside is a comfortable guest house in the heart of Stratford-upon-Avon, where owners Ruth and Peter provide a warm welcome. A refurbishment has left the house in sparkling condition, and the accommodation can suit every need. Choose from the family rooms, one of which is situated on the ground floor, a double, twin or singles. Many rooms have shower rooms en suite, and each room is equipped with a TV, hairdryer and a hospitality tray. Ironing facilities are also available. The choice at breakfast ensures that everyone is satisfied and both the traditional full English breakfast and vegetarian options are freshly cooked. Breakfast is served in the bright and spacious dining room, which looks over the charming front patio garden. Ambleside stands opposite the attractive gardens of Firs Park and is just a short stroll into the town centre where there is a good choice of restaurants, cafés and inns. As well as the Shakespeare attractions, Stratford-upon-Avon offers a wide range of shops and ancient buildings and the benefit of town trails to guide the visitor around this interesting town. Free on-site parking and Wi-fi.

Recommended in the area

Shakespeare's birthplace; The Courtyard Theatre; Anne Hathaway's Cottage; Warwick Castle; Warwick

Arden Way Guest House

★★★ GUEST HOUSE
Address: 22 Shipston Road,
STRATFORD-UPON-AVON, CV37 7LP
Tel/Fax: 01789 205646
Email: info@ardenwayguesthouse.co.uk
Website: www.ardenwayguesthouse.co.uk
Map ref: 3 SP25
Directions: On A3400, S of River Avon, 100mtrs
Rooms: 6 en suite (2GF) S £34-£55
D £56-£68 Notes: Wi-fi ⊗ on premises Parking: 6

A friendly, family-run guest house close to all the amenities of the town centre and just a few minutes from the theatres. To the back of the house there is a large garden with a summer house, while at the front there is ample space for guests' cars. The bedrooms are attractively decorated and all have en suite facilities. All the rooms have Freeview flat-screen TVs, Wi-fi access and tea- and coffee-making equipment. A hearty breakfast is served in the dining room which overlooks the garden. Special diets are catered for on request.

Recommended in the area

Shakespeare properties; The Cotswolds; Warwick Castle

Victoria Spa Lodge

★★★★ GUEST HOUSE
Address: Bishopton Lane, Bishopton,
STRATFORD-UPON-AVON, CV37 9QY
Tel: 01789 267985
Fax: 01789 204728
Email: ptozer@victoriaspalodge.demon.co.uk
Website: www.victoriaspa.co.uk
Map ref: 3 SP25
Directions: A3400 1.5m N to junct A46, 1st left onto
Bishopton Ln, 1st house on right
Rooms: 7 en suite S £50-£55 D £65-£70
Notes: Wi-fi ⊗ on premises Parking: 12

An elegant Victorian Grade II listed building originally opened by Queen Victoria in 1837. It was also the home of cartoonist Bruce Bairnsfather. Overlooking the canal, it is only a 20-minute walk from the town. The beautifully appointed bedrooms offer spacious comfort with quality furniture, stylish fabrics and thoughtful touches as well as Wi-fi. Expect a warm welcome and high standards of service.

Recommended in the area

Warwick Castle; Shakespeare theatres & properties; The Cotswolds

ISLE OF WIGHT

Freshwater Bay

Sandown from Culver Down

Godshill Park Farm House

★★★★★ 🏠 BED & BREAKFAST

Address: Shanklin Road, GODSHILL, PO38 3JF
Tel: 01983 840781
Email: info@godshillparkfarm.uk.com
Website: www.godshillparkfarm.uk.com
Map ref: 3 SZ58
Directions: From ferry teminal towards Newport, onto A3020 & signs to Sandown, at Blackwater Corner right to Godshill, farm on right after Griffin pub
Rooms: 2 en suite D £90-£99 **Notes:** Wi-fi ⊗ on premises 👶 under 8yrs **Parking:** 4

Set on a working organic livestock farm in a hamlet near the picturesque village of Godshill, within an Area of Outstanding Natural Beauty, this delightful 200-year-old stone farmhouse is a perfect base for exploring the island. The en suite bedrooms, one with a four-poster and the other overlooking the mill pond, are beautifully appointed and offer TV, hospitality tray and Wi-fi. Guests can enjoy a delicious full English breakfast, made from local, organic and home-made produce, in the oak-panelled Great Hall.
Recommended in the area
Osborne House; Brading Roman Villa; Godshill Model Village

Enchanted Manor

★ ★ ★ ★ ★ GUEST ACCOMMODATION
Address: Sandrock Road, NITON, PO38 2NG
Tel: 01983 730215
Email: info@enchantedmanor.co.uk
Website: www.enchantedmanor.co.uk
Map ref: 3 SZ57
Rooms: 7 en suite (2GF)
Notes: Wi-fi 🐾
Parking: 15

The Enchanted Manor is a delightful, friendly establishment providing top-class facilities but without the formal atmosphere of some larger hotels. Enviably set within walking distance of the sea, this unique accommodation was inspired by artist Josephine Wall, whose paintings adorn the manor along with crystal chandeliers and sumptuous furnishings. Above all, the ambience is tranquil and very relaxing, thanks in part to the stunning surroundings, overlooking the coastline at the most southern point of the island. All of the suites here are beautifully appointed, and most feature ornate four-posters and have their own lounge and dining area, with thoughtful extras such as LCD TV, DVD, fridge/mini bar and gourmet food basket provided. The en suite bathrooms boast claw-foot baths, jet-spray showers, fluffy robes and luxury toiletries. Outside, the private gardens and enchanting woodlands are the perfect place to enjoy the special fairy grand high teas; on balmy evenings, guests can watch the stars from the spa while sipping champagne. Owner Maggie provides a delicious array of gourmet breakfasts prepared from local produce in the Badger Watch dining room, and a variety of health and beauty treatments are available in the Zodiac suite.

Recommended in the area

Haven Street Steam Railway; Brading Experience; Ventnor Botanic Gardens

The Lawns

★ ★ ★ ★ GUEST ACCOMMODATION
Address: 72 Broadway, SANDOWN, PO36 9AA
Tel: 01983 402549
Email: lawnshotel@aol.com
Website: www.lawnshotelisleofwight.co.uk
Map ref: 3 SZ58
Directions: On A3055 N of town centre
Rooms: 13 en suite (2GF) S £36-£45 D £64-£100
Notes: Wi-fi ⊗ on premises Parking: 13
Closed: Nov-Jan

A warm welcome always awaits you at The Lawns, which has been lovingly upgraded by owners Nick and Stella to provide every home comfort. The Lawns was built in 1865 and stands in its own southwest-facing gardens offering ample parking. Situated in the pleasing area of Sandown, it is just a short walk away from a blue-flag beach, public transport and the town centre, with its restaurants and shops, and is an ideal base from which to explore the rest of the island. Other local attractions on offer include the pier, go-karting, crazy golf and the Tiger and Big Cat Sanctuary, as well as many opportunities to take part in water sports. The Lawns has a comfortable lounge, with Freeview TV and a selection of games available, as well as a bar. Evening meals are available by arrangement. Service is friendly and attentive, and the bedrooms, two of which are on the ground floor, include a four-poster room and two superior rooms. All are comfortably equipped with flat-screen TVs and hospitality trays. All bathrooms are of a very high standard and include wall-mounted hairdryers.

Recommended in the area
Isle of Wight Zoo; Dinosaur Isle; Sandown Pier

The Grange

★★★★ GUEST ACCOMMODATION

Address: 9 Eastcliff Road, SHANKLIN, PO37 6AA
Tel: 01983 867644
Fax: 01983 865537
Email: jenni@thegrangebythesea.com
Website: www.thegrangebythesea.com
Map ref: 3 SZ58
Directions: Off A3055, High St
Rooms: 16 en suite (6GF) S £67-£81 D £84-£112
(Triple £126-£168)
Notes: Wi-fi ⊗ on premises Parking: 8

Situated in the heart of Shanklin's Old Village, and only moments
from its long, sandy beach, The Grange is the perfect retreat from the hectic pace of modern life.
It enjoys a tranquil yet convenient setting and its atmosphere is friendly and relaxed. Built in the 1820s,
it has original features such as the ornate, carved fireplace in the lounge which is now complemented
by a collection of paintings and sculptures ranging in style from bold and striking to classic and elegant.
The beautifully presented bedrooms, some on the ground floor, are decorated in natural tones that
mirror the surrounding environment, and power showers and complimentary luxury toiletries ensure
a great start to each day. In addition, there are a wide range of inspirational courses and activities
available including yoga, massage and beauty treatments, coastline walks, creative writing and art.
The cuisine uses the freshest ingredients, local and organic where possible, and breakfast and morning
coffee can be enjoyed in the garden in fine weather. There is a sauna, and Wi-fi is available.

Recommended in the area

Shanklin Chine; Tiger Sanctuary in Sandown; Brading Roman Villa

The Leconfield

★ ★ ★ ★ ★ ◉ ⌂ GUEST ACCOMMODATION

Address: 85 Leeson Road, Upper Bonchurch,
VENTNOR, PO38 1PU
Tel: 01983 852196
Fax: 01983 856525
Email: enquiries@leconfieldhotel.com
Website: www.leconfieldhotel.com
Map ref: 3 SZ57
Directions: On A3055, 3m from Old Shanklin village
Rooms: 12 en suite (3GF) **S** £48-£180 **D** £96-£200
Notes: Wi-fi ⊗ on premises ⅙ under 16yrs **Parking:** 14

Paul, Cheryl and their small team welcome you to their home on the Isle of Wight. The delightful
Victorian house is elevated 400-feet above sea level and nestles into St Boniface Down in an Area
of Outstanding Natural Beauty. There are views of the sea from nearly all the bedrooms, the sitting
rooms, dining room, conservatory and garden. The Leconfield is on the island's south side and its
unique micro climate is perfect for a break in the quieter winter months, while in the summer months
guests can enjoy the heated outdoor swimming pool in the delightful gardens; a strictly adults-only
oasis. Luxurious, individually designed bedrooms, some at ground-floor level, are equipped with en
suite facilities, TVs with DVD players, hairdryers, hospitality trays, bathrobes and quality complimentary
toiletries. A hearty breakfast prepared from local produce and free-range eggs is served in the
Seascape Dining Room with its panoramic sea views. After a day of exploring the island's many
treasures you'll be welcomed back to an AA rosette standard evening meal with your choice from a
wide selection of wines and other drinks. Your only distraction from this relaxing ambience will be
tranquil shipping activity on the open seas.

Recommended in the area

Ventnor Gardens; Carisbrooke Castle; Osborne House

Flight of Locks, Devizes

Home Farm

★★★★ BED & BREAKFAST

Address: Farleigh Road, Wingfield,
BRADFORD-ON-AVON, BA14 9LG
Tel/Fax: 01225 764492
Email: info@homefarm-guesthouse.co.uk
Website: www.homefarm-guesthouse.co.uk
Map ref: 2 ST86
Directions: 2m S in Wingfield village on A366
Rooms: 3 en suite (1GF)
Notes: ⊗ on premises Parking: 30

Home Farm is an imaginative conversion of what were originally cattle stalls, feeding rooms and a hay loft belonging to Wingfield House. It fronts onto the original farmyard, which provides ample private parking. There is a 2-acre garden and a large, comfortably furnished lounge to relax in. Breakfasts, cooked on an Aga, offer a wide selection including fish dishes, and home-made bread is a feature. Spacious bedrooms comprise a family room, a double, and a ground-floor twin. All en suite rooms have dual-aspect windows, television, radio, hairdryer, trouser press, bathrobes and hospitality tray.

Recommended in the area

Roman Baths, Bath; Longleat; Stonehenge

At the Sign of the Angel

★★★★ 🍴 ☕ GUEST ACCOMMODATION

Address: 6 Church Street, LACOCK,
Chippenham, SN15 2LB
Tel: 01249 730230
Fax: 01249 730527
Email: angel@lacock.co.uk
Website: www.lacock.co.uk
Map ref: 2 ST96
Directions: Off A350 into Lacock, follow 'Local Traffic' sign Rooms: 10 en suite (3GF) S £82
D £120-£145 Notes: Wi-fi Parking: 6 Closed: 23-27 Dec

Log fires, oak panelling and low beams create a wonderful atmosphere in this 15th-century house. The same family has owned this inn for over half a century. The beamed restaurant is renowned for its traditional cooking. Four bedrooms are in the cottage across the footbridge over a stream. Furnished with antiques, one has an enormous bed that was owned by the Victorian engineer Isambard Kingdom Brunel, another has a four-poster, and a third room has a French tented bed.

Recommended in the area

Lacock Abbey (NT); Fox Talbot Museum; Bowood House and Gardens

The George & Dragon

★★★★ ◎◎ RESTAURANT WITH ROOMS
Address: High Street, ROWDE, Devizes, SN10 2PN
Tel: 01380 723053
Email: thegandd@tiscali.co.uk
Website: www.thegeorgeanddragonrowde.co.uk
Map ref: 2 ST96
Directions: 1.5m from Devizes on A350 towards Chippenham
Rooms: 3 (2 en suite) (1 pri facs) £55-£85
Notes: ⊗ on premises **Parking:** 15

A 16th-century coaching inn, the George & Dragon retains many original features, including exposed beams with the carved Tudor rose and large open fireplaces. Wooden floors, antique rugs and candlelit tables create a warm atmosphere in the bar and restaurant. The inn is located on the village high street in Rowde which is only a couple of miles from Devizes and not far from the Caen Hill lock flight on the Kennet & Avon Canal. Accommodation is provided in individually designed bedrooms, furnished with large double beds made up with luxurious bed linens. Two of the bedrooms are en suite while the third has its own private bathroom. All are equipped with flat-screen televisions with DVD players, iPod stations and tea- and coffee-making facilities. The inn has AA Rosettes for its food, so dining in the bar or restaurant should not be missed. The house speciality is fresh fish delivered daily from Cornwall, but a full carte menu is offered featuring local produce, meats and game and is available in both the restaurant and bar. Events are held throughout the year, including the likes of summer barbeques, wine and cheese tastings, games nights and charity quizzes.

Recommended in the area

Bowood House & Gardens; Roman Baths & Pump Room; Stonehenge

The White Horse, Westbury

The Old House

★★★★ GUEST ACCOMMODATION
Address: 161 Wilton Road, SALISBURY, SP2 7JQ
Tel: 01722 333433
Fax: 01722 335551
Map ref: 3 SU12
Directions: 1m W of city centre on A36
Rooms: 7 en suite S £40-£65 D £65-£70
Notes: ⊗ on premises 🐾 under 7yrs **Parking:** 10

Charming accommodation is offered at this 17th-century house that is within walking distance of Salisbury city centre. Ground-floor areas are beautifully furnished in keeping with the building's period character. The mature gardens are a lovely surprise, with three distinct areas providing privacy on summer evenings. Bedrooms have been tastefully decorated and equipped with modern facilities, including bath or shower rooms en suite. There are two rooms at ground-floor level and one room with a sledge bed. All the bedrooms are equipped with hairdryers and hospitality trays.

Recommended in the area
Stourhead (NT); Heale Garden; Wilton House

St Anns House

★ ★ ★ ★ GUEST ACCOMMODATION

Address: 32-34 Saint Ann Street, SALISBURY, SP1 2DP
Tel: 01722 335657
Email: info@stannshouse.co.uk
Website: www.stannshouse.co.uk
Map ref: 3 SU12
Directions: From Brown St turn left onto Saint Ann St
Rooms: 9 en suite (1GF) **S** £55-£70 **D** £70-£120
Notes: Wi-fi
Closed: 23 Dec-2 Jan

St Anns House is a stunning Grade II listed Georgian townhouse offering high quality boutique-style luxury accommodation with friendly, attentive service. A former public house, it sits in a quiet location in one of the oldest parts of Salisbury. Less than two minutes' walk from the main attractions such as the cathedral and the city centre, it is rightly popular with both business and leisure travellers. Today, thanks to a loving and sensitive restoration, it combines many original features, such as cast-iron fireplaces, chandeliers, sash windows and a host of antiques, with modern creature comforts in the en suite bedrooms, including flat-screen TVs, comfortable armchairs, fine Turkish bed linen, good-quality, locally produced lavender toiletries and tea- and coffee-making facilities with fresh milk. A new ground-floor, walking-stick friendly twin room is available for guests with dogs, and storage for bicycles is also available. The freshly prepared breakfasts are not to be missed and owner-chef Michael Riley draws on his wealth of experience to provide private bespoke dining for pre-booked parties of 12 or more in the elegant Georgian dining room. Only the best of seasonal Wiltshire produce is used.

Recommended in the area

Stonehenge; Salisbury Cathedral; Stourhead House and Garden (NT)

Ardecca

★★★★ GUEST ACCOMMODATION

Address: Fieldrise Farm, Kingsdown Lane, Blunsdon, SWINDON, SN25 5DL
Tel: 01793 721238 & 07791 120826
Email: chris-graham.ardecca@fsmail.net
Website: www.ardecca-bedandbreakfast.co.uk
Map ref: 3 SU18
Directions: Off A419, onto B4019 to Blunsdon/
Highworth into Turnpike Rd at Cold Harbour pub.
Then left **Rooms:** 4 en suite (4GF)
S £40-£45 **D** £60-£65 (Family room £85-£95) **Notes:** Wi-fi ⊗ on premises 🍴 under 6yrs ♿ **Parking:** 5

Ardecca (the name is an amalgamation of the names Rebecca and Richard, the owners' children) has been the family home of Chris and Graham Horne for over 25 years. The large modern bungalow is immaculate inside and out and sits in 16 acres of pastureland on the edge of Blunsdon village, in a quiet rural setting in north Wiltshire within easy reach of Swindon and Cirencester, the Cotswolds and the Marlborough downs. A great find and an asset to the area, the bungalow offers spacious first-class accommodation in a friendly and relaxed atmosphere created by Chris and Graham. All the rooms are on the ground floor, larger than average and are equipped with modern amenities including Wi-fi access, TV, hairdryer, radio alarm and tea- and coffee-making facilities. A full English breakfast is provided and freshly cooked evening meals are available by arrangement, alternatively there are many good pubs and restaurants in the area. There is an outdoor patio area with seating and you can explore the immediate area on public footpaths leading through meadows. Ample parking is available. Please note that credit cards are not accepted. Arts and Crafts workshops are available on site.

Recommended in the area

Cotswold Water Park; Avebury stone circle; Marlborough, the Savernake Forest; Lydiard Park; Thames Path; Buscot Park (NT); Stonehenge

The Old Post Office Guest House

★★★★ GUEST HOUSE

Address: Thornhill Road, South Marston,
SWINDON, SN3 4RY
Tel/Fax: 01793 823114
Email: theoldpostofficeguesthouse@yahoo.co.uk
Website: www.theoldpostofficeguesthouse.co.uk
Map ref: 3 SU18
Directions: A420 onto Thornhill Rd at Gablecross
rdbt 0.75m on left before Old Vicarage Lane
Rooms: 5 en suite **S** £45-£55 **D** £55-£75
Notes: Wi-fi ⊗ on premises **Parking:** 5

Sympathetically extended, this attractive property makes an excellent base for touring the West Country.
It has been owned by the Sansum family for four generations, and today guests are welcomed by the
enthusiastic owner. The comfortable and prettily decorated en suite bedrooms include Freeview TV, free
Wi-fi and beverage-making facilities. An extensive choice is offered at breakfast, from a sumptuous full
English to a delicious continental; all dishes are freshly cooked using the best local produce.
Recommended in the area
Cotswold Water Park; Lacock Abbey; Avebury Stone Circle

The Pear Tree Inn

★★★★★ ⊛⊛ RESTAURANT WITH ROOMS

Address: Maypole Group, Top Lane,
WHITLEY, SN12 8QX
Tel: 01225 709131
Fax: 01225 702276
Email: peartreeinn@maypolehotels.com
Website: www.maypolehotels.com
Map ref: 2 ST86
Rooms: 8 en suite (4GF) **S** £95 **D** £125
Notes: Wi-fi **Parking:** 45

This delightful country inn, located just outside Bath, provides cosy, luxurious accommodation and good
food. The chic en suite bedrooms, some housed in an adjoining annexe, combine English and French
influences. The restaurant draws visitors from a wide area thanks to the interesting menu, which
features organic meats, free-range chicken, locally grown vegetables and healthy children's dishes, as
well as the rustic atmosphere and the friendliness of the hosts. Food may be eaten outside, weather
permitting. Real ales, a good wine list and roaring log fires complete the picture.
Recommended in the area
Lacock Abbey; Avebury (NT); Silbury Hill

WORCESTERSHIRE

Worcestershire Beacon, Great Malvern

The Boot Inn

★★★★ ⇔ INN

Address: Radford Road, FLYFORD FLAVELL,
Worcester, WR7 4BS
Tel: 01386 462658
Fax: 01386 462547
Email: enquiries@thebootinn.com
Website: www.thebootinn.com
Map ref: 2 SO95
Directions: In village centre, signed from A422
Rooms: 5 en suite (2GF) **S** £50-£60 **D** £65-£90
Notes: Wi-fi **Parking:** 30

An inn has occupied this site since the 13th century, though 'The Boot' itself, as it is called locally, dates from the Georgian period. It provides an ideal base for anyone wishing to explore Stratford-upon-Avon, the Cotswolds or the Malvern Hills. The award-winning inn has undergone modernisation, yet it has managed to retain much of its historic charm. The comfortable bedrooms in the converted coach house, furnished in antique pine, are equipped with practical extras such as tea- and coffee-making facilities, trouser press and radio-alarm clock, and all have modern bathrooms. Two rooms have disabled access. Guests can relax and indulge in the range of options available at this family-run pub, which prides itself on its friendly staff and lively atmosphere. Traditional ales and an extensive wine list complement the varied and imaginative menus, which are adapted according to availability of ingredients, with everything from sandwiches to bar meals to full carte on offer. The excellent food here, made from fine local produce, can be enjoyed in the cosy public areas, which include an attractive restaurant, a light and airy conservatory and a shaded patio area especially suited to summer dining.

Recommended in the area

Worcester Cathedral; Stratford-upon-Avon; Evesham

The Malvern Hills, Great Malvern

The Dell House

★★★★ BED & BREAKFAST

Address:	Green Lane, Malvern Wells, MALVERN, WR14 4HU
Tel:	01684 564448
Fax:	01684 893974
Email:	burrage@dellhouse.co.uk
Website:	www.dellhouse.co.uk
Map ref:	2 SO74

Directions: 2m S of Great Malvern on A449. Turn left off A449 onto Green Ln. House at top of road on right, just below old church

Rooms: 3 en suite S £35-£45 D £58-£80 Notes: Wi-fi ⊗ on premises 🚼 under 10yrs Parking: 3

The Dell House was built around 1820 when one of Malvern's famous healing springs was diverted to its grounds. Ian and Helen Burrage offer spacious, individually styled bedrooms where period elegance is combined with homely comforts and Wi-fi access; two rooms have wonderful views to the Cotswolds. Breakfast is served in the impressive Morning Room with superb views over the Severn Valley.

Recommended in the area

Malvern Hills; Malvern Theatre; Three Counties Showground; Malvern Springs & Wells

Tower of St Leonard's Church, Clent

Burnby Hall Garden

Burton Mount Country House

★ ★ ★ ★ ★ GUEST ACCOMMODATION

Address: Malton Road, Cherry Burton,
BEVERLEY, HU17 7RA
Tel: 01964 550541
Email: pg@burtonmount.co.uk
Website: www.burtonmount.co.uk
Map ref: 8 TA03
Directions: 2m NW of Beverley. B1248 for Malton,
2m right at x-rds, house on left
Rooms: 3 en suite **S** £64 **D** £91
Notes: Wi-fi ⊗ on premises 👶 under 12yrs **Parking:** 20

Burton Mount is a charming country house three miles from Beverley, set in delightful gardens and offering luxurious accommodation. Nestling in a corner of the Yorkshire Wolds, it sits in its own secluded grounds and small woodland and makes a relaxing retreat for anyone travelling on business or for pleasure. Inside, a spacious hall leads up to the en suite bedrooms, all of which are located on the first floor and are well equipped with thoughtful extra touches, such as TV, hairdryer, tea- and coffee-making facilities, bathrobes and toiletries. Downstairs, the dining room has French windows that open onto a terrace, and this in turn leads through to the spacious and elegant drawing room, which has a blazing fire in the cooler months. A second large and comfortable sitting room has a TV and another log fire. An excellent, Aga-cooked Yorkshire breakfast is served in the morning room and includes smoked bacon, free-range eggs, home-made preserves and delicious bread, or a continental breakfast is available if preferred. The house is home to the Greenwood family, and Pauline Greenwood is renowned locally for her customer care, culinary skills and warm hospitality.

Recommended in the area

Beverley Minster; Bishop Burton Horse Trials; Wilberforce House, Kingston upon Hull

Hornsea Mere

The Royal Bridlington

★★★★ GUEST ACCOMMODATION

Address: 1 Shaftesbury Road, BRIDLINGTON,
YO15 3NP
Tel: 01262 672433
Fax: 01262 672118
Email: info@royalhotelbrid.co.uk
Website: www.royalhotelbrid.co.uk
Map ref: 8 TA16
Directions: A615 N to Bridlington (Kingsgate), right
onto Shaftesbury Rd **Rooms:** 18 (17 en suite) (1 pri
facs) (4GF) **S** £37-£44 **D** £64-£78 **Notes:** Wi-fi ⊗ on premises **Parking:** 7

In an ideal location, just 100 yards from beautiful South Beach, this immaculate property also has a
lovely, enclosed garden. The thoughtfully furnished bedrooms all have bathrooms and are very well
equipped. Some rooms are ground floor with level access to the bar and restaurant. Many rooms have
fine sea views, and Wi-fi is available throughout. Spacious public areas include a dining room serving
breakfasts and dinners, a cosy lounge with plasma TV, a well-stocked bar and open fire.
Recommended in the area
Yorkshire Belle; Burton Agnes; Bridlington South Beach

Thornton Force, Yorkshire Dales National Park

Lucy Cross Farm

★ ★ ★ GUEST ACCOMMODATION

Address: ALDBROUGH ST JOHN,
Richmond, DL11 7AD
Tel: 01325 374319 & 07931 545985
Email: sally@lucycross.co.uk
Website: www.lucycross.co.uk
Map ref: 7 NZ21
Directions: A1 junct 56 onto B6275 at Barton,
white house 3m from Barton rdbt on left
towards Piercebridge

Rooms: 5 (3 en suite) (2 pri facs) (1GF) **S** £35-£45 **D** £65-£75 **Notes:** Wi-fi **Parking:** 10

This working farm is located near the picturesque village of Aldbrough St John, yet is close to major road links and makes a good base for visiting North Yorkshire and the Dales. There is a relaxed atmosphere here, and the traditionally furnished bedrooms are very comfortably equipped; all have free Wi-fi. A lounge is available for guests, and hearty breakfasts are served in the pleasant dining room. Home-cooked evening meals, based on local produce, can be arranged – Aga roasts are a speciality.

Recommended in the area

Yorkshire Dales; Barnard Castle; Croft Racing Circuit

Shallowdale House

★ ★ ★ ★ ★ 🏠 🍽 GUEST ACCOMMODATION

Address: West End, AMPLEFORTH, YO62 4DY
Tel: 01439 788325
Fax: 01439 788885
Email: stay@shallowdalehouse.co.uk
Website: www.shallowdalehouse.co.uk
Map ref: 8 SE57
Directions: Off A170 at W end of village,
on turn to Hambleton

Rooms: 3 (2 en suite) (1 pri facs) **S** £75-£85
D £95-£115 **Notes:** Wi-fi ⊗ on premises 👶 under 12yrs **Parking:** 3 **Closed:** Xmas & New Year

Owned by Anton van der Horst and Phillip Gill, Shallowdale House is in a stunning location overlooking an Area of Outstanding Natural Beauty. The spacious south-facing bedrooms have huge picture windows and lovely views, and the atmosphere is relaxed and friendly. The four-course dinners are a highlight, featuring local and seasonal produce, and equal care is taken with breakfast, which can feature Whitby kippers and local sausages, as well as home-made preserves.

Recommended in the area

Castle Howard; Rievaulx Abbey; Nunnington Hall (NT)

Malham Cove, Yorkshire Dales National Park

Brookhouse Guest House

★ ★ ★ GUEST HOUSE

Address: Station Road, CLAPHAM,
Lancaster, LA2 8ER
Tel: 015242 51580
Email: admin@brookhouseclapham.co.uk
Website: www.brookhouse-clapham.co.uk
Map ref: 6 SD76
Directions: Off A65 into village
Rooms: 3 (2 en suite) (1 pri facs) S £35-£45
D £60-£80 **Notes:** Wi-fi ⊗ on premises ⊚

Situated in a pretty conservation village beside the river, this well-maintained guest house offers comfortable accommodation and good food, served in its popular ground-floor café. The thoughtfully furnished en suite bedrooms, which include a family room, provide a home-from-home, with fluffy towels and bathrobes, TVs and complimentary Wi-fi access as standard. Brookhouse prides itself on the quality of its home-cooked rustic dishes and hearty breakfasts, which are prepared by an experienced chef, using locally sourced meat from an award-winning butcher.
Recommended in the area
Ingleborough Cave; Ingelton Waterfalls Trail; Settle to Carlisle Railway

Muker, Swaledale

Ashfield House

★★★★★ 🏠 ☕ GUEST ACCOMMODATION

Address: Summers Fold, GRASSINGTON,
Skipton, BD23 5AE
Tel: 01756 752584
Fax: 07092 376562
Email: sales@ashfieldhouse.co.uk
Website: www.ashfieldhouse.co.uk
Map ref: 7 SE06
Directions: B6265 to village centre, main street, left onto Summers Fold **Rooms:** 8 en suite **S** £65-£89 **D** £95-£106 **Notes:** Wi-fi ⊗ on premises 👶 under 5yrs **Parking:** 8

This well-maintained Grade II listed 17th-century house is tucked away down a private lane with its own walled gardens. Ashfield House was once a row of miners' cottages, but today it provides luxurious accommodation. There are smart furnishings throughout, from the well equipped en suite bedrooms to the cosy lounges with honesty bar. Guests dine in style, at breakfast time with home-made yoghurt, marmalade, granola, and own-recipe sausages, or from imaginative evening menus.

Recommended in the area

Skipton Castle; Bolton Abbey; Pennine Boat Trips

The Kings Head at Newton

★★★★ GUEST ACCOMMODATION

Address: The Green, GUISBOROUGH,
Nr Great Ayton, TS9 6QR
Tel: 01642 722318
Fax: 01642 724750
Email: info@kingsheadhotel.co.uk
Website: www.kingsheadhotel.co.uk
Map ref: 8 NZ61
Directions: A171 towards Guisborough, at rdbt onto A173 to Newton under Roseberry, under Roseberry Topping landmark
Rooms: 8 en suite (2GF) **S** £59.50-£85 **D** £75-£110
Notes: Wi-fi ⊗ on premises **Parking:** 100 **Closed:** 25 Dec & 1 Jan

This family-owned establishment offers stylish, thoughtfully equipped bedrooms. The restaurant, next door, offers quality food with produce sourced from the local area. A full English or continental breakfast is served in the glass-roofed breakfast area with unspoiled views of Roseberry Topping.

Recommended in the area

Cleveland Way; North York Moors National Park; Whitby

Alexa House

★ ★ ★ ★ GUEST HOUSE

Address: 26 Ripon Road, HARROGATE, HG1 2JJ
Tel: 01423 501988
Email: enquires@alexa-house.co.uk
Website: www.alexa-house.co.uk
Map ref: 8 SE35
Directions: On A61, 0.25m from junct A59
Rooms: 13 en suite (4GF) S £55-£60 D £85-£90
Notes: Wi-fi Parking: 10 Closed: 23-26 Dec

Guests at this beautifully restored detached Victorian property are assured of free parking and a location just a short stroll from the town centre and Harrogate International Centre. All the bright and airy contemporary en suite bedrooms, split between the main house and the cottage rooms, provide a range of complimentary extras such as White Company toiletries, well-stocked refreshment trays and iPod docks. Breakfast is served in the bright dining room and includes an impressive range of fruit, nuts and cereals to accompany the cooked English breakfast. The elegant lounge has a 24-hour honesty bar.
Recommended in the area
Harrogate Turkish Baths; The Valley Gardens; Montpellier Quarter

Laskill Grange

★ ★ ★ ★ GUEST ACCOMMODATION

Address: HELMSLEY, YO62 5NB
Tel: 01439 798268
Email: laskillgrange@tiscali.co.uk
Website: www.laskillgrange.co.uk
Map ref: 8 SE58
Directions: From York A19 to Thirsk, A170 to
Helmsley then B1257 N, after 6m sign on left to
Laskill Grange **Rooms:** 3 (2 en suite) (1 pri facs)
(3GF) S £30-£40 D £77-£80 **Parking:** 20

Laskill is a charming 19th-century house in the North York Moors National Park. There are splendid walks in the surrounding countryside and fishing on the River Seph, which runs through the grounds. The elegant house has exposed beams and open fireplaces, and the immaculate bedrooms are decorated to a very high standard and come with hot-drink trays and flowers. Generous breakfasts are prepared using home-grown produce whenever possible. Hot tubs are available. Across the courtyard from the farmhouse are converted barns for self catering. There is an activity centre for children too.
Recommended in the area
Rievaulx Abbey; Castle Howard; Nunnington Hall (NT)

The New Inn Motel

★ ★ ★ GUEST ACCOMMODATION
Address: Main Street, HUBY, York, YO61 1HQ
Tel/Fax: 01347 810219
Email: enquiries@newinnmotel.freeserve.co.uk
Website: www.newinnmotel.co.uk
Map ref: 8 SE56
Directions: Off A19 E into village centre, motel on
left **Rooms:** 8 en suite (8GF) **S** £40-£55 **D** £70-£80
Parking: 8 **Closed:** mid Nov-mid Dec & part Feb

Located behind the New Inn, this modern family-run motel-style establishment occupies a quiet location in the village of Huby, 9 miles north of York, and is in an ideal spot for visiting the historic city and surrounding countryside. The comfortable en suite chalet bedrooms, all on the ground floor, are spacious and neatly furnished, with TVs and tea and coffee-making facilities. Full English breakfasts, made from locally sourced dry-cured bacon, black pudding and sausages, are served in the cosy dining room. The reception area hosts an array of maps and tourist information, and the resident owners provide a friendly and helpful service.

Recommended in the area

Beningbrough Hall and Gardens (NT); Sutton Bank Visitor Centre; City of York

Newton House

★ ★ ★ ★ 🔔 GUEST ACCOMMODATION
Address: 5-7 York Place, KNARESBOROUGH,
HG5 0AD
Tel: 01423 863539
Fax: 01423 869748
Email: newtonhouse@btinternet.com
Website: www.newtonhouseyorkshire.com
Map ref: 8 SE35
Directions: On A59 in Knaresborough, 200yds from
town centre **Rooms:** 11 (10 en suite) (1 pri facs)
(3GF) **S** £50 **D** £75-£110 **Notes:** Wi-fi **Parking:** 10 **Closed:** 1wk Xmas

This delightfully elegant, Grade II listed former coaching inn is only a short walk from the river, castle and market square. Owners Mark and Lisa Wilson place the emphasis on relaxation, informality and comfort, and the very well equipped bedrooms include four-posters and king-size doubles, as well as family and interconnecting rooms. There is a comfortable lounge too. Breakfasts include eggs Benedict, poached smoked haddock, and porridge with sultanas in malt whisky, as well as the traditional full English.

Recommended in the area

Fountains Abbey; Yorkshire Dales; Newby Hall; RHS Harlow Carr Gardens

Capple Bank Farm

★★★★★ BED & BREAKFAST

Address: West Witton, LEYBURN, DL8 4ND
Tel: 01969 625825
Email: julian.smithers@btinternet.com
Website: www.capplebankfarm.co.uk
Map ref: 7 SE19
Directions: A1 to Bedale. Turn onto A684 to
Leyburn. Through Hawes & Wensley, 1st left in
West Witton. Up hill, left Rooms: 2 en suite S £45
D £65-£70 Notes: ⊗ ⛄ under 10yrs ⊛ Parking: 6

Ideal for exploring the Yorkshire Dales National Park, or just enjoying the peace and quiet, this spacious house, which commands extensive views of Wensleydale, has recently been converted and refurbished. The en suite bedrooms have been finished to a high standard, with quality bed linen and a range of home comforts, and guests have use of a charming lounge with a real fire lit on cooler days. Breakfast, made from fresh local produce and featuring kedgeree and fish cakes as well as full English and continental options, is served at a beautiful table in the open-plan kitchen and impressive dining room.

Recommended in the area

Bolton Castle; Wensleydale; Aysgarth Falls

River House

★★★★ 🏛 ⬡ GUEST HOUSE

Address: MALHAM, Skipton, BD23 4DA
Tel: 01729 830315
Email: info@riverhousehotel.co.uk
Website: www.riverhousehotel.co.uk
Map ref: 7 SD96
Directions: Off A65, N to Malham
Rooms: 8 en suite (1GF) S £45-£65 D £60-£75
Notes: Wi-fi ⛄ under 9yrs Parking: 5

Dating in parts back to 1664, this attractive guest house makes a great base for exploring the Yorkshire Dales. The house combines modern comfort with period elegance, as seen in the bright, comfortable en suite bedrooms, all of which have luxury Scottish toiletries, big fluffy towels and Wi-fi. Some rooms have stunning views of the dales. Public areas include a cosy lounge bar with wood-burning stove and a large, well-appointed dining room. Excellent breakfasts and evening meals offer choice and quality local produce, plus packed lunches are available. Walkers can make use of the drying room to hang wet clothes, the laundry room and there is secure bike storage.

Recommended in the area

Gordale Scar; Settle to Carlisle Railway; Skipton Castle

Bank Villa Guest House

★★★★ 🛏 🍽 GUEST HOUSE
Address: MASHAM, Ripon, HG4 4DB
Tel: 01765 689605
Email: stay@bankvilla.com
Website: www.bankvilla.com
Map ref: 7 SE28
Directions: Enter on A6108 from Ripon, property on right
Rooms: 6 (4 en suite) (2 pri facs)
Notes: ⊗ on premises 🚼 under 5yrs **Parking:** 6

All the delights of Masham are within walking distance and the Yorkshire Dales are within easy reach of this guest house. Take into account the award-winning food and the delight of staying in a comfortable, historic Georgian home, and a visit here becomes a must. Graham and Liz's welcome is relaxed and friendly. The comfortable accommodation is immaculate and full of character, with crisp, fresh linen and fluffy white towels. The food is served in the licensed dining room using home-grown and locally sourced produce whenever possible.

Recommended in the area

Black Sheep & Theakstons breweries; Rievaulx Abbey; Fountains Abbey; Yorkshire Dales

17 Burgate

★★★★★ 🛏 GUEST ACCOMMODATION
Address: 17 Burgate, PICKERING, YO18 7AU
Tel: 01751 473463
Email: info@17burgate.co.uk
Website: www.17burgate.co.uk
Map ref: 8 SE78
Directions: From A170 follow sign to Castle. 17 Burgate on right **Rooms:** 5 en suite **S** £70-£75 **D** £80-£110 **Notes:** Wi-fi ⊗ on premises 🚼 under 10yrs **Parking:** 7

This elegant market town house, close to the town centre and the castle, has been expertly renovated, and the owners have gone the extra mile to make sure you enjoy your stay here. The comfortable, individually designed bedrooms all have modern facilities including free broadband, flat-screen TV, DVD player and a range of spa cosmetics and aromatic candles. Public areas include a comfortable lounge bar with a log-burning stove and well-stocked bar, and breakfast includes a wide choice of local, healthy foods. The peaceful garden includes a terrace on which to relax and enjoy a bottle of wine.

Recommended in the area

Flamingo Land; Castle Howard; North Yorkshire Moors Railway

Fangdale beck, Bilsdale

Low Skibeden House

★ ★ ★ FARMHOUSE

Address: Harrogate Road, SKIPTON, BD23 6AB
Tel: 01756 793849 & 07050 207787
Website: www.yorkshirenet.co.uk/accgde/
lowskibeden/index.html

Map ref: 7 SE35
Rooms: 4 en suite D £60-£64
Notes: ⊗ on premises ✠
Parking: 4

Surrounded by open countryside, on the edge of the Yorkshire Dales National Park and enjoying fine views, Low Skibeden House is an attractive stone-built 16th-century farmhouse. It is located just a mile from Skipton, which has many amenities. Guests are greeted with tea or coffee and cake, before settling into the traditionally furnished bedrooms, (all en suite). Family accommodation is available, and there is also a spacious and comfortable visitors' lounge with TV where guests are invited to enjoy suppertime drinks. A separate dining room is the setting for hearty farmhouse breakfasts.

Recommended in the area

Bolton Abbey; Harrogate; York

The Blackwell Ox Inn

★ ★ ★ ★ ◉ 🛏 INN

Address: Huby Road, SUTTON-ON-THE-FOREST,
Y061 1DT
Tel: 01347 810328 & 01904 690758
Fax: 01904 691529
Email: enquiries@blackwelloxinn.co.uk
Website: www.blackwelloxinn.co.uk
Map ref: 8 SE56
Directions: Off A1237, onto B1363 to Sutton-on-the-Forest. Left at T-junct, 50yds on right
Rooms: 7 en suite **S** £65 **D** £95-£110
Notes: ⊗ on premises **Parking:** 18

A picturesque village just seven miles from the centre of York is the location of this friendly, renovated inn, which dates back to around 1823 and is named after a memorable 2,278lb, 6ft-tall (at the shoulders) animal that was bred locally. The finest local meat and produce still figures prominently in the inn's renowned restaurant, where Head Chef Tom Kingston and his team create serious gastro-pub food. There's a separate area where you can relax with an aperitif and browse the menu before being served in the traditional-style dining room. For less formal eating, a selection from the restaurant menu is also available in the bar, where logs blaze in an open fireplace in winter and fine, hand-pulled ales are kept in top condition (children are allowed in the bar until 8pm). There's also a pleasant terrace for alfresco dining on warm summer days. Accommodation at the inn offers stylish en suite bedrooms which have been individually designed – you could even opt for a four-poster room with a big, claw-foot bathtub right in the bedroom, and perhaps upgrade to the Champagne Break for a really romantic stay. All of the rooms include a television with DVD player and the bathrooms have Molton Brown toiletries.

Recommended in the area

Sutton Park and Gardens; the City of York; Beningbrough Hall (NT)

Spital Hill

★★★★★ 🛏 🚪 GUEST ACCOMMODATION
Address: York Road, THIRSK, YO7 3AE
Tel: 01845 522273
Fax: 01845 524970
Email: spitalhill@spitalhill.entadsl.com
Website: www.spitalhill.co.uk
Map ref: 8 SE48
Directions: 1.5m SE of town, set back 200yds from A19, driveway marked by 2 white posts
Rooms: 5 (4 en suite) (1 pri facs) (1GF) S £62-£69 D £94-£106 Notes: ⊗ on premises 👣 under 12yrs Parking: 6

Robin and Ann Clough are passionate about offering their guests genuine hospitality at their beautiful home set in gardens and surrounded by open countryside. Ann produces an excellent set dinner each evening as an optional extra, using good fresh produce; usually the couple will join their guests at the table. Breakfast is also a highlight. Bedrooms are furnished with quality and style, and thoughtfully equipped with many extras; there is no tea-making equipment as Ann prefers to offer tea as a service.
Recommended in the area
Herriott Centre, Thirsk; Byland Abbey; Revaulx Abbey

Woodhouse Farm

★★★★ FARMHOUSE
Address: WESTOW, York, YO60 7LL
Tel: 01653 618378 & 07904 293422
Fax: 01653 618378
Email: stay@wood-house-farm.co.uk
Website: www.wood-house-farm.co.uk
Map ref: 8 SE76
Directions: Off A64 to Kirkham Priory & Westow. Right at T-junct, farm drive 0.5m out of village on right Rooms: 2 en suite S £40-£45 D £60-£70
Notes: Wi-fi ⊗ on premises 🐾 Parking: 6 Closed: Xmas, New Year & mid Mar-mid Apr

This 500-acre family-run working farm is set in rolling countryside nestled between the Vale of York, the Yorkshire Wolds and the Howardian Hills. The 18th-century farmhouse has been sympathetically restored retaining original beams and open log fires to provide a homely feel. All rooms are well equipped and consist of king-size and family rooms. Start the day with a delicious country breakfast sourced from locally produced sausages and bacon, plus home-made preserves, cakes and scones.
Recommended in the area
Castle Howard; York Minster; North Yorkshire Moors

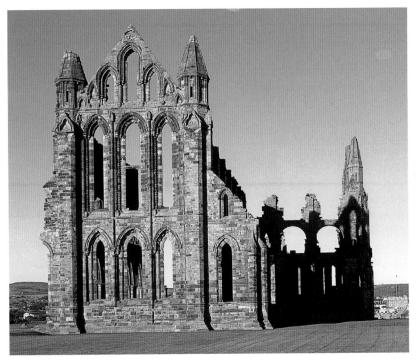

Whitby Abbey

Corra Lynn

★★★★ GUEST ACCOMMODATION
Address: 28 Crescent Avenue, WHITBY, YO21 3EW
Tel/Fax: 01947 602214
Map ref: 8 NZ81
Directions: Corner A174 & Crescent Av
Rooms: 5 en suite S £30 D £64
Notes: ⊗ on premises ☺ **Parking:** 5
Closed: 21 Dec-5 Jan

Bruce and Christine Marot have a passion for what
they do, mixing traditional values of cleanliness, comfort and friendly service with a modern trendy
style. The house is set in a prominent corner position on the West Cliff within easy walking distance
of the town of Whitby and its picturesque harbour. The bedrooms are thoughtfully equipped with
colour TV, radio alarm and hospitality tray, and are individually furnished and colourfully decorated.
The delightful dining room, with a corner bar and a wall adorned with clocks, really catches the eye.
Breakfasts at Corra Lynn are hearty, with a vegetarian option, and the menu changes with the seasons.
There is off-street parking.

Recommended in the area

Whitby Abbey; Captain Cook Memorial Museum; Robin Hood's Bay

Estbek House

★ ★ ★ ★ ◉◉ ≋ RESTAURANT WITH ROOMS

Address: East Row, Sandsend, WHITBY, YO21 3SU
Tel: 01947 893424
Fax: 01947 893625
Email: info@estbekhouse.co.uk
Website: www.estbekhouse.co.uk
Map ref: 8 NZ81
Directions: On Cleveland Way, within Sandsend, next to East Beck
Rooms: 4 (3 en suite) (1 pri facs)
Notes: Wi-fi ⊗ on premises ⚲ under 14yrs **Parking:** 6

Estbek House, a beautiful Georgian establishment located in a small coastal village north-west of Whitby, is a restaurant with rooms that specialises in seafood. Here, diners can indulge themselves in the first-floor restaurant while listening to the relaxing break of the waves from the nearby Yorkshire Moors coastline. Chef/co-proprietor Tim Lawrence has nearly 30 years' experience of seafood cookery and he and his team present a range of mouth-watering dishes, including non-fish alternatives, on daily-changing menus. An innovative wine chalk board shows a large selection of bottles and wines by the glass, especially notable for the large Australian contingent, with over 100 wines listed. Surroundings in the restaurant are modern and stylishly simple – airy and bright by day, thoughtfully lit in the evenings; when the weather allows, diners may eat outside in the flower-bordered courtyard. On the ground floor is a small bar and breakfast room, while above are the individually decorated and luxurious bedrooms. Each has its own name – such as Florence or Eva – and character, and comes with a wealth of thoughtful extras such as flat-screen TV, CD/radio alarm clock, hairdryer, tea and coffee-making facilities and complimentary guest pack.

Recommended in the area

Mulgrave castles; Mulgrave woods; Cleveland Way

Keld, Swaledale

Netherby House

★ ★ ★ ★ 🏠 ☕ GUEST ACCOMMODATION

Address: 90 Coach Road, Sleights,
WHITBY, YO22 5EQ
Tel/Fax: 01947 810211
Email: info@netherby-house.co.uk
Website: www.netherby-house.co.uk
Map ref: 8 NZ81
Directions: In village of Sleights, off A169 (Whitby-Pickering road)
Rooms: 11 en suite (5GF) **S** £37-£46.50 **D** £74-£93
Notes: ⊗ on premises 🐾 under 2yrs **Parking:** 17 **Closed:** 25-26 Dec

For owners Lyn and Barry Truman their bed and breakfast business is a labour of love; the beautifully kept gardens and the delightful day rooms and bedrooms, all contribute to a restful stay. Hospitality is another strength of Netherby House, and imaginative evening meals using fresh garden produce are served in the candlelit dining room. There are twin, double and family rooms, and a four-poster room adds that extra touch of luxury. There is a lounge-bar and a conservatory for relaxing in.

Recommended in the area

Historic Whitby; North Yorkshire Moors National Park; North Yorkshire Moors Railway

Ascot House

★★★★ GUEST ACCOMMODATION

Address: 80 East Parade, YORK, YO31 7YH
Tel: 01904 426826
Fax: 01904 431077
Email: admin@ascothouseyork.com
Website: www.ascothouseyork.com
Map ref: 8 SE65
Directions: 0.5m NE of city centre. Off A1036
Heworth Green onto Mill Ln, 2nd left
Rooms: 13 (12 en suite) (1 pri facs) (2GF)
S £55-£70 D £70-£80 Notes: Wi-fi Parking: 13 Closed: 21-28 Dec

This Victorian villa was built for a prominent family in 1869 close to the city centre. The owners have retained many original features, yet they have improved the building to provide modern standards of comfort. Most of the spacious rooms on the ground and first floors have period furniture and four-poster or canopy beds. The top-floor rooms have now been completely refurbished and come with superb bathrooms; all rooms have hospitality trays, hairdryers, radio alarms and TVs. The curved stained-glass window on the landing is a particularly attractive feature. There is a spacious and comfortable lounge where you can relax, watch television or enjoy a drink from the Butlers Pantry. Tea and coffee are also served in the lounge throughout the day. Delicious traditional, vegetarian and continental breakfasts are served in the dining room; the generous portions are sure to set you up for the day. Ascot House is a welcoming property that can be reached from the city by bus in just a few minutes, or by a short brisk walk. It has an enclosed car park, and the public park next door has two tennis courts and two bowling greens. A nearby pub serves good food, and there are also many restaurants, wine bars and theatres within walking distance.

Recommended in the area

Jorvik Viking Centre; National Railway Museum; York Minster

Lake Gormire, North York Moors National Park

The Heathers Guest House

★★★★ GUEST ACCOMMODATION

Address: 54 Shipton Rd, Clifton-Without, YORK,
YO30 5RQ
Tel/Fax: 01904 640989
Email: aabbg@heathers-guest-house.co.uk
Website: www.heathers-guest-house.co.uk
Map ref: 8 SE65
Directions: N of York on A19, halfway between
A1237 ring road & York city centre
Rooms: 6 (4 en suite) (2 pri facs) **S** £52-£126
D £56-£130 **Notes:** Wi-fi ⊗ on premises ⋈ under 10yrs **Parking:** 9 **Closed:** Xmas

Remodelling and refurbishment at this large 1930s house has resulted in a most comfortable and welcoming establishment. Heather and Graham Fisher have designed each room individually using quality fabrics and decor and there is a feeling of luxury in the bedrooms, all of which have en suite or private facilities and benefit from TV, Wi-fi and well-stocked tea- and coffee-making facilities. The light and airy breakfast room looks out onto a well-tended garden area, and off-street parking is guaranteed.
Recommended in the area
North York Moors; Castle Howard; Ryedale Folk Museum

WEST YORKSHIRE

Rochdale Canal

Stoodley Pike on Pennine Way

The Huddersfield Central Lodge

★★★★ GUEST ACCOMMODATION

Address: 11/15 Beast Market,
HUDDERSFIELD, HD1 1QF
Tel: 01484 515551
Fax: 01484 432349
Email: angela@centrallodge.com
Website: www.centrallodge.com
Map ref: 7 SE11
Directions: In town centre off Lord St, signs for
Beast Market from ring road **Rooms:** 22 en suite
S £52-£58 D £58-£68 **Notes:** Wi-fi **Parking:** 50

This friendly, family-run operation is located in the town centre, close to amenities and transport links. Some of the smart, spacious bedrooms are in the main building, while others, many with kitchenettes, are situated across a courtyard. All are well equipped, with Freeview TVs. Public rooms include a bar with a plasma-screen TV and a conservatory. Breakfasts are based on local and organic produce. For evening meals, ask about Woks Cooking. There are smoking rooms available and children and pets are welcome.

Recommended in the area

Galpharm Stadium; Holmfirth; The National Coal Mining Museum for England

CHANNEL ISLANDS

St Peter Port

The Panorama

★ ★ ★ ★ ★ GUEST ACCOMMODATION
Address: La Rue du Crocquet, ST AUBIN, JE3 8BZ
Tel: 01534 742429
Fax: 01534 745940
Email: info@panoramajersey.com
Website: www.panoramajersey.com
Map ref: 13
Directions: In village centre
Rooms: 14 en suite (3GF) S £44-£68 D £88-£135
Notes: Wi-fi ⊗ on premises ❌ under 18yrs
Closed: mid Oct-mid Apr

The Panorama is aptly named indeed, with its spectacular views across St Aubin's Bay. A long established favourite with visitors, not least because of the genuinely warm welcome, it is situated on a pretty seafront street. Inside are antiques aplenty, including a number of elegant fireplaces, and it is well known for its collection of over 500 teapots. Wireless internet access is now also available. A feature of the recently upgraded bedrooms is the luxurious pocket-sprung beds, most well over six feet long. The breakfasts, each individually cooked to order, are another draw, with dishes such as Grand Slam and Elegant Rarebit among the inventive choices on the lengthy menu. For lunch or dinner there are many restaurants in close proximity, providing ample opportunity to sample the best produce that Jersey has to offer. Many are within walking distance, and the owners will happily make recommendations. A good base for walking, cycling (a cycle track along the promenade leads to St Helier) or travelling around the island by bus. Day trips by boat are available to the neighbouring islands of Guernsey, Herm and Sark, and also to St Malo in Brittany. The accommodation is unsuitable for children.

Recommended in the area

Picturesque village of St Aubin; Railway Walk to Corbière; Beauport and Les Creux Country Park

ISLE OF MAN

Snaefell Mountain Railway, Laxey

'Lady Isabella' working water wheel

Aaron House

★★★★★ ≋ GUEST HOUSE

Address: The Promenade, PORT ST MARY, IM9 5DE
Tel: 01624 835702
Fax: 01624 837731
Website: www.aaronhouse.co.uk
Map ref: 5 SC26
Directions: Follow signs for South & Port St Mary, left at Post Office. House in centre of Promenade
Rooms: 4 (3 en suite) (1 pri facs) **D** £70-£118
Notes: ⊗ on premises ✻ under 12yrs ⊜
Closed: 21 Dec-3 Jan

Overlooking Chapel Bay's stunning harbour, this family-run establishment lovingly recreates the property's original Victorian style, with exquisite interior design, cast-iron fireplaces in the public rooms and sparklingly polished period furniture. Delicious home-made cakes served on arrival and the luxurious bedrooms have a hot water bottle placed in your bed at night. Breakfast is a treat and evening meals are offered in the winter only (Monday–Friday). There is free parking 70 yards away.

Recommended in the area

Cregneash Folk Village; Victorian Steam Railway; Sound and Calf of Man (bird sanctuary)

SCOTLAND

Kilchurn Castle, Loch Awe

Callater Lodge Guest House

★★★★ GUEST HOUSE

Address: 9 Glenshee Road, BRAEMAR,
Aberdeenshire, AB35 5YQ
Tel: 013397 41275
Email: info@hotel-braemar.co.uk
Website: www.callaterlodge.co.uk
Map ref: 12 NO19
Directions: Next to A93, 300yds S of Braemar centre
Rooms: 6 en suite **S** £40-£45 **D** £75-£80
Notes: ⊗ on premises **Parking:** 6 **Closed:** Xmas

A warm welcome is assured at Callater Lodge which stands in spacious, attractive grounds. Sink into deep leather chairs after a day spent walking, climbing, golfing, cycling, fishing or skiing. The individually-styled, en suite bedrooms have lovely soft furnishings, TV, and tea- and coffee-making facilities. A wide choice is offered at breakfast, and later, soup of the day, snacks and sandwiches are served. Surrounded by fine hills, Braemar Castle can be reached via a pretty walk, and a number of local trails includes the Whisky Trail. There is a drying room, plus storage for bicycles, golf clubs and skis for guests.
Recommended in the area
Balmoral Castle; Cairngorm National Park; Glenshee Ski Centre, Cairnwell

Kirkton House

★★★★★ GUEST ACCOMMODATION

Address: Darleith Road, CARDROSS,
Argyll & Bute, G82 5EZ
Tel: 01389 841951
Fax: 01389 841868
Email: aa@kirktonhouse.co.uk
Website: www.kirktonhouse.co.uk
Map ref: 9 NS37
Directions: 0.5m N of village. Turn N off A814 onto Darleith Rd at W end of village. Kirkton House 0.5m on right
Rooms: 6 en suite (2GF) **S** £30-£45 **D** £60-£70 **Notes:** Wi-fi **Parking:** 10 **Closed:** Dec-Jan

Guests feel at ease here thanks to Gillian and Stewart Macdonald's warm hospitality and their comfortable home. The converted 18th-century farmhouse stands in peaceful countryside with panoramic views of the River Clyde. Stone walls and large fireplaces give a cosy, rustic atmosphere, while the mainly spacious bedrooms are individually styled. The full Scottish breakfast is a high point.
Recommended in the area
Loch Lomond; The Hill House, Helensburgh (NTS); Burrell Collection, Glasgow

Glenburnie House

★ ★ ★ ★ GUEST HOUSE

Address: The Esplanade, OBAN,
Argyll & Bute, PA34 5AQ
Tel/Fax: 01631 562089
Email: graeme.strachan@btinternet.com
Website: www.glenburnie.co.uk
Map ref: 9 NM82
Directions: On Oban seafront. Follow signs for
Ganavan **Rooms:** 12 en suite (2GF) **S** £45-£50
D £80-£100 **Notes:** Wi-fi ✪ on premises ✿ under
12yrs **Parking:** 12 **Closed:** Nov-Mar

This impressive Victorian house, which sits on Oban's seafront just a few minutes' stroll from the town
centre, has breathtaking views over the bay down to the Sound of Lorn. Inside, it has been lovingly
restored to a high standard. The en suite bedrooms (including a four-poster room and a mini-suite) are
beautifully decorated and very well equipped. There is also a cosy ground-floor lounge and an elegant
dining room, where hearty traditional breakfasts, which include home-made preserves, are served.
Recommended in the area
McCaig's Tower; Dunstaffnage Castle; Trips to the Isle of Mull

Craigadam

★ ★ ★ ★ 🛏 🍴 GUEST HOUSE

Address: Craigadam, CASTLE DOUGLAS,
Dumfries & Galloway, DG7 3HU
Tel: 01556 650233 & 650100
Fax: 01556 650233
Email: inquiry@craigadam.com
Website: www.craigadam.com
Map ref: NX76
Directions: From Castle Douglas E on A75 to
Crocketford. Turn left on A712 for 2m. **Rooms:** 10
en suite (7GF) **S** £45-£80 **D** £90-£100 **Notes:** Wi-fi **Parking:** 12 **Closed:** Xmas & New Year

Set on a working farm, this elegant country house offers gracious living in a relaxed environment.
The strikingly individual and large en suite bedrooms are housed in a converted 18th-century
farmstead, with antique furnishings and French windows opening out onto a courtyard. Public areas
include a well-furnished lounge with a log fire and a snooker room with comprehensive honesty bar.
The dining room features a magnificent 15-seater table, the setting for Celia Pickup's delightful meals.
Recommended in the area
Dalton Pottery; Cream o' Galloway; Mill on the Fleet

Wallamhill House

★ ★ ★ ★ BED & BREAKFAST

Address: Kirkton, DUMFRIES,
Dumfries & Galloway, DG1 1SL
Tel: 01387 248249
Email: wallamhill@aol.com
Website: www.wallamhill.co.uk
Map ref: 5 NX97
Directions: 3m N of Dumfries. Off A701 signed
Kirkton, 1.5m on right
Rooms: 3 en suite **S** £38 **D** £60
Notes: Wi-fi 🚫 on premises **Parking:** 6

Hospitality is a real strength at Wallamhill House, an attractive house set in well-tended gardens and peaceful countryside three miles from Dumfries. The large bedrooms are extremely well equipped and there is a drawing room and a mini health club, with sauna, steam shower and gym equipment. Evening meals (by arrangement) are served in the dining room around one large table, and you can bring your own wine. The area offers great walking, cycling, or mountain biking in the Ae and Mabie forests.

Recommended in the area

Nithdale; Sweetheart Abbey, New Abbey; Caerlaverock Castle

Hartfell House & The Limetree Restaurant

★ ★ ★ ★ ⚜ GUEST HOUSE

Address: Hartfell Crescent, MOFFAT,
Dumfries & Galloway, DG10 9AL
Tel: 01683 220153
Email: enquiries@hartfellhouse.co.uk
Website: www.hartfellhouse.co.uk
Map ref: 10 NT00

Directions: Off High St at war memorial onto Well St & Old Well Rd. Hartfell Crescent on right **Rooms:** 7 en suite (1GF) **S** £35-£40 **D** £60-£70 **Notes:** Wi-fi 🚫 on premises **Parking:** 6 **Closed:** Xmas

A stunning Victorian manor house standing in gardens with commanding countryside views. Offering spacious and tastefully furnished bedrooms, and a large, first-floor guest lounge. The choice of a continental breakfast or a full Scottish breakfast is served in the magnificent dining room. A memorable meal can be enjoyed in the restaurant where the Scottish and international menus use local produce.

Recommended in the area

Galloway Forest Park; Dumfries; Carlisle

Gillbank House

★★★★★ GUEST ACCOMMODATION

Address: 8 East Morton Street, THORNHILL,
Dumfries & Galloway, DG3 5LZ
Tel: 01848 330597
Fax: 01848 331713
Email: hanne@gillbank.co.uk
Website: www.gillbank.co.uk
Map ref: 5 NX89
Directions: In town centre off A76
Rooms: 6 en suite (2GF) **S** £50 **D** £70
Notes: ⊗ on premises ✗ under 8yrs **Parking:** 8

Gillbank is a charming late Victorian house located close to the town centre; shops, pubs and restaurants are two minutes' walk away. Bedrooms are comfortable, spacious and well presented, with smart en suite shower rooms and tea- and coffee-making facilities. Breakfast is served at individual tables in the bright dining room, next to the comfortable lounge. There's bicycle storage, and if you are a keen angler the River Nith, famous for sea trout and salmon fishing, is just half a mile away.

Recommended in the area

Drumlanrig Castle Gardens & Country Park; Thornhill Golf Course; Morton Castle

Bonnington Guest House

★★★★ GUEST HOUSE

Address: 202 Ferry Road, EDINBURGH, EH6 4NW
Tel/Fax: 0131 554 7610
Email: booking@thebonningtonguesthouse.com
Website: www.thebonningtonguesthouse.com
Map ref: 10 NT27
Directions: On A902, near corner of Ferry Rd & Newhaven Rd
Rooms: 7 (5 en suite) (2 pri facs) (1GF) **S** £45 **D** £60-£90
Notes: Wi-fi ⊗ on premises **Parking:** 9

An impressive three-storey property, this guest house is situated just 10 minutes from Edinburgh city centre, with its own off-road parking and good public transport links. Built in 1840, the house backs onto Victoria Park and is close to Leith and the Botanical Gardens The individually furnished bedrooms are located on two floors. All are equipped with fridges, bottled water, a decanter of sherry, tea- and coffee-making facilities and TVs with Freeview; Wi-fi access is also available. A substantial breakfast is served in the dining room.

Recommended in the area

Edinburgh Castle; Dynamic Earth; Museum of Scotland

Elmview

★★★★★ GUEST ACCOMMODATION
Address: 15 Glengyle Terrace, EDINBURGH, EH3 9LN
Tel: 0131 228 1973
Email: nici@elmview.co.uk
Website: www.elmview.co.uk
Map ref: 10 NT27
Directions: 0.5m S of city centre. Off A702 Leven St onto Valleyfield St, one-way to Glengyle Terrace
Rooms: 3 en suite (3GF) **S** £60-£100 **D** £80-£130
Notes: Wi-fi ⊗ on premises 👶 under 15yrs **Closed:** Dec-Mar

Elmview is situated in the heart of Edinburgh in a delightful Victorian terrace within easy walking distance of Edinburgh Castle and Princes Street. The spacious and quiet en suite bedrooms have been furnished to include everything a guest could want. Fresh flowers, complimentary sherry and elegant furnishings all add to the feeling of a personal home. Elmview overlooks a large urban park, which includes a free, 36-hole pitch and putt golf course. The highlight of a stay is the excellent breakfast taken at one large table.
Recommended in the area
Edinburgh Castle; Edinburgh Old Town; Museum of Scotland; Royal Mile

The International Guest House

★★★★ GUEST HOUSE
Address: 37 Mayfield Gardens,
EDINBURGH, EH9 2BX
Tel: 0131 667 2511 & 0845 241 7551
Fax: 0131 667 1112
Email: intergh1@yahoo.co.uk
Website: www.accommodation-edinburgh.com
Map ref: 10 NT27
Directions: On A701 1.5m S of Princes St
Rooms: 9 en suite (1GF) **S** £35-£75 **D** £65-£130
Notes: Wi-fi ⊗ on premises **Parking:** 3

This attractive Victorian terrace house, on the south side of the city, 1.5 miles from Edinburgh Castle, is on a main bus route to the city centre. All the bedrooms, decorated and fitted in matching period floral prints, have fresh flowers and modern en suites. Some rooms have magnificent views across to the extinct volcano known as Arthur's Seat. A hearty Scottish breakfast is served on fine bone china at separate tables in the dining room which features a lovely marble fireplace.
Recommended in the area
Edinburgh Castle; Palace of Holyroodhouse; University of Edinburgh

Kew House

★ ★ ★ ★ ★ GUEST ACCOMMODATION

Address: 1 Kew Terrace, Murrayfield,
EDINBURGH, EH12 5JE
Tel: 0131 313 0700
Fax: 0131 313 0747
Email: info@kewhouse.com
Website: www.kewhouse.com
Map ref: 10 NT27
Directions: 1m W of city centre A8
Rooms: 6 en suite (2GF) **S** £75-£95 **D** £85-£180
Notes: Wi-fi **Parking:** 6

Kew House forms part of a listed Victorian terrace dating from 1860, located a mile west of the city centre, convenient for Murrayfield Rugby Stadium, and just a 15-minute walk from Princes Street. Regular bus services from Princes Street pass the door. The house is ideal for both business travellers and holidaymakers, with secure private parking. While many period features have been retained, the interior design is contemporary, and the standards of housekeeping are superb. Expect complimentary sherry and chocolates on arrival, and you can order supper in the lounge. Full Scottish breakfast with an alternative vegetarian choice is included in the room tariff, and light snacks, with room service, are available all day. Bedrooms, including some on the ground floor, are en suite and well equipped with remote control TV with digital channels, direct-dial telephones, modem points, hairdryers, trouser presses, fresh flowers and tea and coffee facilities. The superior rooms also have their own fridge. Kew House also offers a luxurious serviced apartment accommodating up to three people.

Recommended in the area

Edinburgh Castle; Edinburgh International Conference Centre; Murrayfield Rugby Stadium

Arthur's Seat

23 Mayfield

★ ★ ★ ★ 🏨 GUEST ACCOMMODATION

Address: 23 Mayfield Gardens,
            EDINBURGH, EH9 2BX
Tel: 0131 667 5806
Fax: 0131 667 6833
Email: info@23mayfield.co.uk
Website: www.23mayfield.co.uk
Map ref: 10 NT27
Directions: A720 bypass S, follow city centre signs.
Left at Craigmillar Park, 0.5m on right

Rooms: 9 en suite (2GF) **S** £55-£65 **D** £65-£130 **Notes:** Wi-fi ⊗ on premises **Parking:** 10

A great location just a mile from the city centre, adds to the charms of this family-run guest house.
It occupies a detached Victorian villa that retains many original features, and has spacious rooms.
Individual decor in each room is colour-coordinated. The Four Poster Room boasts a huge, hand-carved
mahogany bed, Egyptian cottons, flat-screen TV and Bose sound system. Other amenities include free
Wi-fi, an elegant lounge and an exceptional breakfast menu, which includes Scottish smoked salmon.

Recommended in the area

Edinburgh Castle; Holyrood Palace; Princes Street

Southside Guest House

★ ★ ★ ★ 🛏 GUEST HOUSE

Address: 8 Newington Road, EDINBURGH, EH9 1QS
Tel: 0131 668 4422
Fax: 0131 667 7771
Email: info@southsideguesthouse.co.uk
Website: www.southsideguesthouse.co.uk
Map ref: 10 NT27
Directions: E end of Princes St onto North Bridge to Royal Mile, continue S, 0.5m, house on right
Rooms: 8 en suite (1GF) **S** £60-£80 **D** £80-£140
Notes: Wi-fi ⊗ on premises 🧒 under 10yrs

Built in 1865, Southside Guest House is an elegant Victorian sandstone terraced house in the centre of Edinburgh, only a few minutes from Holyrood Park. The owners Lynne and Franco have been involved in the hospitality trade for many years and have happily made their home in the capital. Lynne is from the Highlands, and Franco hails from Florence. They offer individually designed, stylish, well-equipped bedrooms, with direct-dial telephones, DVD players, free wireless internet access, and many other comforts including quality mattresses and crisp fine linen. Two of the rooms have four-poster beds and comfortable sofas, and the remaining rooms come in a variety of colour schemes and bed sizes. Breakfast at Southside is guaranteed to satisfy with its great choice of traditional freshly cooked Scottish dishes, cheeses, oatcakes, fresh fruit and real coffee. Guests sit at separate tables in the attractive dining room. Southside Guest House has recently enhanced its facilities with a new self-contained apartment.

Recommended in the area

Edinburgh Castle; Edinburgh Festival Theatre; The Palace of Holyroodhouse; Old Town; Holyrood Park; Princes Street shops and gardens

The Spindrift

★ ★ ★ ★ ☕ 🛏 GUEST HOUSE

Address: Pittenweem Road,
ANSTRUTHER, Fife, KY10 3DT
Tel/Fax: 01333 310573
Email: info@thespindrift.co.uk
Website: www.thespindrift.co.uk
Map ref: 10 NO50
Directions: Enter town from W on A917, 1st building
on left
Rooms: 8 (7 en suite) (1 pri facs)
S £40-£55 **D** £64-£80
Notes: Wi-fi 🐾 under 10yrs **Parking:** 12 **Closed:** Xmas-late Jan

A unique feature of this house is the top-floor Captain's Room, made to resemble a shipmaster's cabin by the original owner – the east-facing window looks towards Anstruther harbour. All the individually furnished, spacious bedrooms are brightly decorated and have a wide range of extras. The lounge has an honesty bar for a pre-dinner drink, and enjoyable, home-cooked fare is served in the dining room.
Recommended in the area
Scottish Fisheries Museum; St Andrews; East Neuk coastal villages

The Kelvingrove

★ ★ ★ ★ GUEST ACCOMMODATION

Address: 944 Sauchiehall Street, GLASGOW, G3 7TH
Tel: 0141 339 5011
Fax: 0141 339 6566
Email: info@kelvingrovehotel.com
Website: www.kelvingrove-hotel.co.uk
Map ref: 9 NS56
Directions: M8 junct 18, 0.5m along road signed
Kelvingrove Museum, on left
Rooms: 22 en suite (3GF) **S** £40-£70 **D** £70-£100

This friendly terraced establishment is in Glasgow's lively West End and close to the town centre. Run by three generations of the same family it is very well maintained. All of the bedrooms, including triples and several good family rooms, are well equipped for guest comfort and convenience. The en suite bathrooms have power showers and luxuriously soft towels. Free wireless internet connection is also available. Breakfast is served in the bright breakfast room and the reception lounge is always open.
Recommended in the area
Kelvingrove Museum and Art Gallery; Botanic Gardens; SECC

Loch Scavaig towards The Cullin Hills, Isle of Skye

Loch Ness Lodge

★ ★ ★ ★ ★ ◉◉ 🍴 RESTAURANT WITH ROOMS

Address: Brachla, Loch Ness-Side,
INVERNESS, Highland, IV3 8LA
Tel: 01456 459469
Fax: 01456 459439
Email: escape@lodgeatlochness.com
Website: www.lodgeatlochness.com
Map ref: 12 NH53
Directions: A9 Inverness onto A82 signed Fort
William, in 9m & 30mph speed sign, Lodge on right
after Clansman Hotel **Rooms:** 7 en suite (1GF) **S** £120-£180 **D** £190-£280
Notes: Wi-fi ⊗ on premises 🐾 under 12yrs **Parking:** 10 **Closed:** 2-31 Jan

This house overlooks Loch Ness and each of the individually designed bedrooms enjoys loch views. The
bedrooms are of the highest standard, and beautifully presented with a mix of traditional luxury and
modern technology. There is a spa with a hot tub, sauna and a variety of treatments. Impressive meals
are served in the award-winning restaurant. AA Guest Accommodation for Scotland 2009-2010.
Recommended in the area
Loch Ness Exhibition Centre, Drumnadrochit; Culloden Battlefield; Tomatin Distillery

Foyers Bay Country House

★★★ GUEST HOUSE

Address: Lochness, FOYERS,
Highland, IV2 6YB
Tel: 01456 486624
Email: enquiries@foyersbay.co.uk
Website: www.foyersbay.co.uk
Map ref: 12 NH42
Directions: Off B852 into Lower Foyers
Rooms: 6 en suite (1GF) **S** £45-£55 **D** £60-£95
Notes: Wi-fi ⊗ on premises ⚹ under 16yrs
Parking: 6

Set on the quiet, undeveloped side of Loch Ness, midway between Inverness and Fort Augustus, among hillside woodlands with a colourful abundance of rhododendrons, this delightful house offers stunning views as well as forest walks and nature trails. It makes a perfect choice for a relaxing break away from it all. Foyers Bay Country House was originally built as a family home in the late 1890s and today it still offers many of the delights of a Victorian villa, though it has been thoughtfully refurbished. There is a comfortable residents' bar and lounge adjacent to an airy, plant-filled conservatory restaurant, where traditional Scottish breakfasts and delicious evening meals are served against a backdrop of magnificent, unspoilt views of the loch. The attractive bedrooms, which vary in size and one of which is on the ground floor, all have en suite shower rooms, hairdryer, TV and tea- and coffee-making facilities. Some of the rooms have loch views.

Recommended in the area

Inverness; Loch Ness; Glen Affric

An Cala Guest House

★★★★★ GUEST HOUSE

Address: Woodlands Terrace,
GRANTOWN-ON-SPEY, Highland, PH26 3JU
Tel: 01479 873293
Email: ancala@globalnet.co.uk
Website: www.ancala.info
Map ref: 12 NJ02
Directions: From Aviemore on A95 left onto B9102 at rdbt outside Grantown. After 400yds, 1st left, An Cala opposite **Rooms:** 4 en suite **D** £76-£84
Notes: Wi-fi ⊗ on premises 🐾 under 3yrs **Parking:** 6 **Closed:** Xmas

A large Victorian house set in well-tended gardens and overlooking woods that makes an attractive setting in which to relax, and yet is just a 12-minute walk from the town centre. The house is in the Cairngorms National Park and has on-site parking. Beautifully decorated bedrooms with king or super king-size double beds – one room has a lovely king-size four-poster bed from Castle Grant. All rooms have smart en suites and antique furniture. Freeview television and free Wi-Fi access.

Recommended in the area

The Malt Whisky Trail; Ballindalloch Castle; Osprey Centre at Abernethy

The Ghillies Lodge

★★★★ 🏠 BED & BREAKFAST

Address: 16 Island Bank Road, INVERNESS, Highland, IV2 4QS
Tel: 01463 232137
Fax: 01463 713744
Email: info@ghillieslodge.com
Website: www.ghillieslodge.com
Map ref: 12 NH64
Directions: 1m SW from town centre on B862, pink house facing river
Rooms: 3 en suite (1GF)
Notes: Wi-fi **Parking:** 3

Built in 1847 as a fisherman's lodge, the Ghillies Lodge lies on the River Ness with fine views over the Ness Islands and just a mile from Inverness centre, making it an ideal base for touring the Highlands. The attractive and peaceful en suite bedrooms, (including one on the ground floor) are individually styled, well equipped and wireless internet connection is available. There is a comfortable lounge-dining room and a conservatory overlooks the river.

Recommended in the area

Loch Ness; Speyside distilleries; Isle of Skye

Moonen Bay from Neist Point, Isle of Skye

Lyndon Guest House

★★★★ GUEST HOUSE

Address: 50 Telford Street, INVERNESS,
Highland, IV3 5LE
Tel: 01463 232551
Fax: 01463 225827
Email: lyndonguesthouse@btopenworld.com
Website: www.lyndon-guest-house.co.uk
Map ref: 12 NH64
Directions: From A9 onto A82 over Friars Bridge,
right at rdbt onto Telford St. House on right **Rooms:**

6 en suite (2GF) **S** £25-£38 **D** £50-£70 **Notes:** Wi-fi ⊗ on premises **Parking:** 5 **Closed:** 20 Dec-5 Jan

Guests are well catered for at this friendly family-run establishment, just 10 minutes' walk from the centre of Inverness. All of the spacious en suite bedrooms, four of which are family rooms, include flat-screen TVs, hairdryers and tea- and coffee-making facilities. Free Wi-fi is available throughout the house. Continental and full Scottish breakfasts are served in the dining room at separate tables, with vegetarian and special dietary meals available on request. There is ample off-street parking.

Recommended in the area

Loch Ness; Inverness Floral Hall; Culloden Battlefield

Moyness House

★ ★ ★ ★ GUEST ACCOMMODATION
Address: 6 Bruce Gardens, INVERNESS, Highland, IV3 5EN
Tel/Fax: 01463 233836
Email: stay@moyness.co.uk
Website: www.moyness.co.uk
Map ref: 12 NH64
Directions: Off A82 (Fort William road), almost opp Highland Regional Council headquarters
Rooms: 6 en suite (2GF) S £55-£75 D £68-£100
Notes: Wi-fi Parking: 10

Built in 1880 this gracious villa, once the home of acclaimed Scottish author Neil Gunn, has been sympathetically restored to its full Victorian charm by Jenny and Richard Jones, and has many fine period details. The six stylish en suite bedrooms, named after Gunn's novels, are enhanced by contemporary amenities and thoughtful extra touches. Breakfasts served in the elegant dining room include a wide range of delicious Scottish choices, as well as vegetarian and healthy options, using fresh local produce. The inviting sitting room overlooks the garden to the front, and a pretty walled garden to the rear is a peaceful retreat in warm weather. Free wireless internet connection is available throughout the house. Moyness House has ample parking within the grounds, and is well located in a quiet residential street, less than 10 minutes' walk from the city centre where there are several highly recommended restaurants, the Eden Court Theatre and delightful riverside walks. Jenny and Richard are happy to advise on local eateries and to make dinner reservations for their guests. They will also be glad to provide touring advice and help guests make the most of their stay in the beautiful Highlands.

Recommended in the area

Culloden Battlefield; Loch Ness and the Caledonian Canal; Urquhart Castle and Cawdor Castle

Urquhart Castle, Loch Ness

Trafford Bank

★★★★★ ☕ GUEST HOUSE

Address: 96 Fairfield Road, INVERNESS, Highland, IV3 5LL
Tel: 01463 241414
Email: enquiries@invernesshotelaccommodation.co.uk
Website: www.traffordbank.co.uk
Map ref: 12 NH64
Directions: Off A82 at Kenneth St, Fairfield Rd 2nd left, 600yds on right
Rooms: 5 en suite **S** £60-£90 **D** £80-£120
Notes: Wi-fi ⊗ on premises **Parking:** 10

Luxurious accommodation and Highland hospitality go hand-in-hand at this guest house, run by Lorraine Freel and Koshal Pun. This multilingual pair can welcome you in Italian, French, Hindi and Swahili. Located within walking distance of the city centre and the Caledonian Canal, Trafford Bank, built in 1873, was once the local bishop's home. Lorraine's flair for interior design has produced a pleasing mix of antique and contemporary; some furnishings she has designed herself. The dining-room chairs are a special feature, and there is unusual lighting and original art throughout the house. The bright bedrooms are individually themed; all are en suite and have enticing extras like Arran aromatic products and organic soap from the Strathpeffer Spa soap company. Each bedroom is superbly decorated with fine bed linen, hairdryers, Fairtrade tea and coffee, flat-screen digital TVs, DVD players, CD/radio alarms, iPod docking stations and silent fridges. Breakfast is prepared using the best Highland produce and served on Anta pottery in the stunning conservatory. There are two spacious lounges and the house is surrounded by mature gardens that you are welcome to enjoy. Wi-fi is available throughout the house.

Recommended in the area

Cawdor Castle; Culloden Battlefield (NTS); Loch Ness; Moniack Castle (Highland Winery)

Calgary Bay, Isle of Mull

Craiglinnhe House

★ ★ ★ ★ GUEST HOUSE
Address: Lettermore, BALLACHULISH,
Highland, PH49 4JD
Tel: 01855 811270
Email: info@craiglinnhe.co.uk
Website: www.craiglinnhe.co.uk
Map ref: 9 NN05
Directions: From village A82 onto A828, Craiglinnhe
1.5m on left **Rooms:** 5 en suite S £42-£64
D £56-£85 **Notes:** Wi-fi ⊗ on premises ⚑ under
13yrs **Parking:** 5 **Closed:** 24-26 Dec

Craiglinnhe House was built in 1885 and while retaining its Victorian style and character, it has been modernised to provide the utmost comfort with stylish, well-equipped bedrooms. This is the perfect base for walking, climbing, skiing and exploring the West Highlands. The elegant lounge has stunning views of Loch Linnhe and is a lovely place to relax, while the dining room provides a fine setting for the superb meals cooked by owner David Hughes. A fine selection of single malts whiskies is available.
Recommended in the area
Glencoe; Fort William; Whisky distillery

Lyn-Leven Guest House

★★★★ GUEST HOUSE
Address: West Laroch, SOUTH BALLACHULISH,
Highland, PH49 4JP
Tel: 01855 811392
Fax: 01855 811600
Email: macleodcilla@aol.com
Website: www.lynleven.co.uk
Map ref: 9 NN05
Directions: Off A82 signed on left West Laroch
Rooms: 12 en suite (12GF) **S** £30-£45 **D** £50-£64
Parking: 12 **Closed:** Xmas

Beautifully situated, this guest house maintains high standards in all areas. Highland hospitality puts guests at their ease, and the spectacular views of Loch Leven guarantee plenty to talk about. Bedrooms vary in size, are prettily decorated, and have showers and some thoughtful extras. The spacious lounge and smart dining room make the most of the scenic outlook, and the lounge has Sky TV. Delicious home-cooked evening meals and breakfasts are served at separate tables. There is ample parking.
Recommended in the area
Ballachulish Country House Golf Course; Glencoe Visitor Centre and Museum

Corriechoille Lodge

★★★★ ☕ GUEST HOUSE
Address: SPEAN BRIDGE, Highland, PH34 4EY
Tel: 01397 712002
Website: www.corriechoille.com
Map ref: 12 NN28
Directions: Off A82 signed Corriechoille, 2.5m,
left at fork (10mph sign). At end of tarmac, turn right
up hill & left
Rooms: 4 en suite (1GF) **S** £40-£46 **D** £60-£72
Notes: Wi-fi ⊗ on premises ❦ under 7yrs
Parking: 7 **Closed:** Nov-Mar, Sun & Mon

Standing above the River Spean, Corriechoille Lodge is an extensively renovated former fishing lodge near Spean Bridge. There are magnificent views of the Nevis range and surrounding mountains from the comfortable first-floor lounge and some of the bedrooms. Guest rooms are spacious and well-appointed, with en suite facilities, TVs and tea and coffee facilities. Enjoy traditional breakfasts, with evening meals available by arrangement. The house is licensed and stocks many single malt whiskies.
Recommended in the area
Glenfinnan Monument; Viaduct & Station Museum; Ben Nevis footpath/Glen Nevis; Creag Meagaidh

Tobermory, Isle of Mull

Smiddy House

★★★★ ◉◉ ♨ RESTAURANT WITH ROOMS

Address: Roy Bridge Road, SPEAN BRIDGE,
Highland, PH34 4EU
Tel: 01397 712335
Fax: 01397 712043
Email: enquiry@smiddyhouse.co.uk
Website: www.smiddyhouse.co.uk
Map ref: 12 NN28
Directions: In village centre, A82 onto A86
Rooms: 4 en suite S £60-£85 D £70-£90
Notes: Wi-fi **Parking:** 15

Ideally located for exploring the Highlands, Smiddy House offers genuine Scottish hospitality in luxurious surroundings. The guest rooms, named after places in Scotland, are well appointed with luxury linen and towels. The restaurant, Russell's, is awarded two AA Rosettes and provides fine Scottish cuisine in a relaxed and informal setting; there is a garden room where guests can enjoy a pre-dinner drink whilst perusing the evening's menu.

Recommended in the area

Ben Nevis and the Nevis range; Loch Ness; Glenfinnan Monument

Glenan Lodge Guest House

★★★★ GUEST HOUSE
Address: TOMATIN, Highland, IV13 7YT
Tel: 01808 511217
Email: enquiries@glenanlodge.co.uk
Website: www.glenanlodge.co.uk
Map ref: 12 NH82
Directions: Off A9 to Tomatin,
signed to Lodge
Rooms: 7 en suite S £30 D £60
Notes: Wi-fi ⊗ on premises ⭑ under 5yrs
Parking: 7

Tomatin's best kept secret, Glenan Lodge is situated on the edge of the village just two miles from the Caingorms National Park and only 15 miles from Inverness to the north or Aviemore to the south. The house provides the perfect base from which to explore the Highlands or visit the many malt whisky distilleries in the area. For the fly fisher, the guest house has a two-mile beat on the River Finhorn for salmon and wild brown trout fishing. The Finhorn Valley is a haven for wildlife; red deer, mountain goats, golden eagles, red kites and many more birds of prey are regularly spotted, and red squirrels are daily visitors to the garden. The location is ideal for golf, cycling, walking or even skiing on Cairngorm. All the bedrooms are decorated to a high standard with en suite facilities (bath or shower), televisions and tea and coffee making equipment. There is also a guests' lounge with an open fire, piano and a selection of games and puzzles to while away the winter nights. The premises are licensed so you can enjoy a drink as you sit and relax. Home-cooked evening meals are available by prior arrangement.

Recommended in the area

Culloden; Strathspey Steam Railway; Cawdor Castle; Loch Ness

Tigh Na Leigh Guesthouse

★★★★★ ⚜ 🍴 GUEST ACCOMMODATION

Address: 22-24 Airlie Street, ALYTH,
Perth & Kinross, PH11 8AJ
Tel: 01828 632372
Fax: 01828 632279
Email: bandcblack@yahoo.co.uk
Website: www.tighnaleigh.co.uk
Map ref: 10 NO24
Directions: In town centre on B952
Rooms: 5 en suite (1GF) **S** £47 **D** £95-£120
Notes: Wi-fi 🐾 under 12yrs **Parking:** 5 **Closed:** Dec-Feb

Previous winner of the AA Guest Accommodation of the Year for Scotland award, this guest house in the heart of the country town of Alyth is an absolute delight. Tigh Na Leigh is Gaelic for 'The house of the Doctor or Physician', and although it may look rather sombre from the outside, the property is superbly modernised and furnished with an eclectic mix of modern and antique furniture. The large, luxurious and individually decorated bedrooms, one of which is on the ground floor, are very well equipped, and most rooms have spa baths. All rooms have TV/DVD player, tea and coffee-making facilities, hairdryer and bathrobes. For extra luxury, one room has a grand four-poster, while the suite has its own lounge with a very comfortable sofa. The public rooms comprise three entirely different lounges, one of which has a log fire for cooler evenings and another of which provides broadband internet connection. Delicious home-cooked dinners have an international flavour, and these, as well as the hearty breakfasts, are all made from the best of Scottish produce – vegetables come from the kitchen garden or surrounding (organic) farms where possible. Meals are served in the huge conservatory/dining room overlooking the spectacular landscaped garden.

Recommended in the area

Scone Palace; Glamis Castle; Dunkeld Cathedral

Bla Bheinn and the Cuillin Hills, Isle of Skye

Gilmore House

★ ★ ★ ★ BED & BREAKFAST

Address: Perth Road, BLAIRGOWRIE,
Perth & Kinross, PH10 6EJ

Tel/Fax: 01250 872791

Email: jill@gilmorehouse.co.uk

Website: www.gilmorehouse.co.uk

Map ref: 10 NO14

Directions: On A93 S

Rooms: 3 en suite D £56-£70

Notes: Wi-fi **Parking:** 3 **Closed:** Xmas

Built in 1899, this deceptively spacious late-Victorian detached house is the perfect base from which to explore all that Perthshire has to offer, being conveniently located for Glamis Castle, Scone Palace and Dunkeld. The three comfortable en suite rooms include a cosy king, a twin and a very spacious superking. There are two beautiful lounges for guests' use, with plenty of reading material to plan your activities. A full Scottish breakfast or a lighter option is served in the elegant dining room overlooking the front garden, and the owners pride themselves on the relaxed, warm and friendly ambience.

Recommended in the area

Glamis Castle; Blair Castle; Perth races

The Anglers Inn

★ ★ ★ ❀ INN

Address: Main Road, Guildtown, PERTH,
Perth & Kinross, PH2 6BS
Tel: 01821 640329
Email: info@theanglersinn.co.uk
Website: www.theanglersinn.co.uk
Map ref: 10 NO12
Directions: 6m N of Perth on A93
Rooms: 5 en suite **S** £50 **D** £100
Notes: Wi-fi 🐾 **Parking:** 40

This charming country inn, which has been extensively renovated and totally refurbished by experienced restaurateurs Shona and Jeremy Wares, occupies a peaceful rural setting in Guildtown, yet is only a short drive from Perth city centre. It provides a perfect base for sports and nature enthusiasts, and for those who wish to take advantage of Perthshire's many golf courses or the local racecourse. Fishing and shooting parties will find storage rooms and cases for equipment, and cold rooms for catches. Inside the inn, all is warm and traditional, with comfortable leather chairs and a wood-burning stove, yet combined with a contemporary twist. Residents will find tastefully styled en suite bedrooms with flatscreen TVs, complimentary Wi-fi, comfortable beds and fine views of the surrounding countryside. Food is a major draw here thanks to Jeremy's culinary expertise, and the award-winning restaurant has a loyal following, thanks to the impressive freshly prepared dishes made using local ingredients and accompanied by a superb selection of wines. The dinner menu is supplemented by chalkboard seasonal specials, plus the famous fishcakes and local game dishes. There's also ample space in the bar in which to relax with a pint of locally produced ale or enjoy popular bar sports.

Recommended in the area

Scone Palace; Glamis Castle; Perth racecourse

Edinburgh Castle and St Cuthbert's Church

Crailing Old School

★★★★ 🏠 🍽 GUEST HOUSE

Address: CRAILING, Nr Jedburgh,
Scottish Borders, TD8 6TL
Tel: 01835 850382
Email: jean.player@virgin.net
Website: www.crailingoldschool.co.uk
Map ref: 10 NT62
Directions: A698 onto B6400 signed Nisbet,
Crailing Old School also signed
Rooms: 4 (2 en suite) (1 pri facs) (1GF) **S** £38.50-£40
D £60-£80 **Notes:** Wi-fi 🐾 under 9yrs **Parking:** 6 **Closed:** 24 Dec-2 Jan, 1wk Feb & 2wks Autumn

This delightful Victorian village school has been imaginatively renovated to combine original features with modern comforts. Jean Leach-Player was a runner-up in the AA's Landlady of the Year award on three occasions. This is a good area for outdoor pursuits including fishing, walking and golf. Breakfasts (and dinner by arrangement) are served in the stylish lounge/dining room and the best local ingredients are used. The lodge annexe, 10 metres from the house, offers ground floor access. Wi-fi is available.
Recommended in the area
St Cuthbert's Way; The Teviot and Tweed Rivers; Roxburghe Championship Golf Course

The Horseshoe Inn

★ ★ ★ ★ ◉◉◉ RESTAURANT WITH ROOMS

Address: EDDLESTON, Peebles,
Scottish Borders, EH45 8QP
Tel: 01721 730225
Fax: 01721 730268
Email: reservations@horseshoeinn.co.uk
Website: www.horseshoeinn.co.uk
Map ref: 10 NT24
Directions: A703, 5m N of Peebles
Rooms: 8 en suite (6GF) S £70 D £100
Notes: Wi-fi Parking: 20 Closed: 25 Dec & Mon

Originally a blacksmith's smiddy, located just 30 minutes from Edinburgh, the inn underwent a complete transformation in 2005. Vivienne Steele has stamped her identity throughout the place, creating an informal and relaxed bistro area, a warm and cosy lounge and the impressive, award-winning Bardoulet's Restaurant. The following year the adjacent Horseshoe Lodge was refurbished, providing high quality accommodation in a Victorian former primary school. Each room is individually decorated and equipped with en suite facilities and either double or twin beds. Guests at the lodge are on hand to enjoy all the delights of the inn, and while the decor sets the mood it is the food that leaves customers wanting to return time and time again. Patrick Bardoulet revels in having his own restaurant and uses his French flair to combine his native cuisine with local ingredients to provide a host of unique dishes that blend the modern and the traditional. The front of house team, headed by Vivienne, provide friendly service, advice on dishes and wines, and cater for your every need, so you can sit back, relax and enjoy the company, the food and the surroundings.

Recommended in the area

Dawyck Botanic Gardens; Robert Smail's Printing Works; Traquair House

Fauhope House

★ ★ ★ ★ ★ 🛏 GUEST HOUSE

Address: Gattonside, MELROSE,
Scottish Borders, TD6 9LU
Tel/Fax: 01896 823184
Email: info@fauhopehouse.com
Map ref: 10 NT53
Directions: 0.7m N of Melrose over River Tweed.
N off B6360 at Gattonside 30mph sign (E) up
long driveway **Rooms:** 3 en suite
Notes: ⊗ on premises **Parking:** 10

Fauhope House is a fine example of the Arts and Crafts style of architecture of the 1890s, designed by Sidney Mitchell, who was also responsible for Edinburgh's much-admired Ramsey Gardens property. It is perched high on a hillside on the north-east edge of the village of Gattonside, and provides the kind of breathtaking views of the River Tweed and the Eildon Hills that have inspired artists and writers down the years. It offers discerning guests comfortable seclusion and the space to relax, yet is just a ten-minute walk from the Borders town of Melrose, with its shops, restaurant and small theatre. A short drive will take you to Abbotsford, home of Sir Walter Scott, and the Robert Adam-designed Mellerstain House. The hospitality provided by experienced host Sheila Robson is first class, and the delightful country house boasts a splendid interior, furnished and decorated to the highest possible standard. Stunning floral displays enhance the overall interior design, and lavish drapes and fine furniture grace the drawing room and the magnificent dining room, where full Scottish or a continental breakfast is served. The generously sized bedrooms are luxurious and superbly equipped, each with individual furnishings and thoughtful extras. Fauhope House was AA Guest Accommodation of the Year for Scotland 2008/2009.

Recommended in the area

Melrose Abbey; Roxburghe Golf Course; River Tweed; Fantastic walks

The Falkirk Wheel

Daviot House

★★★★ GUEST HOUSE

Address: 12 Queens Terrace, AYR,
South Ayrshire, KA7 1DU
Tel: 01292 269678
Email: daviothouse@hotmail.com
Website: www.daviothouse.com
Map ref: 9 NS32
Directions: Off A719 onto Wellington Sq & Bath Place,
turn right **Rooms:** 5 (4 en suite) (1 pri facs) **S** £35-£45
D £60-£85 **Notes:** Wi-fi ⊗ on premises ⛄

In a peaceful residential area, a short distance from the beach
and town centre, Daviot House is a comfortable Victorian
terrace home that retains many original features. Bedrooms are bright and modern, and equipped with
thoughtful extras. In the dining room, guests congregate around one big table to start the day with a
hearty, cooked Scottish breakfast. The hosts are happy to book a round of golf for guests on the local
municipal courses.

Recommended in the area

Burns Cottage; Royal Troon & Turnberry golf courses; Culzean & Country Park

Annfield Guest House

★ ★ ★ ★ GUEST HOUSE

Address: 18 North Church Street,
CALLANDER, Stirling, FK17 8EG
Tel: 01877 330204
Fax: 01877 330674
Email: reservations@annfieldguesthouse.co.uk
Website: www.annfieldguesthouse.co.uk
Map ref: 9 NN60
Directions: Off A84 Main St onto North Church St,
at top on right

Rooms: 7 (4 en suite) (1 pri facs) **S** £35-£45 **D** £60-£70 😊 **Notes:** Wi-fi ⊗ on premises
🧒 under 6yrs **Parking:** 7 **Closed:** Xmas

Quietly situated just two minutes' walk from Callander's bustling main street, this is a beautiful Victorian villa. Recently fully renovated to the highest standards, Annfield retains all the charm of a bygone age. The owners pride themselves on their attention to detail, from fresh flowers and goose-down duvets to silver cutlery and soft fluffy towels. Breakfast is a highlight, all prepared with local ingredients.

Recommended in the area

Falkirk Wheel; Loch Lomond and Trossachs National Park; Stirling Castle; Loch Katrine

Arden House

★ ★ ★ ★ 🏠 GUEST ACCOMMODATION

Address: Bracklinn Road, CALLANDER,
Stirling, FK17 8EQ
Tel: 01877 330235
Email: ardenhouse@onetel.com
Website: www.ardenhouse.org.uk
Map ref: 9 NN60
Directions: Off A84 Main St onto Bracklinn Rd,
house 200yds on left

Rooms: 6 en suite (2GF) **S** £40 **D** £70-£80
Notes: Wi-fi ⊗ on premises 🧒 under 14yrs **Parking:** 10 **Closed:** Nov-Mar

This is the fictional home of Doctors Finlay and Cameron and is peacefully located in the town's most beautiful setting. Ian and William offer guests a genuine welcome with tea and home-made cakes in their stylish sitting room, on arrival. The house has been tastefully and lovingly refurbished to reflect its Victorian heritage. Beautifully presented Scottish breakfasts, prepared using locally sourced produce, supplemented by daily specials, are the perfect start to the day.

Recommended in the area

Loch Lomond & Trossachs National Park; Stirling Castle; Loch Katrine; The Falkirk Wheel

Creagan House

★★★★★ ⊛⊛ RESTAURANT WITH ROOMS
Address: STRATHYRE, Callander, Stirling, FK18 8ND
Tel: 01877 384638
Fax: 01877 384319
Email: eatandstay@creaganhouse.co.uk
Website: www.creaganhouse.co.uk
Map ref: 9 NN51
Directions: 0.25m N of Strathyre on A84 **Rooms:** 5
en suite (1GF) **S** £70-£90 **D** £120-£140 **Notes:** Wi-fi
Parking: 25 **Closed:** 4-19 Nov, Xmas & 21 Jan-5 Mar

This 17th-century farmhouse has been the home of Gordon and Cherry Gunn for over 20 years and has operated as a restaurant-with-rooms for most of those. Situated by Queen Elizabeth Forest Park, it has been lovingly restored to retain its original period features. The charming en suite bedrooms provide satellite TV, CD/radio alarm and good-quality toiletries. Food is at the heart of the house, with the baronial-style dining room providing a wonderful setting for Gordon's classical French cooking with Scottish influences, made from locally sourced produce and complemented by a thoughtful wine list.
Recommended in the area
Loch Katrine boat trips; Falls of Dochart; Stirling Castle

Arden Country House

★★★★★ ≜ GUEST ACCOMMODATION
Address: Belsyde, LINLITHGOW, West Lothian, EH49 6QE
Tel/Fax: 01506 670172
Email: info@ardencountryhouse.com
Website: www.ardencountryhouse.com
Map ref: 10 NS97
Directions: 1.3m SW of Linlithgow. A706 over Union Canal,
entrance 200yds on left at Lodge Cottage
Rooms: 3 en suite (1GF) **S** £50-£100 **D** £80-£110 **Notes:** Wi-fi
⊗ on premises ⚲ under 12yrs **Parking:** 4 **Closed:** 25-26 Dec

Situated in the grounds of the Belsyde Country Estate, this award-winning B&B offers guests a picturesque rural retreat with all the conveniences and comforts of a modern country house. As well as spacious, stylishly furnished en suite bedrooms, residents can enjoy complimentary afternoon tea with home baking, free Wi-fi and a cosy lounge. The charming dining room is the setting for wonderful breakfasts using the best of local produce. Beth Cruickshank was a finalist for AA Friendliest Landlady of the Year 2008 Award.
Recommended in the area

Linlithgow Palace (birth place of Mary Queen of Scots); Blackness Castle; Hopetoun House

Belsyde House

★ ★ ★ ★ 🏛 GUEST ACCOMMODATION

Address: Lanark Road, LINLITHGOW,
West Lothian, EH49 6QE
Tel/Fax: 01506 842098
Email: info@belsydehouse.com
Website: www.belsyde.com
Map ref: 10 NS97
Directions: 1.5m SW on A706, 1st left over Union
Canal **Rooms:** 3 en suite D £70-£90 **Notes:** Wi-fi
⊗ on premises (ex assist dogs) 👶 under 12yrs
Parking: 10 **Closed:** Xmas

A tree-lined driveway leads to this welcoming 18th-century farmhouse, peacefully situated in attractive grounds with horse and sheep pastures and views of the Ochil Hills beyond. Close to the Union Canal and halfway between Glasgow and Edinburgh, it makes a good touring base. Inside, well-proportioned bedrooms are individually furnished and well equipped, with complimentary Wi-fi. The breakfast includes a vegetarian menu. Belsyde has also won a Green Tourism award.

Recommended in the area

Hopetoun House; Linlithgow Palace; The Falkirk Wheel, Falkirk

Lumsdaine House

★ ★ ★ ★ BED & BREAKFAST

Address: Woodcockdale Farm, Lanark Road,
LINLITHGOW, West Lothian, EH49 6QE
Tel: 01506 845001
Email: margaret@lumsdainehouse.co.uk
Website: www.lumsdainehouse.co.uk
Map ref: 10 NS97
Directions: 1.5m SW on A706 **Rooms:** 3 en suite
S £35-£40 D £55-£60 **Notes:** Wi-fi ⊗ on premises
👶 under 14yrs **Parking:** 3 **Closed:** 20 Dec-1 Jan

Just a few minutes' drive from historic Linlithgow, this property offers modern, comfortable and spacious accommodation in a rural setting with some wonderful open views. Guests are greeted with tea and home baking before being shown to their rooms, two of which feature four-poster beds. All bedrooms provide en suite shower rooms, TVs, free Wi-fi, hairdryers and hospitality trays. Lumsdaine House prides itself on its healthy breakfasts, served in the spacious dining room. There's a lounge area as well as large gardens for guests to enjoy.

Recommended in the area

Linlithgow Palace; Royal Yacht Britannia; Bo'ness Steam Railway

Portree Harbour, Isle of Skye

Shorefield House

★ ★ ★ ★ ≙ GUEST HOUSE

Address: Edinbane, PORTREE, Isle of Skye, IV51 9PW
Tel: 01470 582444
Email: stay@shorefield-house.com
Website: www.shorefield-house.com
Map ref: 11 NG35
Directions: 12m from Portree & 8m from Dunvegan, off A850 into Edinbane, 1st on right
Rooms: 4 en suite (3GF) **D** £80-£90 Family £95-£140 **Notes:** Wi-fi ⊗ on premises **Parking:** 10
Closed: Xmas & New Year

Customer care and comfort are priority at Shorefield House which offers spacious, high quality accommodation. There are en suite double, twin and family rooms, each well decorated and furnished with homely extras. An à la carte Highland breakfast or a continental buffet are on offer to suit all tastes. Peacefully situated looking across Loch Greshornich, Shorefield House enables easy exploration of all areas of Skye, and access to the excellent local restaurants for evening meals.

Recommended in the area

Dunvegan Castle & seal colony; The Three Chimneys Restaurant, Colbost; Talisker Whisky Distillery

The Old Man of Hoy, Orkney Islands

WALES

Rhossili Bay

Lastra Farm

★★★★ GUEST ACCOMMODATION

Address: Penrhyd, ALMWCH, Isle of Anglesey,
LL68 9TF
Tel: 01407 830906
Fax: 01407 832522
Email: booking@lastra-hotel.com
Website: www.lastra-hotel.com
Map ref: 5 SH49
Directions: On A5025 turn left after Welcome sign.
Follow signs to leisure centre, Lastra Farm signed
Rooms: 8 en suite (3GF) **Notes:** Wi-fi **Parking:** 50

Lastra Farm is conveniently located for the coast road, making it a good holiday base. A 17th-century Welsh farmhouse, it retains many original features, such as the warm wood panelling. The en suite bedrooms, which vary in size, are all pine-furnished and colourfully decorated. Three double rooms are housed separately in the Victorian Lodge for extra privacy. There is also a comfortable lounge and a cosy bar, while a wide range of good-value meals is available in the restaurant and bistro.

Recommended in the area

Anglesey Sea Zoo; Plas Newydd (NT); Beaumaris Castle

Sarnau Mansion

★★★★ GUEST ACCOMMODATION

Address: Llysonnen Road, CARMARTHEN,
Carmarthenshire, SA33 5DZ
Tel/Fax: 01267 211404
Email: fernihough@so1405.force9.co.uk
Website: www.sarnaumansion.co.uk
Map ref: 1 SN42
Directions: 5m W of Carmarthen. Off A40 onto
B4298 & Bancyfelin road, Sarnau on right
Rooms: 4 (3 en suite) (1 pri facs) **S** £45-£50
D £70-£80 **Notes:** ⊗ on premises ✗ under 5yrs **Parking:** 10

This fine Grade II listed country house, built in 1765, is set in the heart of the Carmarthen countryside, in 16 acres of grounds, which include a tennis court. It's not far from here to the many attractions and beaches of south and west Wales, and it is a delightful place to return to each evening. Many original features have been retained and the public areas are both comfortable and elegant. Bedrooms are large and nicely decorated, and all of the rooms have stunning rural views.

Recommended in the area

National Botanic Garden of Wales; Aberglasney Gardens; Dylan Thomas Boathouse, Laugharne

Allt Y Golau Farmhouse

★ ★ ★ ★ 🏠 FARMHOUSE

Address: Allt Y Golau Uchaf, FELINGWM UCHAF,
Carmarthenshire, SA32 7BB
Tel: 01267 290455
Email: alltygolau@btinternet.com
Website: www.alltygolau.com
Map ref: 1 SN52
Directions: A40 onto B4310, N for 2m. 1st on left
after Felingwm Uchaf
Rooms: 3 (2 en suite) (1 pri facs) (2GF) S £45 D £65
Notes: ⊗ on premises ☺ Parking: 3 Closed: 20 Dec-2 Jan

Beautifully renovated by owners Colin and Jacquie Rouse, this Georgian stone farmhouse offers the epitome of gracious country living and a welcome that earned Jacquie a place in the finals of the AA Friendliest Landlady of the Year Awards in 2008. The owners are knowledgeable about the heritage and nature of the area, and are always happy to advise their guests on how to get the best out of their visit. The setting of the farmhouse, with views over the Tywi Valley towards the Black Mountain, is glorious, and the two acres of gardens include a fine orchard. Snowdrops, daffodils and bluebells successively carpet the ground in spring, and ducks, geese, turkeys, and the hens that provide the breakfast eggs roam free here. Inside the house there are cosy sofas and easy chairs around the lovely old fireplace in the lounge. The traditional dining room features one big elm table and an eclectic display of antiques, including a stately grandfather clock. Breakfast here is a real highlight, with home baking and the finest local produce accompanying those fresh eggs. The bright, comfortable bedrooms are in traditional style, with pine furniture and patchwork quilts.

Recommended in the area

National Botanic Garden of Wales; Aberglasney Gardens; Dynefwr Castle and Park

Coedllys Country House

★ ★ ★ ★ ★ BED & BREAKFAST

Address: Coedllys Uchaf, Llangynin, ST CLEARS,
Carmarthenshire, SA33 4JY
Tel: 01994 231455
Fax: 01994 231441
Email: coedllys@btinternet.com
Website: www.coedllyscountryhouse.co.uk
Map ref: 1 SN21
Directions: A40 St Clears rdbt, take 3rd exit, at lights
turn left. After 100yds turn right, 3m to Llangynin,
pass village sign. 30mph sign on left, turn immediately down track (private drive) Rooms: 3 en suite
S £57.50-£62.50 D £90-£100 Notes: Wi-fi 🐾 under 12yrs Parking: 6 Closed: Xmas

Set in 11 acres of grounds, Coedllys is the ultimate country hideaway, tucked away in a tranquil spot
and surrounded by farmland with far-reaching views and a pretty woodland dell. Guests are invited to
amble around and enjoy the abundant wildlife. Owners Valerie and Keith Harber are serious about
conservation and nature and they provide a refuge for countless animals, including sheep, donkeys and
ponies. Inside, this large, beautiful house has been tastefully restored to provide elegant bedrooms with
antique furniture and luxurious fabrics, as well as a host of thoughtful extras such as chocolates, fruit,
flowers and magazines alongside soft bathrobes, slippers, flat-screen TV/DVD, free Wi-fi, iPod player,
comfortable sofas and large, inviting antique beds – all of which combine to make a stay here truly
memorable. Energetic guests are welcome to make use of the fitness suite, or they can simply relax in
the Hydro swimming pool (available April–September only) and sauna. An extensive breakfast menu,
from lighter choices through to a full breakfast, uses the finest local produce, including free-range eggs
from Coedllys's own chickens.

Recommended in the area

Dylan Thomas Boathouse, Laugharne; Millennium Coastal Path; National Botanical Gardens

Lake Llyn Idwal beneath Carnedd Dyfydd, Snowdonia

Bryn Bella Guest House

★ ★ ★ ★ GUEST HOUSE

Address: Lon Muriau, Llanrwst Road,
BETWS-Y-COED, Conwy, LL24 0HD
Tel: 01690 710627
Email: welcome@bryn-bella.co.uk
Website: www.bryn-bella.co.uk
Map ref: 5 SH75
Directions: A5 onto A470, 0.5m right onto driveway
signed Bryn Bella **Rooms:** 5 en suite (1GF)
Notes: Wi-fi ⊗ on premises **Parking:** 5

Situated in a quiet elevated position, with stunning views of the picturesque village of Betws-y-Coed, this elegant Victorian house makes a perfect base from which to explore Snowdonia and North Wales. Priding itself on its eco-friendly credentials and awards, this establishment offers a range of thoughtfully equipped bedrooms with modern en suite bathrooms. The public areas include an attractive dining room and a comfortable lounge; there's also a peaceful garden and terraced patio area. Guest services include a daily weather forecast, drying and ironing facilities, and free parking.

Recommended in the area

Bodnant Garden (NT); Conwy Castle; Snowdon Mountain Railway

Cwmanog Isaf Farm

★ ★ ★ ★ FARMHOUSE
Address: Fairy Glen, BETWS-Y-COED,
Conwy, LL24 0SL
Tel: 01690 710225 & 07808 421634
Email: heather.hughes3@tesco.net
Website: www.cwmanogisaffarmholidays.co.uk
Map ref: 5 SH75
Directions: 1m S of Betws-y-Coed off A470 by Fairy
Glen Hotel, 500yds on farm lane
Rooms: 3 (2 en suite) (1 pri facs) (1GF) S £45
D £58-£66 Notes: ⊗ on premises ⊀ under 15yrs ☻ Parking: 4 Closed: 15 Dec-7 Feb

Hidden away, yet only a 20-minute stroll from the Victorian village of Betws-y-Coed, Cwmanog Isaf, a 200-year-old house on a working livestock farm, is set in 30 acres of undulating land, including the renowned Fairy Glen, and has stunning views of the surrounding countryside. It provides comfortably furnished and well equipped bedrooms (one on the ground floor). and serves wholesome Welsh farmhouse cuisine using home-reared and local organic produce, home-made bread and preserves.
Recommended in the area
Bodnant Garden (NT); Fairy Glen; Portmeirion

Park Hill

★ ★ ★ ★ GUEST HOUSE
Address: Llanrwst Road, BETWS-Y-COED,
Conwy, LL24 0HD
Tel/Fax: 01690 710540
Email: welcome@park-hill.co.uk
Website: www.park-hill.co.uk
Map ref: 5 SH75
Directions: 0.5m N of Betws-y-Coed on A470
(Llanrwst road)
Rooms: 9 en suite S £53-£80 D £60-£84
Notes: ⊗ on premises ⊀ under 8yrs Parking: 11

The Park Hill, a fine Victorian building, is situated in the Snowdonia National Park, and has breathtaking views over the River Conwy. It makes an ideal base for walkers. You will find teddy bears here, there and everywhere, as the owners have a collection of 200. Guests can enjoy a swim in the splendid indoor heated pool, relax in the whirlpool bath or take a sauna, before retiring to the bar or the comfortable and well-equipped en suite bedrooms. Breakfasts and dinners are made from local produce.
Recommended in the area
Mount Snowdon; Tree Top Adventure, Snowdonia; Conwy Castle

Penmachno Hall

★★★★★ 🛏 GUEST ACCOMMODATION

Address: Penmachno, BETWS-Y-COED, Conwy, LL24 0PU
Tel/Fax: 01690 760410
Email: stay@penmachnohall.co.uk
Website: www.penmachnohall.co.uk
Map ref: 5 SH75
Directions: 4m S of Betws-y-Coed. A5 onto B4406 to
Penmachno, over bridge, right at Eagles pub signed Ty Mawr.
500yds at stone bridge
Rooms: 3 en suite **D** £80-£95 **Notes:** Wi-fi ⊗ on premises
Parking: 5 **Closed:** Xmas & New Year

Penmachno Hall, a lovingly restored Victorian rectory, is situated
in over two acres of mature grounds in the secluded Glasgwm Valley in Snowdonia National Park. With
its breathtaking views and quiet forest tracks leading to waterfalls, the valley is a haven of tranquillity
within easy reach of bustling Betws-y-Coed. This is an establishment that prides itself on catering
for the visitor's every need. Stylish decor and quality furnishings highlight the many original features
throughout the ground-floor areas, while the bedrooms come with a wealth of thoughtful extras, and
each benefits from panoramic views. The spacious Morning Room has comfortable sofas and large
bay windows overlooking the garden; it houses a large collection of books, maps, walking guides and
tourist information, as well as games and puzzles. The slightly more formal dining room is the venue
for evening meals, served dinner-party style around a central dining table. Supper is available from
Tuesday to Friday (£15 per person), and a 5-course set dinner on Saturday (£35 per person), based on
guests' preferences and using only the finest, fresh local produce. An extensive wine list complements
the meal, and expert advice is available to help guests select the most appropriate wine.

Recommended in the area

Snowdon; Bodnant Garden (NT); Portmeirion

Tan-y-Foel Country House

★ ★ ★ ★ ★ ❀❀❀ GUEST HOUSE

Address: Capel Garmon, BETWS-Y-COED,
Conwy, LL26 0RE
Tel: 01690 710507
Fax: 01690 710681
Email: enquiries@tyfhotel.co.uk
Website: www.tyfhotel.co.uk
Map ref: 5 SH75
Directions: 1.5m E of Betws-y-Coed. Off A5 onto
A470 N, 2m right for Capel Garmon, establishment
signed 1.5m on left
Rooms: 5 en suite (1GF) **S** £115-£140 **D** £125-£190 (Junior Suite £240)
Notes: ⊗ on premises ✝ under 12yrs **Parking:** 14 **Closed:** Dec

The 17th-century Welsh stone exterior of this country house gives no hint of the interior, where a series
of intimate and immaculately designed rooms unfold. Bold ideas fuse the traditional character of the
building with contemporary style, giving it an elegant simplicity that goes hand-in-hand with luxurious
facilities. Tan-y-Foel is aimed at the discerning traveller looking for a gourmet hideaway in a peaceful,
location in the heart of Snowdonia National Park. The surrounding countryside is delightful, with the
opportunity for some lovely walks. Independent and family-run, this place offers a highly original
country-house experience, with the owners' influence clearly in evidence throughout. There is a range
of options, not only in bedroom size but in the style of decor too, and many of the regular guests have
their own favourites. Naturally, each bedroom has its own bathroom, and each is well decorated and
furnished, with a selection of welcoming extras. A major highlight of a stay here is the food, and dinner
is a memorable occasion, consisting of carefully chosen fresh ingredients, skilfully prepared.

Recommended in the area

Bodnant Garden (NT); Snowdon Mountain Railway; Conwy Castle

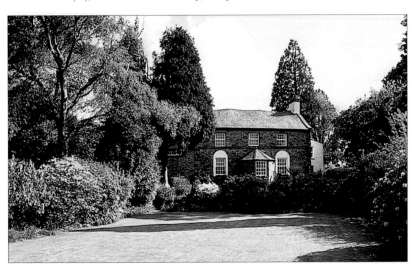

Conwy Castle and Telford's Suspension Bridge

Ty Gwyn Inn

★ ★ ★ INN

Address: BETWS-Y-COED, Conwy, LL24 0SG

Tel/Fax: 01690 710383

Email: mratcl1050@aol.com

Website: www.tygwynhotel.co.uk

Map ref: 5 SH75

Directions: Junct of A5 & A470, by Waterloo Bridge

Rooms: 13 (10 en suite) (1GF) **S** £40-£70

D £54-£120

Notes: Wi-fi **Parking:** 14 **Closed:** Mon-Wed in Jan

Originally a coaching inn, the Ty Gwyn dates back to 1636 and is situated on the edge of the village, close to the Waterloo Bridge. The inn retains many original features and the quality and style of the furnishings and the collections of memorabilia throughout enhance its intrinsic charm. Bedrooms, some of which feature antique and four-poster beds, are equipped with thoughtful extras. The en suite rooms have been refurbished with new bath and shower rooms, and two rooms have spa tubs. The imaginative international dishes are prepared from fresh local produce.

Recommended in the area

Portmeirion Village; Snowdon Mountain Railway; Swallow Falls

Sychnant Pass Country House

★★★★★ @ GUEST ACCOMMODATION

Address: Sychnant Pass Road, CONWY, LL32 8BJ
Tel/Fax: 01824 790732
Email: info@pentremawrcountryhouse.co.uk
Website: www.sychnantpasscountryhouse.co.uk
Map ref: 5 SH77
Directions: 1.75m W of Conwy. Off A547 Bangor Rd in town onto Mount Pleasant & Sychnant Pass Rd, 1.75m on right near top of hill
Rooms: 12 en suite (2GF) **S** £75-£160 **D** £95-£180
Notes: Wi-fi **Parking:** 30
Closed: 24-26 Dec & Jan

There are fine views from this Edwardian house, set in 3 acres of wonderful gardens with lawns, trees and a wild garden with ponds and a stream. Nestling in the foothills of the Snowdonia National Park, guests at this exceptional establishment, which offers country-house luxury, can unwind and enjoy the superb health and leisure facilities, with salt-treated (no chlorine) indoor pool, fitness equipment, sauna, and hot tub. The range of bedrooms are imaginative and stylish, and include four-poster rooms, suites with galleried bedrooms and two suites with their own private terrace and hot tub. They are all superbly comfortable and equipped with a range of thoughtful extras such as dressing gowns, big fluffy towels and refrigerator. Lounges, warmed by open fires in chillier months, are comfortable and inviting, and imaginative meals created from locally sourced seasonal produce by owner Graham, a trained chef who has worked at Gleneagles and Turnberry, are served in the attractive dining room. High teas are available for younger children.

Recommended in the area

Conwy; Bodnant Garden (NT); Penrhyn Castle

Abbey Lodge

★ ★ ★ ★ GUEST HOUSE

Address: 14 Abbey Road, LLANDUDNO,
Conwy, LL30 2EA
Tel/Fax: 01492 878042
Email: enquiries@abbeylodgeuk.com
Website: www.abbeylodgeuk.com
Map ref: 5 SH78
Directions: A546 to N end of town, onto Clement Av,
right onto Abbey Rd
Rooms: 4 en suite **S** £37.50 **D** £70-£75
Notes: Wi-fi ⊗ on premises ∦ under 12yrs ✉
Parking: 4 **Closed:** Dec-1 Mar

Built in 1840 and set in a quiet leafy avenue within easy walking distance of the promenade, Abbey Lodge retains all the charm of a Victorian townhouse. This Grade II listed building is under the personal supervision of Dennis and Janet, who welcome guests with a complimentary pot of tea or coffee in the comfortable lounge; they will even meet you from the train. The pretty walled garden that shelters beneath the Great Orme is the perfect place to relax. The charming en suite bedrooms are well equipped with hospitality trays, hairdryers, TV, magazines, books, towels and bathrobes. Free wi-fi is available throughout the house. A collection of local interest books and maps are available to help guests plan excursions. Breakfast is mostly sourced from the farmers market, and packed lunches can be ordered. Abbey Road is quiet, yet only 5 minutes' walk from the pier and the Victorian High Street with a good choice of shops, cafés and a variety of restaurants.

Recommended in the area

Bodnant Garden (NT); Conwy Castle; Snowdonia Mountains

Brigstock House

★★★★ GUEST HOUSE

Address: 1 St David's Place, LLANDUDNO,
Conwy, LL30 2UG
Tel: 01492 876416
Email: simon.hanson4@virgin.net
Website: www.brigstockhouse.co.uk
Map ref: 5 SH78
Directions: A470 into Llandudno, left onto The
Parade promenade, left onto Lloyd St, left onto St
David's Rd & left onto St David's Place **Rooms:** 9 (8
en suite) (1 pri facs) **S** fr £30 **D** fr £30 **Notes:** Wi-fi ⊗ on premises 🕍 under 12yrs **Parking:** 6

This impressive Edwardian property is situated in a quiet tree-lined road just a short level walk to the
amenities of Llandudno, such as the theatre and Venue Cymru. All of the bedrooms have been decorated
to a high standard, providing many home comforts, such as flatscreen digital TVs. Two of the suites have
their own lounge area. Substantial breakfasts, and dinners by arrangement, are served in the elegant
dining room. Guests can also make use of a comfortable lounge, a secluded garden area and patio.

Recommended in the area

Great Orme Tramway & Copper Mines; Snowdonia National Park; Bodnant Garden (NT)

Can-Y-Bae

★★★★ GUEST ACCOMMODATION

Address: 10 Mostyn Crescent, Central Promenade,
LLANDUDNO, Conwy, LL30 1AR
Tel: 01492 874188
Fax: 01492 868376
Email: canybae@btconnect.com
Website: www.can-y-baehotel.com
Map ref: 5 SH78 **Directions:** A55 junct 10 onto
A470, signed Llandudno/Promenade. Can-Y-Bae on
promenade between Venue Cymru & Band Stand
Rooms: 16 en suite (2GF) **S** £35–£45 **D** £80 **Notes:** Wi-fi 🕍 under 12yrs

Can-Y-Bae is an attractively renovated 19th-century property, centrally located on the promenade of
this seaside resort, just 300 yards from the theatre, and five minutes' walk from the town centre and
new shopping complex. Bedrooms are equipped with both practical and homely extras, including tea-
and coffee-making facilities, and the upper floors are serviced by a lift. Day rooms include a lounge with
sea views, a cosy bar and an attractive basement dining room where home-cooked meals are served.

Recommended in the area

Great Orme Tramway or Cable Car; Happy Valley Gardens; Festiniog and West Highland Railways

Rhossili beach

St Hilary Guest House

★★★★ GUEST ACCOMMODATION

Address: The Promenade, 16 Craig-Y-Don Parade,
LLANDUDNO, Conwy, LL30 1BG
Tel: 01492 875551
Fax: 01492 877538
Email: info@sthilaryguesthouse.co.uk
Website: www.sthilaryguesthouse.co.uk
Map ref: 5 SH78
Directions: 0.5m E of town centre. On B5115
seafront road near Venue Cymru Theatre

Rooms: 9 en suite (1GF) **S** £38-£65 **D** £58-£75 **Notes:** Wi-fi ⊗ **Closed:** end Nov-early Feb

This elegant Grade II listed Victorian seafront guest house has spectacular views of Llandudno's sweeping bay and the Great and Little Orme Headlands. Proprietors Anne-Marie and Howard provide you with a welcoming and friendly atmosphere. Delicious breakfasts, tastefully decorated comfortable bedrooms with flatscreen TV, a well stocked drinks tray, free Wi-fi, and little extras make your stay special. For the theatre, or for conference delegates, Venue Cymru is only a 5 minute walk.

Recommended in the area

The Great Orme Country Park; Conwy Castle; Snowdonia

Plas Rhos

★★★★★ ⌂ GUEST ACCOMMODATION

Address: Cayley Promenade, RHOS-ON-SEA,
Conwy, LL28 4EP
Tel: 01492 543698
Fax: 01492 540088
Email: info@plasrhos.co.uk
Website: www.plasrhos.co.uk
Map ref: 5 SH88
Directions: A55 junct 20, B5115 for Rhos-on-Sea,
right at rdbt onto Whitehall Rd to promenade
Rooms: 7 en suite **S** £50-£65 **D** £75-£100
Notes: Wi-fi ⊗ on premises ⋔ under 12yrs **Parking:** 4 **Closed:** 21 Dec-Jan

A yearning to live by the sea and indulge their passion for sailing brought Susan and Colin Hazelden to the North Wales coast. Running a hotel in Derbyshire for many years was the ideal preparation for looking after guests at their renovated Victorian home. Built as a gentleman's residence in the late 19th century, Plas Rhos is situated on Cayley Promenade, where it enjoys panoramic views over the bay, beach and coast. Breakfast, a particularly memorable meal, is taken overlooking the pretty patio garden. It consists of cereals, fresh fruit, juices and yoghurt followed by free-range eggs cooked to your liking with Welsh sausage, local back bacon, tomato, mushrooms, beans and fried bread or your choice of a number of other hot options including kippers or scrambled eggs with smoked salmon. The two sumptuous lounges have spectacular sea views, comfy chairs and sofas, and interesting memorabilia, while the modest-size bedrooms are individually decorated and have plenty of thoughtful extras. One period room is furnished with a romantic half-tester and antiques, and enjoys those same stunning views. Wi-fi broadband internet access is available in all rooms – just bring your laptop.

Recommended in the area

Conwy Castle; Bodnant Garden (NT); Snowdonia National Park

Castle House

★★★★★ BED & BREAKFAST
Address: Bull Lane (Love Lane), DENBIGH,
Denbighshire, LL16 3LY
Tel: 01745 816860
Fax: 01745 817214
Email: c.hobson@virgin.net
Website: www.castlehousebandb.co.uk
Map ref: 5 SJ06 **Directions:** A55 junct 27 onto A525 to
Denbigh. From Vale St take 1st exit at rdbt, pass supermarket,
1st left to T-junct then right. 20yds on left onto unmarked drive
Rooms: 3 en suite **S** £50 **D** £150 **Notes:** ⊗ on premises
Parking: 6 **Closed:** 20-30 Dec

Located within Denbigh's medieval town walls, this substantial Grade II listed former gentleman's residence dates back to 1820. As well as enjoying magnificent views across the Clwyd Valley towards the Clwydian range of mountains, designated an Area of Outstanding Natural Beauty, it enjoys prime position within the tranquil grounds of Plas Castell Estate, with two acres of landscaped gardens at guests' disposal, including a croquet lawn and fish pond. Also within the grounds is the 16th-century Leicester's Church, an unfinished cathedral built by the nobleman Robert Dudley. Inside Castle House, with its grand entrance reception hall and feature mirror lending a sense of days gone by, all has been lovingly restored to provide high standards of comfort and facilities. Spacious, individually themed and evocatively named bedrooms are equipped with quality furnishings, a wealth of thoughtful extras and smart, efficient en suite bathrooms with floor lighting and underfloor heating. There is also a romantic lounge and a formal dining room with ornate ceiling plasterwork and log fires in winter, where guests can enjoy delicious breakfasts through to scrumptious afternoon teas and candlelit dinners.

Recommended in the area

Offa's Dyke; Loggerheads Country Park; Snowdonia

Pentre Mawr Country House

★ ★ ★ ★ ★ 🍽 GUEST ACCOMMODATION
Address: LLANDYROG, Denbighshire, LL16 4LA
Tel: 01824 790732
Fax: 01824 790441
Email: info@pentremawrcountryhouse.co.uk
Website: www.pentremawrcountryhouse.co.uk
Map ref: 5 SJ16
Directions: From Denbigh follow signs to Bodfari/
Llandyrnog. Left at rdbt to Bodfari, after 50yds
turn left onto country lane, follow road and Pentre
Mawr on left **Rooms:** 5 en suite **S** £75-£130 **D** £95-£150
Notes: Wi-fi 🐾 under 13yrs ⊗ **Parking:** 8

This property, owned by the same family for 400 years, is a unique destination, bursting with character. Tucked away in an unspoilt corner of North Wales, in an Area of Outstanding Natural Beauty, this former farmhouse is set in nearly 200 acres of meadows, park and woodland. A true Welsh country house, it features well-appointed en suite bedrooms and suites, some with hot tubs and all very spacious and thoughtfully equipped. As well as large drawing rooms, there is also a formal dining room, ideal for family gatherings and special occasions, and a less formal dining area in the conservatory by the saltwater swimming pool in the walled garden. The daily-changing menu includes carefully sourced local meats and cheeses as well as homemade breads and sorbets. Full Welsh breakfasts with Buck's fizz are served in the morning room. Influenced by a love of the outdoors and Africa, owners Bre and Graham have introduced a number of luxurious canvas safari lodges to bring guests closer to nature without compromising on comfort; all are fully heated, have super king-size beds, oak floors and decks with hot tubs plus bathrooms with free-standing baths and showers.

Recommended in the area

Snowdonia National Park; Denbigh Castle; Moel Fammau mountain walk

Firgrove Country House B & B

★★★★★ 🏚 🍴 BED & BREAKFAST

Address: Firgrove, Llanfwrog, RUTHIN,
Denbighshire, LL15 2LL
Tel/Fax: 01824 702677
Email: meadway@firgrovecountryhouse.co.uk
Website: www.firgrovecountryhouse.co.uk
Map ref: 5 SJ15
Directions: 0.5m SW Ruthin. A494 onto B5105,
0.25m **Rooms:** 3 en suite **S** £50-£75 **D** £60-£90
Notes: Wi-fi ⊗ 📍 **Parking:** 4 **Closed:** Nov-Feb

This Grade II listed building, with its inspiring views across the Vale of Clwyd, has well-equipped bedrooms and modern comforts. The well-proportioned bedrooms retain many original period features and have smart bathrooms. One of the bedrooms has an attractive four-poster bed, while another is a self-contained ground-floor suite with an open fire, small kitchen and a private sitting room. Home-made and locally sourced produce features in the splendid breakfasts; evening meals can be enjoyed by prior arrangement. The delightful garden provides a charming setting for the house.

Recommended in the area

Offa's Dyke Path; Bodnant Garden (NT); Chester

Bach-Y-Graig

★★★★ FARMHOUSE

Address: Tremeirchion, ST ASAPH,
Denbighshire, LL17 0UH
Tel/Fax: 01745 730627
Email: anwen@bachygraig.co.uk
Website: www.bachygraig.co.uk
Map ref: 5 SJ07
Directions: 3m SE of St Asaph. Off A525 at Trefnant onto A541 to x-rds with white railings, left down hill, over bridge & then right
Rooms: 3 (2 en suite) (1 pri facs) **S** £45-£50
D £70-£75 **Notes:** Wi-fi ⊗ on premises **Parking:** 3 **Closed:** Xmas & New Year

The wealth of oak beams and panelling, and Grade II listing, testify to the historic character of this farmhouse set in 200 acres with private fishing rights on the River Clwyd. Bedrooms are furnished with fine period pieces and quality soft fabrics – some rooms have antique brass beds. The ground floor has a quiet lounge and a sitting-dining room where a scrumptious breakfast is served.

Recommended in the area

Bodnant Garden (NT); The Old Gaol, Ruthin; Tweedmill Factory Outlets, St Asaph

Tan-Yr-Onnen Guest House

★ ★ ★ ★ ★ GUEST HOUSE

Address: Waen, ST ASAPH,
Denbighshire, LL17 0DU
Tel/Fax: 01745 583821
Email: tanyronnenvisit@aol.com
Website: www.northwalesbreaks.co.uk
Map ref: 5 SJ07
Directions: W on A55 junct 28, turn left in 300yds
Rooms: 6 en suite (4GF) S £60-£80 D £75-£100
Notes: Wi-fi **Parking:** 8

Set in the heart of North Wales, in the verdant Vale of Clwyd, Patrick and Sara Murphy's guest house, Tan-Yr-Onnen, is perfectly located for exploring this beautiful area and nearby Chester. Now awarded the AA's highest B&B rating, quality is the keyword here, with very high standards throughout. The house has been extensively refurbished and the separately accessed bedrooms newly constructed; all are modern and well equipped. The en suite ground-floor rooms feature king-size beds and some have French doors opening onto the patio, while those on the first floor offer suite accommodation. All provide home comforts such as bathrobes, fluffy towels, comfy beds, flat-screen TVs (with Freeview and DVD players), and tea and coffee-making facilities, plus all little touches to make your stay feel extra special. Free Wi-fi is available. The hearty breakfast table will set you up for a day's exploration and features fruit juices, fresh fruit salad, yoghurts, cereals, home-baked bread and a full Welsh breakfast. Adjacent to the dining room is the lounge and large conservatory. Here you can enjoy a cool glass of wine in the evening as you admire the grounds and gardens at the foot of the Clwydian range. Private parking is available.

Recommended in the area

St Asaph; Bodelwyddan Castle; Offa's Dyke Path

13th century Valle Crucis Abbey ruins, Llangollen

Llwyndu Farmhouse

★★★★ ➴ GUEST ACCOMMODATION
Address: Llanaber, BARMOUTH, Gwynedd, LL42 1RR
Tel: 01341 280144
Email: intouch@llwyndu-farmhouse.co.uk
Website: www.llwyndu-farmhouse.co.uk
Map ref: 5 SH61
Directions: A496 towards Harlech where street lights
end, on outskirts of Barmouth, take next right
Rooms: 7 en suite D £84-£100
Parking: 10 Closed: 25-26 Dec

This converted 16th-century farmhouse stands overlooking Cardigan Bay in Llanaber, near Barmouth and the Mawddach Estuary, in an Area of Outstanding Natural Beauty. Noted for its fine ale and hospitality as far back as 1600, Llwyndu maintains the centuries-old tradition by providing good food, wines and local beers as well as comfortable accommodation. Many attractive elements of the original building have also survived the centuries, including inglenook fireplaces, exposed beams and timbers. Bedrooms offer all the modern comforts, with en suite facilities, televisions and tea- and coffee-making equipment, though some reflect earlier influences with their four-poster beds. Some rooms are located in the main house and four are in a converted granary, each with their own external door. There is a cosy lounge, where you might socialise with fellow guests and plan trips out. Quality Welsh produce is to the fore in the enjoyable meals served at individual tables in the character dining room. The setting for the two or three course dinners is wonderfully atmospheric by night, with candles and old lamps lighting up the exposed stone and timber. A good choice is offered for breakfast, and vegetarian and special diets can be catered for with prior notice.

Recommended in the area
RNLI Visitor Centre; Harlech Castle; Portmeirion Village

Precipice Walk at Dolgellau, Snowdonia National Park

Tyddynmawr Farmhouse

★★★★★ FARMHOUSE

Address: Cader Road, Islawrdref, DOLGELLAU,
Gwynedd, LL40 1TL
Tel: 01341 422331
Website: www.wales-guesthouse.co.uk
Map ref: 2 SH71
Directions: From town centre left at top of square,
left at garage onto Cader Rd for 3m, 1st farm on left
after Gwernan Lake **Rooms:** 3 en suite (1GF) **S** £55
D £68-£70 **Notes:** ⊗ ⛄ ☻ **Parking:** 8 **Closed:** Jan

Birdwatchers, ramblers, photographers and artists see these spectacular surroundings as a paradise, and the farmhouse accommodation appeals equally to those just happy to sit and look. Olwen Evans prides herself on her home cooking and warm hospitality. Oak beams and log fires lend character to the stone house, and bedrooms are spacious and furnished with Welsh oak furniture; one room has a balcony, and a ground-floor room benefits from a patio. The en suites are large and luxurious. This breathtaking mountain setting is about three miles from the historic market town of Dolgellau.

Recommended in the area

Walking – Cader Idris, Precipice Walk, Torrent Walk, Maddach Estuary Walk; steam railways

Cyfathfa Castle, Merthyr Tydfil

Penrhadw Farm

★★★★ GUEST HOUSE
Address: Pontsticill, MERTHYR TYDFIL, CF48 2TU
Tel: 01685 723481 & 722461
Fax: 01685 722461
Email: treghotel@aol.com
Website: www.penrhadwfarm.co.uk
Map ref: 2 SO00
Directions: 5m N of Merthyr Tydfil. (Please see map on website) **Rooms:** 10 en suite (1GF) **S** £45-£60
D £70-£100 **Notes:** Wi-fi ⊗ **Parking:** 20

This former Victorian farmhouse, located in the heart of the glorious Brecon Beacons National Park and with spectacular mountain views, has been totally refurbished to provide high-quality modern accommodation. The well-equipped, spacious bedrooms include two large suites in cottages adjacent to the main building. All rooms are en suite and come with hospitality tray, TV and trouser press. There is also a comfortable guest lounge with a TV and video recorder. Separate tables are provided in the cosy breakfast room, where hearty Welsh breakfasts are served.

Recommended in the area

The Brecon Mountain Railway; Brecon Beacons National Park; Millennium Stadium, Cardiff

The Crown at Whitebrook

★★★★★ ⚜⚜ 🍴 RESTAURANT WITH ROOMS

Address: WHITEBROOK, Monmouthshire, NP25 4TX
Tel: 01600 860254
Fax: 01600 860607
Email: info@crownatwhitebrook.co.uk
Website: www.crownatwhitebrook.co.uk
Map ref: 2 SO50
Directions: 4m from Monmouth on B4293, left at sign to Whitebrook, 2m on unmarked road, Crown on right
Rooms: 8 en suite **S** £80-£100 **D** £125-£150 **Notes:** Wi-fi ⊗ on premises 👶 under 12yrs **Parking:** 20 **Closed:** 22 Dec-4 Jan

In a secluded spot in the wooded valley of the River Wye, yet just five miles from the town of Monmouth, this former drover's cottage dates back to the 17th century and boasts five acres of tranquil, landscaped gardens in which guests can wander and relax. A restaurant with rooms, its refurbished and individually decorated bedrooms boast a contemporary feel and have the latest in smart facilities. The executive rooms boast the added luxury of walk-in power showers, and two rooms have double-ended baths. All have outstanding views across the rolling countryside and offer a whole host of thoughtful extras such as individually controlled heating, flat-screen TV, internet/email and tea and coffee-making facilities. In addition, the 'comfort-cool' system helps keep the rooms cool and comfortable on hot summer days. Downstairs, the lounge combines many original features with a bright, fresh look, but it is the smart, modern restaurant that lies at the heart of the whole operation. For the outstanding cooking is the draw here, with memorable cuisine featuring locally sourced ingredients skilfully prepared by head chef James Sommerin, and all accompanied by a seriously good wine list.

Recommended in the area

Brecon Beacons; Tintern Abbey; Offa's Dyke

Labuan Guest House

★★★★ GUEST HOUSE
Address: 464 Chepstow Road, NEWPORT, NP19 8JF
Tel/Fax: 01633 664533
Email: patricia.bees@ntlworld.com
Website: www.labuanhouse.co.uk
Map ref: 2 ST38
Directions: M4 junct 24, 1.5m on B4237
Rooms: 5 (3 en suite) (2 pri facs) (1GF)
S £38-£45 D £68-£75
Notes: Wi-fi 🐾 **Parking:** 6

John and Patricia Bees have created a warm and friendly home-from-home atmosphere at their fine Victorian house with its lovely garden, set on the main road into Newport. Golfers will find kindred spirits in these keen players, who will arrange tee times for their guests at any of the 45 courses within a 40-minute drive; it's just a mile away from Celtic Manor Resort which will host the 2010 Ryder Cup. After a day on the course or exploring the area, the high comfort levels in the stylish en suite bedrooms are very welcome indeed. Each good-sized room is well equipped with TV/DVD, tea- and coffee-making facilities, hairdryers, fluffy bathrobes and Wi-fi. Bathrooms feature a wide range of extras. On the ground floor there is a twin room and a comfortable lounge where guests can relax, and in winter a log fire makes for a cosy atmosphere. There is a good choice from the menu for hearty breakfasts that include home-made bread and preserves, and are taken in the welcoming dining room at separate tables. Evening meals can be arranged, as can lunches to go, packed in a cool bag. Labuan is just a few minutes drive from the M4 so it makes an ideal location for business people visiting Newport. Off-street parking is available.

Recommended in the area

Tredegar House; Caerleon Roman Site & History Museum; Newport Wetlands

Erw-Lon Farm

★ ★ ★ ★ ≜ FARMHOUSE
Address: Pontfaen, FISHGUARD,
        Pembrokeshire, SA65 9TS
Tel: 01348 881297
Email: lilwenmcallister@btinternet.com
Website: www.erwlonfarm.co.uk
Map ref: 1 SM93
Directions: 5.5m SE of Fishguard on B4313
Rooms: 3 en suite **S** £40 **D** £62-£66 **Notes:** ⊗ ⼓
under 10yrs ◉ **Parking:** 5 **Closed:** Dec-Mar

This lovely old house is at the heart of a working sheep and cattle farm, and its landscaped gardens overlook the stunning Gwaun Valley towards Carningli, the Mountain of the Angels. Lilwen McAllister is an exceptional hostess, providing a very homely feel to the farmhouse. The lounge is a lovely place to relax, while the bedrooms are comfortable and well equipped. Mrs McAllister's traditional farmhouse cooking uses fresh local produce and meals are served in generous portions. Erw–Lon Farm is well situated as a base to explore Pembrokeshire and Cardigan Bay.

Recommended in the area

Castell Henllys; Strumble Head; St David's Cathedral; Pembrokeshire Coastal Path

Crug-Glas Country House

★★★★★ ≜ ⌒ GUEST HOUSE
Address: SOLVA, Haverfordwest,
        Pembrokeshire, SA62 6XX
Tel: 01348 831302
Email: janet@crugglas.plus.com
Website: www.crug-glas.co.uk
Map ref: 1 SM82
Rooms: 7 en suite (2GF) **S** £70 **D** £100-£150
Notes: Wi-fi ⊗ on premises ⼓ under 12yrs
Parking: 10 **Closed:** 24-27 Dec

Crug-Glas is a family-run country house situated about a mile inland from the breathtaking Pembrokeshire coast. On a dairy, beef and cereal farm of roughly 600 acres, this delightful property has a history dating back to the 12th century. Guests today can expect comfort, relaxation and flawless attention to detail. Each spacious bedroom has the hallmarks of assured design, with grand furnishings and luxury en suite bathrooms. One suite on the top floor provides great views. AA award-winning breakfasts and dinners use the finest local produce. The sunsets in the evening are stunning.

Recommended in the area

Abereiddy beach; Porthgain; St David's

Ramsey House

★★★★★ 🛏 🍽 GUEST HOUSE

Address: Lower Moor, ST DAVID'S, Haverfordwest,
Pembrokeshire, SA62 6RP
Tel: 01437 720321
Email: info@ramseyhouse.co.uk
Website: www.ramseyhouse.co.uk
Map ref: 1 SM72
Directions: From Cross Sq in St David's towards
Porthclais, house 0.25m on left
Rooms: 6 (5 en suite) (1 pri facs) (3GF) **S** £60-£110
D £90-£110 **Notes:** Wi-fi ⊗ on premises **Parking:** 10

Family-run by Suzanne and Shaun Ellison, Ramsey House is just a gentle stroll from the centre of Britain's smallest city, St David's, a place with a rich historical heritage surrounded by beautiful countryside, with the Pembrokeshire coastal path nearby. The Ellisons provide the ideal combination of professional hotel management and the warmth of a friendly guest house with a relaxed atmosphere. They are happy to advise guests on the many activities and places of interest nearby, and there are plenty of books and leaflets too, to help you plan your excursions. All bedrooms have been refurbished in a luxury boutique style; first-floor rooms have views out to sea, over countryside or towards the cathedral, and those on the ground-floor look out over the gardens. Accommodation includes a licensed bar, next to the dining room, secure bicycle storage, a wet room, light laundry facilities and ample off-street parking. Shaun is an accomplished chef who champions quality local produce, so you can expect a real flavour of Wales from your meals. Breakfast provides a choice of home-made items including breads and preserves, and a three-course dinner is served in the restaurant. Freshly prepared picnics can also be arranged for your day out.

Recommended in the area

Pembrokeshire islands; St David's Cathedral; Pembrokeshire Coast National Park

The Waterings

★★★★ BED & BREAKFAST

Address: Anchor Drive, High Street, ST DAVID'S,
Pembrokeshire, SA62 6QH
Tel/Fax: 01437 720876
Email: enquiries@waterings.co.uk
Website: www.waterings.co.uk
Map ref: 1 SM72
Directions: On A487 on E edge of St David's
Rooms: 5 en suite (5GF) **S** £50-£80 **D** £75-£85
Notes: ⊗ not in bedrooms ✦ under 5yrs ☻
Parking: 20

The Waterings is set in an acre of beautiful landscaped grounds in a quiet location close to the Pembrokeshire Coast National Park Visitor Centre and only a short walk from St David's 800-year-old cathedral, which is the setting for an annual music festival at the end of May. The magnificent coastline with its abundance of birdlife is also within easy reach. The en suite bedrooms in this spacious accommodation are all on the ground floor and are set around an attractive courtyard. All the bedrooms are equipped with TV and have tea- and coffee-making facilities. The accommodation includes two family rooms with lounge, two double rooms with lounge and a double room with small sitting area. Breakfast, prepared from a good selection of local produce, is served in a smart dining room in the main house. Outside amenities at The Waterings include a picnic area with tables and benches, a barbecue and a croquet lawn. The nearest sandy beach is just a 15-minute walk away; other activities in the area include walking, boat trips to Ramsey Island, an RSPB reserve a mile offshore, sea fishing, whale and dolphin spotting boat trips, canoeing, surfing, rock climbing and abseiling.

Recommended in the area

Ramsey Island boat trips; Pembrokeshire Coast National Park; Whitesands Beach

Panorama

★ ★ ★ ★ 🛏 GUEST ACCOMMODATION

Address: The Esplanade, TENBY,
Pembrokeshire, SA70 7DU
Tel/Fax: 01834 844976
Email: mail@tenby-hotel.co.uk
Website: www.tenby-hotel.co.uk
Map ref: 1 SN10
Directions: A478 follow South Beach & Town Centre
signs. Sharp left under railway arches, up Greenhill
Rd, onto South Pde then Esplanade

Rooms: 8 en suite **S** £45-£50 **D** £80-£110 **Notes:** ⊗ on premises 🧒 under 5yrs **Closed:** 22-28 Dec

Right on the Esplanade overlooking Tenby's fine South Beach and across Carmarthen Bay, the friendly, family-run Panorama is part of a handsome terrace of Victorian properties. It provides the perfect location for exploring the Pembrokeshire coastline and the ancient town with its harbour and medieval wall. The well appointed bedrooms have been decorated and furnished to the highest standard, all en suite, with tea- and coffee-making facilities. A good selection of dishes is available at breakfast.

Recommended in the area

Caldy monastic island; Tudor Merchant's House; Tenby Museum & Art Gallery

Canal Bank

★ ★ ★ ★ ★ BED & BREAKFAST

Address: Ty Gardd, Canal Bank, BRECON,
Powys, LD3 7HG
Tel: 01874 623464
Email: enquiries@accommodation-
breconbeacons.co.uk
Website: www.accommodation-breconbeacons.co.uk
Map ref: 2 SO02
Directions: B4601 signed Brecon, left over bridge
before fuel station, right, to end of road

Rooms: 3 en suite **S** £50-£60 **D** £70-£90 **Notes:** Wi-fi 🧒 ♿ **Parking:** 5

Once a row of canal workers' cottages this is now a stylish home, full of warmth and comfort. Peacefully situated by the canal and with lovely views over the fields and hills, Canal Bank is within minutes of all Brecon's attractions. No need to drive in the evening, the restaurants are just a pleasant stroll away. Quality is the essence here from the Welsh slate and oak furnishings to posture-sprung mattresses, goose-down duvets and revitalising spa baths with lashings of hot water.

Recommended in the area

Brecon & Monmouth Canal; Dan yr Ogaf Show Caves; Brecon Beacons National Park

Cribyn, Pen-y-Fan, Corn Du mountains from Fan-y-Big, Brecon Beacons National Park

Llanddetty Hall Farm

★★★★ FARMHOUSE
Address: Talybont-on-Usk, BRECON,
Powys, LD3 7YR
Tel/Fax: 01874 676415
Map ref: 2 SO02
Directions: SE of Brecon. Off B4558
Rooms: 4 (3 en suite) (1 pri facs) (1GF)
S £35 **D** £60-£62
Notes: ⊗ on premises 🐾 under 12yrs ⊕
Parking: 6 **Closed:** 16 Dec-14 Jan

This listed farmhouse is part of a sheep farm in the Brecon Beacons National Park. The Brecon and Monmouth Canal flows through the farm at the rear, while the front of the house overlooks the River Usk. Bedrooms, including one on the ground floor, feature exposed beams and polished floorboards. Three rooms are en suite and one has a private bathroom – all have radio alarms and tea- and coffee-making facilities. There is a lounge with a television, and a dining room where breakfast is served at an oak refectory table.

Recommended in the area

Brecon Beacons National Park; Hay-on-Wye; Aberglasney

Glangrwyney Court

★★★★★ BED & BREAKFAST

Address: CRICKHOWELL, Powys, NP8 1ES
Tel: 01873 811288
Fax: 01873 810317
Email: info@glancourt.co.uk
Website: www.glancourt.co.uk
Map ref: 2 SO21
Directions: 2m SE of Crickhowell on A40 (near county boundary)
Rooms: 10 en suite (1GF) S £65-£85
Notes: Wi-fi **Parking:** 12

A privately-owned, Georgian Grade II listed country house, Glangrwyney Court offers delightful luxury accommodation. Forming part of a small country estate on the edge of the beautiful Brecon Beacons and the Black Mountains, it stands in 4 acres of walled gardens and makes an ideal base for touring this lovely area. The house throughout is tastefully decorated and furnished with period pieces. Guests are encouraged to relax in the cosy sitting room in front of a roaring log fire in the winter months. Glangrwyney Court has been home to the same family for the last 17 years, during which time the main house and the cottages have been sympathetically restored to provide excellent modern comforts. The accommodation comprises eight bedrooms in the main house, one ground-floor room in the Garden Courtyard, and three cottages which are available on a bed and breakfast basis or for self-catering. All rooms have TV and DVD players, hairdryers, clock radios, quality toiletries, fluffy bath towels and robes plus tea and coffee making facilities.

Recommended in the area

Brecon Beacons National Park; Dan-Yr-Ogof Caves; Big Pit National Mining Museum of Wales

Guidfa House

★★★★★ 🛏 🍽 GUEST ACCOMMODATION

Address: Crossgates, LLANDRINDOD WELLS,
Powys, LD1 6RF
Tel: 01597 851241
Fax: 01597 851875
Email: guidfa@globalnet.co.uk
Website: www.guidfa-house.co.uk
Map ref: 2 SO06
Directions: 3m N of Llandrindod Wells, at junct of
A483 & A44
Rooms: 6 en suite (1GF) **S** £65 **D** £80-£105 **Notes:** Wi-fi ⊗ on premises 🚼 under 10yrs **Parking:** 10

Expect a relaxed stay at Anne and Tony Millan's charming Georgian house, set within picturesque gardens and located in the village of Crossgates, just north of Llandrindod Wells. All rooms come well equipped with comfortable beds, fluffy towels, soft bathrobes and quality toiletries. The luxurious Coach House suite has a super-king double bed and a large, separate sitting room and spa bath. Free Wi-fi is available. The meals at Guidfa House are both delicious and imaginative, prepared from local produce.

Recommended in the area

Elan Valley RSPB Red Kite Feeding Station; Royal Welsh Showground; Builth Wells

Moors Farm B&B

★★★★★ BED & BREAKFAST

Address: Oswestry Road, WELSHPOOL,
Powys, SY21 9JR
Tel: 01938 553395 & 07957 882967
Email: moorsfarm@tiscali.co.uk
Website: www.moors-farm.com
Map ref: 2 SJ20
Directions: 1.5m NE of Welshpool off A483
Rooms: 5 en suite **Notes:** ⊗ on premises

This farmhouse is still at the heart of a working farm that raises sheep and cattle; the building is full of character, with lots of old beams and log fires that are as warm as the welcome. The accommodation is both spacious and comfortable, and the luxury Gate House barn conversion offers self-catering accommodation suitable for larger groups. Wholesome breakfasts are served around a huge family table, where guests sit together in the traditional manner; house party dinners are available by prior arrangement. Moors Farm is just a mile from the bustling market town of Welshpool where you'll find cafés, restaurants and traditional pubs.

Recommended in the area

Powis Castle & Gardens (NT); Welshpool & Llanfair Light Railway; Offa's Dyke Path

Maen Llia (Llia's Stone), Fforest Fawr, Brecon Beacons National Park

MAPS

KEY TO ATLAS PAGES

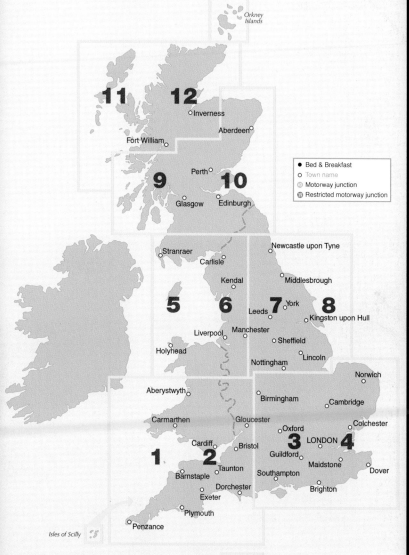

Shetland Islands

13

Orkney Islands

11 **12**

Inverness

Aberdeen

Fort William

Bed & Breakfast
Town name
Motorway junction
Restricted motorway junction

9 Perth **10**

Glasgow Edinburgh

Stranraer

Carlisle

Newcastle upon Tyne

Kendal

Middlesbrough

5 **6** **7** York **8**

Leeds

Kingston upon Hull

Liverpool Manchester

Sheffield

Holyhead

Lincoln

Nottingham

Norwich

Aberystwyth

Birmingham

Cambridge

Carmarthen

Gloucester

Colchester

Oxford

3 LONDON **4**

Cardiff Bristol

Guildford

1 **2**

Maidstone

Dover

Taunton

Southampton

Barnstaple

Brighton

Dorchester

Exeter

Plymouth

Isles of Scilly

Penzance

13

Channel Islands

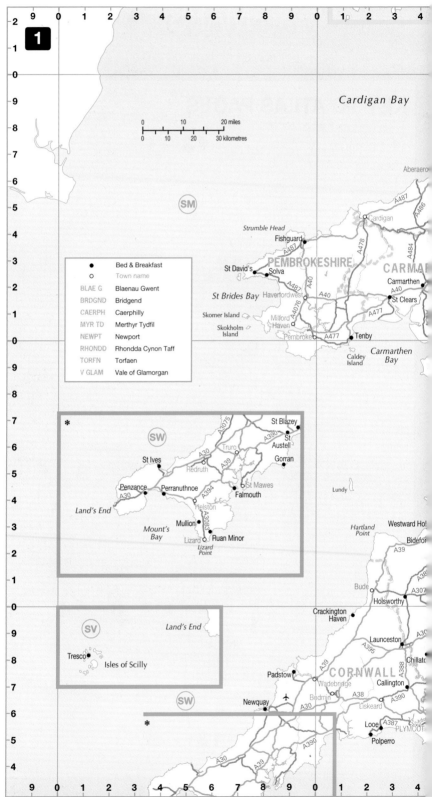

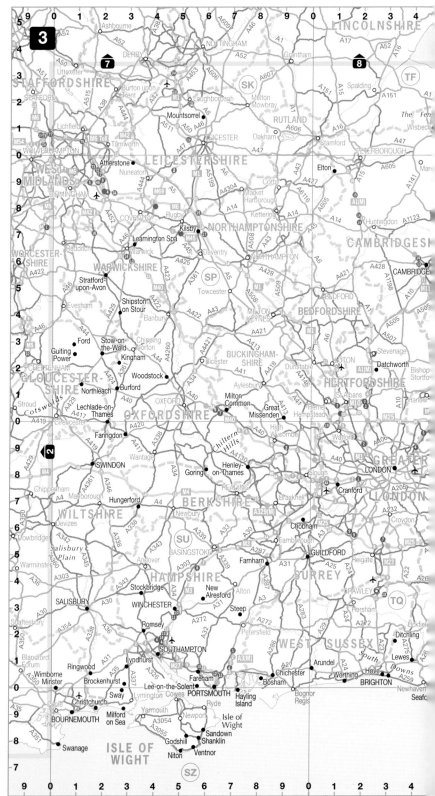

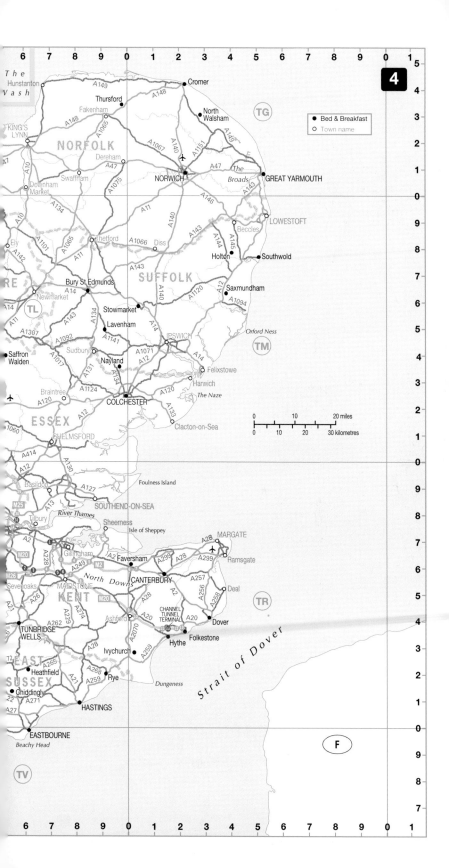

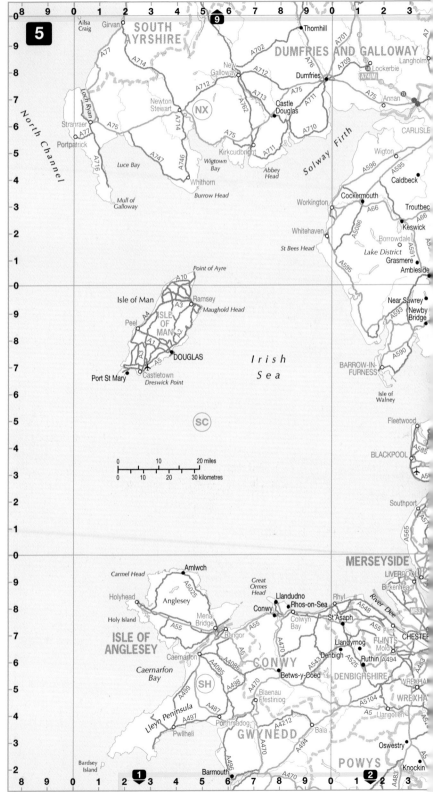

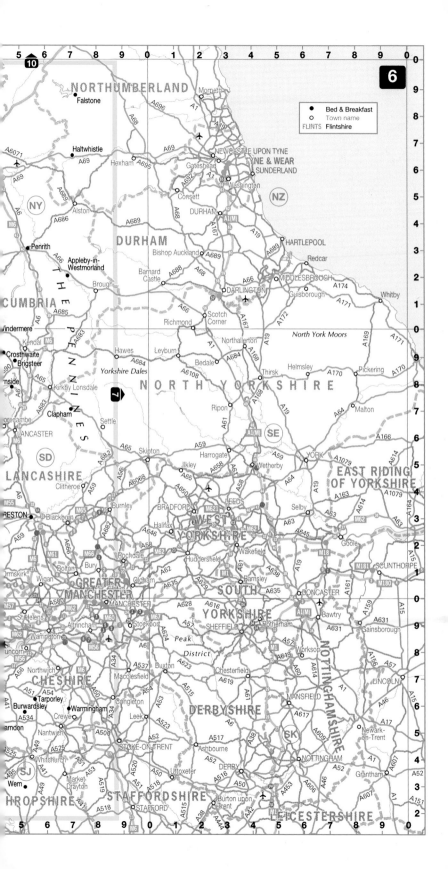

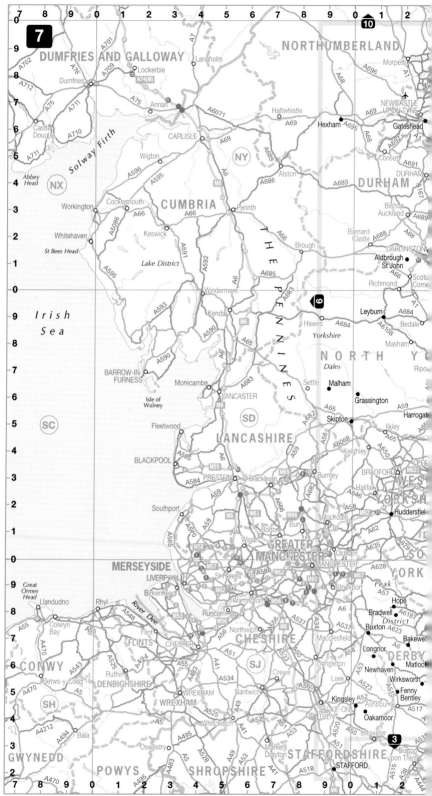

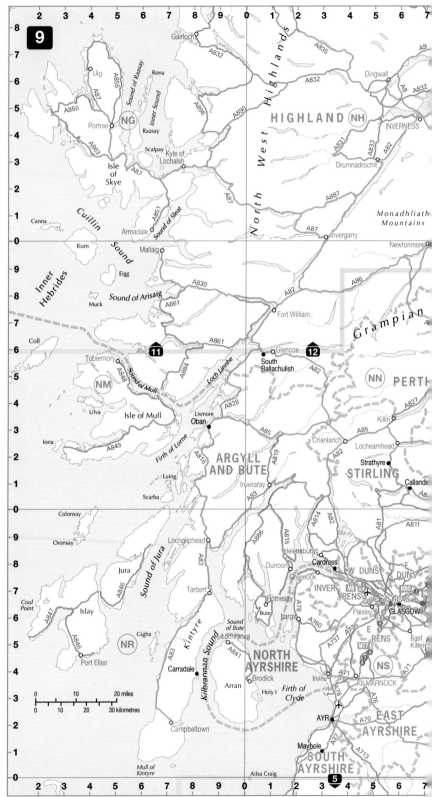

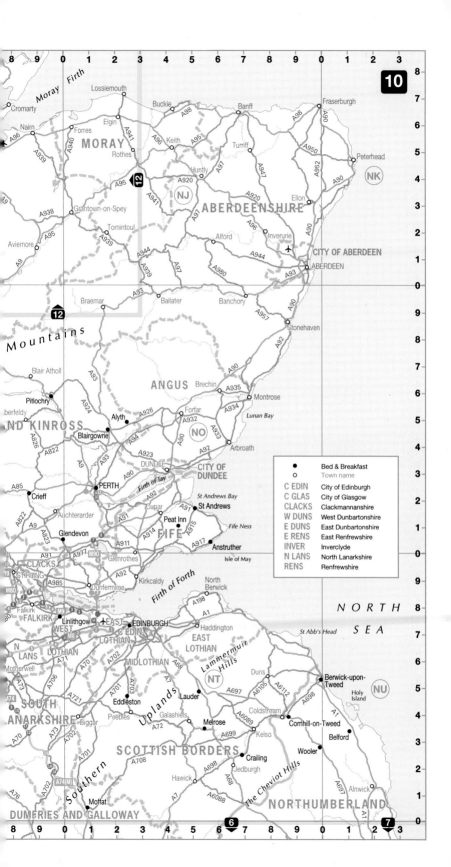

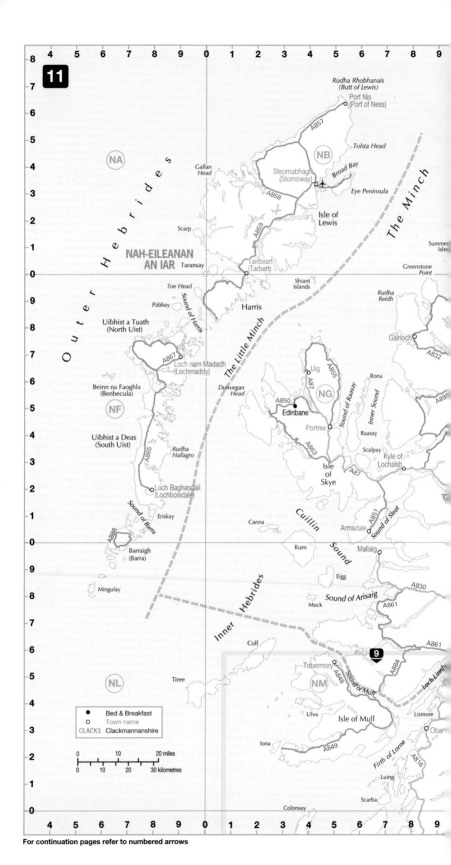

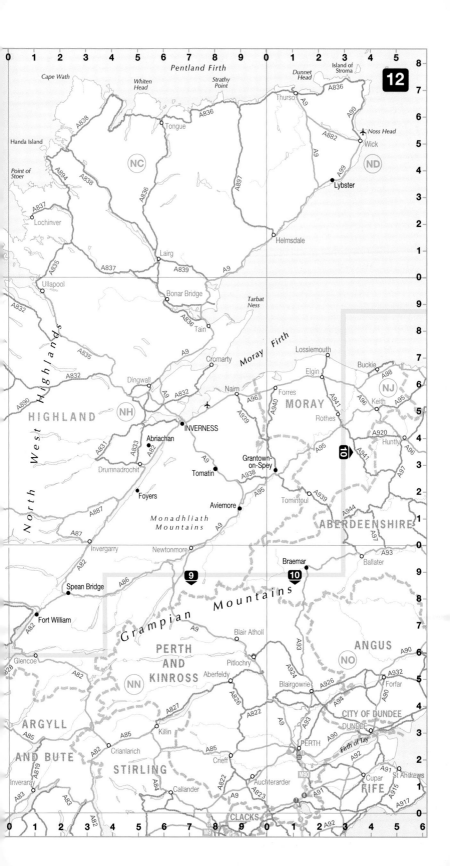

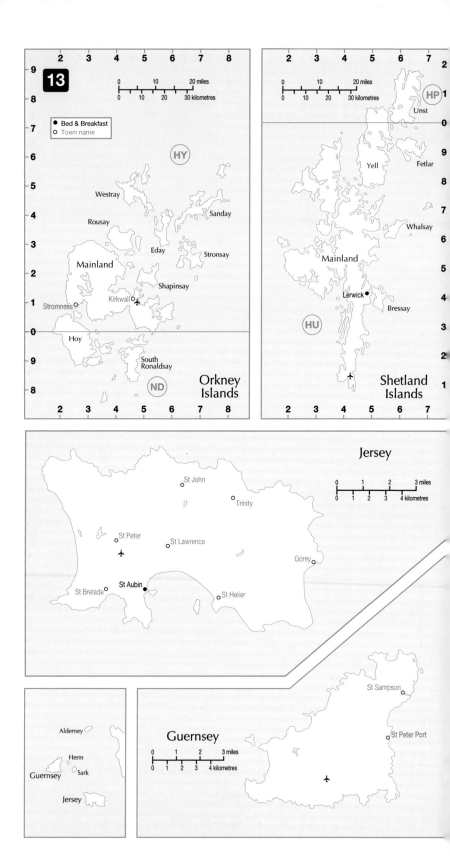

County Map

England				**Wales**	
1	Bedfordshire	14	Warwickshire	**Wales**	
2	Berkshire	15	West Midlands	26	Blaenau Gwent
3	Bristol	16	Worcestershire	27	Bridgend
4	Buckinghamshire			28	Caerphilly
5	Cambridgeshire	**Scotland**		29	Denbighshire
6	Greater Manchester	17	City of Glasgow	30	Flintshire
7	Herefordshire	18	Clackmannanshire	31	Merthyr Tydfil
8	Hertfordshire	19	East Ayrshire	32	Monmouthshire
9	Leicestershire	20	East Dunbartonshire	33	Neath Port Talbot
10	Northamptonshire	21	East Renfrewshire	34	Newport
11	Nottinghamshire	22	Perth & Kinross	35	Rhondda Cynon Taff
12	Rutland	23	Renfrewshire	36	Torfaen
13	Staffordshire	24	South Lanarkshire	37	Vale of Glamorgan
		25	West Dunbartonshire	38	Wrexham

Location Index

Location Index

Location Index

Location Index

B&B Index

B&B Index

B&B Index

The Automobile Association would like to thank the following photographers, companies and picture libraries for their assistance in the preparation of this book.

Abbreviations for the picture credits are as follows: (t) top; (b) bottom; (l) left; (r) right; (c) centre; (AA) AA World Travel Library.

4 Royalty Free Photodisc; 5 Royalty Free Photodisc; 7 Stockbyte Royalty Free; 8 AA/N Hicks; 9 TongRo Image Stock/Alamy; 10 Royalty Free Photodisc; 14/15 AA/A Lawson; 16 AA/J Tims; 18 AA/A Lawson; 21 AA/T Souter; 22 AA/M Moody; 24 AA/C Coe; 25t AA/J Tims; 26 AA/M Birkitt; 32t AA/J Welsh; 33 AA/J Wood; 34t AA/R Tenison; 39t AA/J Wood; 44/45 AA/J Wood; 52t AA/J Wood; 55t AA/C Jones; 56t AA/C Jones; 61 AA/A Mockford & N Bonetti; 74t AA/S Day; 76 AA/A Midgley; 77t AA/M Birkitt; 80t AA/T Mackie; 84t AA/T Mackie; 85 AA/P Baker; 89t AA/C Jones; 92t AA/G Edwardes; 96t AA/N Hicks; 98t AA/N Hicks; 100t AA/C Jones; 107t AA/P Baker; 108 AA/R Ireland; 109t AA/R Newton; 113t AA/R Ireland; 115t AA/M Jourdan; 117t AA/A Burton; 121t AA/M Jourdan; 122 AA/N Setchfield; 124 AA/W Voysey; 125t AA/S Day; 128t AA/H Palmer; 132t AA/S Day; 134t AA/M Moody; 135 AA/S Day; 140t AA/A Burton; 141 AA/M Moody; 142t AA/A Burton; 144t AA/M Moody; 146t AA/M Moody; 148 AA/H Williams; 149t AA/I Burgum; 153 AA/C Jones; 154 AA/M Moody; 155t AA/M Moody; 156 AA/N Setchfield; 158t AA/N Setchfield; 162t AA/P Baker; 163 AA/N Setchfield; 164 AA/J Beazley; 165t AA/S Day; 166 AA/J Tims; 167t AA/J Tims; 168 AA/T Mackie; 172t AA/T Mackie; 174 AA/J Tims; 179 AA/S&O Mathews; 184t AA/T Mackie; 185 AA/T Mackie; 186 AA/M Birkitt; 188 AA/J Beazley; 189t AA/R Coulam; 191t AA/R Coulam; 196t AA/T Woodcock; 197 AA/C Jones; 200t AA/S Day; 204 AA/M Morris; 207t AA/C Jones; 210t AA/C Jones; 212 AA/M Birkitt; 219t AA/J Tims; 225 AA/J Tims; 227t AA/J Tims; 228 AA/A Tryner; 231 AA/T Mackie; 235t AA/T Mackie; 236 AA/J Tims; 238t AA/J Tims; 239 AA/J Miller; 243 AA/J Miller; 244t AA/J Miller; 250t AA/J Miller; 253 AA/J Miller; 254t AA/J Miller; 260 AA/R Coulam; 262t AA/R Coulam; 263 AA/V Greaves; 266 AA/C Jones; 269 AA/A Burton; 270t AA/A Burton; 275 AA/M Moody; 278t AA/M Moody; 282 AA/C Jones; 284t AA/M Moody; 285 AA/C Jones; 286 AA; 288t AA/M Adelman; 289 AA/T Mackie; 291t AA/T Mackie; 292 AA/T Mackie; 298t AA/M Kipling; 301t AA/L Whitwam; 303t AA/T Mackie; 305t AA/M Kipling; 306 AA/J Tims; 307t AA/J Tims; 308 AA/S Abraham; 310 AA; 311t AA; 312/313 AA/S Day; 320t AA/J Smith; 323t AA/N Hicks; 326t AA/R Weir; 328 AA/S Anderson; 330t AA/S Whitehorne; 332t AA/S Whitehorne; 335t AA/S Whitehorne; 337t AA/J Smith; 340t AA/J Smith; 344t AA/S Whitehorne; 345 AA/S Whitehorne; 346/347 AA/M Moody; 351t AA/A J Hopkins; 355t AA/G Munday; 359t AA/C Molyneux; 365 AA/N Jenkins; 367t AA/D Croucher; 368t AA/I Burgum; 375t AA/N Jenkins; 378 AA/C&A Molyneux

Every effort has been made to trace the copyright holders, and we apologise in advance for any accidental errors. We would be happy to apply any corrections in the following edition of this publication.